STAGESTRUCK: THE ROMANCE

OF ALFRED LUNT AND LYNN FONTANNE

STAGESTRUCK:

The Romance of Alfred Lunt and Lynn Fontanne

MAURICE ZOLOTOW

HARCOURT, BRACE & WORLD, INC., NEW YORK

To Stephen Zolotow

Who borrows every changing shape to find expression

CONTENTS

Contents

LIST OF ILLUSTRATIONS

List of Illustrations

(Between pages 182 and 183)

Lynn Fontanne in *The Wooing of Eve* (1916), with Violet Kemble Cooper and Laurette Taylor

Alfred Lunt in *Romance and Arabella* (1917)

Alfred in *Clarence* (1919)

Lynn as Dulcy (1921), with John Westley and George Alison

Alfred and Lynn in *Arms and the Man* (1925)

Alfred with Carol Dempster in *Sally of the Sawdust* (1925)

Lynn beating Alfred in *At Mrs. Beam's* (1926)

Alfred cajoles Lynn in *Caprice* (1928)

Lynn and Alfred in *Meteor* (1929), with Edward Emery

The Lunts in *Elizabeth the Queen* (1930)

Alfred, Noel Coward, and Lynn in *Design for Living* (1933), with Campbell Gullan

Alfred and Lynn in *Point Valaine* (1935)

Alfred with Les Blondes on the set of *Idiot's Delight* (1936), with Lynn

The Lunts in *Amphitryon 38* (1937)

As Trigorin and Madame Arkadina in *The Sea Gull* (1938)

The beginning of the most passionate love scene ever played by the Lunts, in *O Mistress Mine* (1946)

The Lunts in *The Great Sebastians* (1955)

In *The Visit* (1958)

STAGESTRUCK: THE ROMANCE

OF ALFRED LUNT AND LYNN FONTANNE

ONE

THE MYSTERY

OF THEIR MARRIAGE

*A*SKED TO reveal his secrets of dramaturgy, Robert E. Sherwood once replied, "It's really quite simple. I just write plays for the Lunts. All you have to do to have a Broadway hit is write a play in which there is a good part for Alfred Lunt and an equally good part for Lynn Fontanne." Now there are other formulas for writing hit plays, but the Sherwood system was sure-fire between 1925 and 1950, when the Lunts reigned as the most spectacular box-office attraction in the theatre. In the golden age of Broadway, the decade after World War I, they incarnated the romance and glamour of theatre. They were synonymous with theatre. It was known, even by persons who knew them only from a distance, that the Lunts were passionately dedicated to the acting art. They lived only to act. They had, in the words of Sherwood, "a plain, simple, childish relish for the theatre." Their conversations revolved around the theatre—and especially the play they were in at the moment.

During their run in *The Great Sebastians*, Noel Coward, their oldest and dearest friend, happened to be in New York for several months. He was in the habit of meeting them after their performance several nights a week and having supper with them. Every night they talked and talked about how well or how badly the performance had gone that night or how they were working on a marvelous new piece of business to put into the second act or what did he think was the better reading of some speech or other. After several weeks, Coward found the problems of playing in *The Great Sebastians*, however interesting they might be to Lynn and Alfred, quite unbearable. One night in the middle of one of their enthusiastic discussions about acting problems, Coward, who felt left out and didn't want to be in anyway, got up and said, "Listen, darlings, if either of you ever mentions *The Great Sebastians* again while I am in your house, I swear I am going to knock your heads together until your brains rattle. Let's change the subject." But that is hopeless really. No matter what subject is being discussed, Lynn and Afred will get the conversation back to the theatre in general, and to whatever play they are playing in at the moment or rehearsing or considering as a future vehicle.

Actors' Equity limits rehearsals to eight hours daily. The Lunts say this is ridiculous. Even twelve hours a day is not enough for them. When he was directing *The Taming of the Shrew* for the Theatre Guild, Alfred wanted to make the cast work ten to fourteen hours a day. Equity refused permission. Alfred pleaded with the union leaders to change the rules.

"Miss Fontanne and I rehearse all the time," he pointed out. "Even after we leave the theatre, we rehearse. We sleep in the same bed. We have a script in our hands when we go to bed. You can't come and tell us to stop rehearsing after eight hours. Why, we wouldn't allow you in the bedroom!"

The Duchess of Windsor once asked Lynn: "Is it true that you and your husband sleep in separate bedrooms?"

"Alfred and I don't even sleep in separate beds!" she replied.

Moss Hart, while staying at the Savoy in London, once complained about the drabness of his suite. "But," protested the manager, "we have given you the same suite that was recently occupied by Miss Fontanne and Mr. Lunt."

"The Lunts never notice *where* they are," Hart explained. "They spend the night talking only about what happened to them in the theatre that day."

Their friends and colleagues are astonished that they have remained happily married to each other for so long. One cynical theory is that only by staying legally wedded could they have got away with the indelicate episodes they played so brazenly to respectable audiences in the provinces, for they toured the length and breadth of the country in such immoral comedies as *The Guardsman* and *Design for Living*. In *O Mistress Mine* there was a highly erotic scene during which Lynn, who played the kept woman of a cabinet minister, and Alfred, who played the minister, made love on a couch so realistically that the audience felt like *voyeurs* at a small orgy. At one matinee, a lady, disgusted by what can only be described as the "deep necking" taking place on the stage, got up to leave. Her friend made her sit down. "It's perfectly all right," she said. "They're married in private life, you know."

How, one wonders, can they stand so much of each other? They act together. They live together. They are together all day long and most of the night. They don't take separate vacations. They don't have separate sets of friends. They don't even have separate diversions, like golf or contract bridge, which might cleave them asunder for at least one afternoon a week. Once, Lady Juliet Duff invited Lynn to have lunch with her and Lady Cynthia Asquith.

"I couldn't, I'm afraid, unless you ask Alfred too," Lynn said. "I don't go anywhere without him."

Alfred directed *Ondine,* that loveliest of all the Giraudoux plays, in which Audrey Hepburn starred. Alfred and Lynn did not play in *Ondine.* Lynn was at rehearsals frequently. She sat out front until it was time to go home with Alfred. Just before *Ondine* was to go to Boston for its tryout, somebody asked Alfred whether Lynn was going along.

"Of course, she's going along," he said incredulously. "She's going to be in Boston every minute I'm there. Wherever I go in Boston, she'll go with me. She's leaving with me—on the same train—and in the next seat to me."

Alexander Woollcott, a dear friend, regarded marriage as a senseless custom. He hated to invite married couples to his dinner parties and weekends. He might invite either the wife or the husband—but not both. Most of his married friends resigned themselves to his annoying habit. The Lunts refused. If Woollcott wanted Lynn he would have to swallow Alfred, and vice versa. Woollcott stormed and raged—but he gave in. Eventually he admitted they were better as a couple. He confided to Lily Bonner that Lynn and Alfred were the only married couple whose company he enjoyed more together than separately.

Woollcott had finally become aware of something Noel Coward learned years before. For a long time, Coward had been troubled by whether he liked the company of one more than the company of the other. Then one day he had a revelation: they really were not two different people. "They were one person and now I realized why I'd never been able to decide between them," he says.

W. Graham Robertson, an English writer, painter, and professional recluse who was almost as bizarre a personality as Woollcott, got to know the Lunts and when they were playing in London he would

5

come up from his pastoral retreat to see them act and enjoy the pleasures of their repartee. He once attempted to explain their mystery in a letter:

They are strange and wonderful personalities—very difficult to understand until you realize that they are not two, but one personality. Each is the other's complement. Together they are marvelous, their artistry amazing. Apart, they are oddly ineffectual. Alfred, a vaguely wandering soul who looks at you like a lost dog who is afraid of being washed; Lynn (like "Maud")—splendidly null, a sort of highly intellectual ice-maiden. Alfred's genius illuminates Lynn; Lynn's strong brain and well balanced judgement keep Alfred within bounds and bring him back to earth when he soars skyward. I love them both, but the Alfred-Lynn combination is the real person, not the component parts.

Vivien Leigh, attempting to clarify the mystery, told me, during a long interview in her Eton Square flat at the time her divorce from Sir Laurence Olivier was pending: "Why cannot Larry and I be like Lynn and Alfred? I don't think it's because we don't act together as frequently. No, I think it's something they have in their temperaments and we don't. I think it is that Lynn and Alfred have angelic natures."

Another theory has it that the Lunts do not have the customary division between work and personal life in their marriage and that everything that happens to one happens to the other. Coward has often wondered whether they love each other so much because they act so well together, or act so well together because they love each other so much. "Sometimes I've thought that they are in the theatre so intensely because the theatre makes it possible for them to be together more often and in more ways than they might be if they were in some other line of work," he says.

Alfred himself says: "People always want to know why we get on so well together, and the answer is I've never been bored. She's the most exciting person I've ever known and I'm in love with her. The answer is so simple nobody believes it. Married life is spending all your time with a charming person who makes life more interesting because you can spend so much time with her." Lynn remembers admiring Alfred's voice and acting technique the very first time she met him. She at once fell madly in love with him and has continued to feel intoxicated by his presence ever since. "I suppose it is rather unusual, but there it is," she says, shrugging helplessly.

So they are lovers in their own strange and romantic ways. And they share many interests and passions in common, although all of the roads lead to the same end, the theatre, those three hours when their existence expresses itself most fully in the unreal existence of phantoms on a stage. But this unreality is their reality.

Among the qualities they have in common is a great physical exuberance. Jean Giraudoux first saw them play in 1937 in his *Amphitryon 38*. S. N. Behrman, the English adapter, asked his opinion of the acting team. Giraudoux threw up his hands and cried, *"Quelle vitalité!"*

This explosive life-force combines with a powerful sensual receptivity. Once I was having tea at their country estate, Ten Chimneys, in Genesee Depot, Wisconsin. It was served in an alcove on a balcony between the first and second floors of the main house. The table was set with a tea service and trays of cookies and sandwiches. We could look out of a French window. I heard a bird cry.

"What kind of bird was that?" I asked.

"A catbird," Lynn replied.

"He always screams *HarriET, HarriET, HarriET*," Alfred said.

"When Alfred's mother was alive, we were always amused by the coincidence," Lynn said.

"My mother's name was Harriet. She lived on the farm with us."

Lynn cocked her head. She listened to another bird call.

"That's a cardinal," she said. "He says *fierce, fierce, fierce*. I guess he finds life fierce."

"Actually," corrected Alfred, "it's more like the name of that old servant in *The Cherry Orchard*. Y'know, Firs."

"Yes," Lynn agreed, "you've got to give it more of a hissing. *Fiersss. Fiersss.*"

She sang the notes of the cardinal. She even assumed the fluttering movements of a bird. Then Alfred described how during the last dry spell he'd seen a robin bathing in the shallow end of the swimming pool. Alfred dabbled his fingers in the air and became a robin cooling himself. This reminded Lynn of the time a cardinal had gone into the deep end and drowned. His mate had hovered around the pool for several days. The cardinals became real to you. You almost saw the scene. This is the heart of the acting genius—the ability, first, to respond sensitively to experience, and then to reproduce what has been felt so vividly in physical terms that an audience shares the original experience. I was watching it in a raw state, as they played at being birds, but I could see how they felt something, remembered something, stimulated each other as they went along.

Lynn poured the tea. I bit into a cookie. It was a marvelous tidbit—soft and melting. I had another one.

"Do you like them?"

"The best I ever tasted."

"Alfred baked them," she said happily.

He beamed with pleasure.

"He also baked the bread." I had a slice—buttered with unsalted butter, home-churned.

And now, with hardly a transition, and unconscious of what they were doing because it was as natural as breathing, they were playing two different roles.

"There's an amusing little pub here we'd love to get our hands on," she said. "The things we could do. We'd love to have a restaurant. We have grand ideas about food and service. And the liquor—we'd serve only the best of drinks, use the finest gin in our martinis. And decent coffee. And fresh baked beans and fresh vegetables. We're against frozen things. And Alfred would do all the baking and prepare the sauces. He's marvelous at sauces."

"Lynnie, do you think we should serve steaks?"

"I'd adore to."

"But steaks are awfully risky. If the slightest thing goes wrong, it tastes awful. A few seconds too long—and the meat's overdone. We like our steaks medium rare with a Béarnaise sauce."

"You must taste Alfred's Béarnaise sauce. You never get food at a restaurant like you do at home. Even the best restaurants have lost their quality."

"They're too crowded and too crowded with people who've got no taste. I remember a dinner we had at Voisin's. We'd gone to much trouble, ordering some specialties in advance. Well, the place was full of a new sort of person, loud and vulgar, and you felt they didn't really love good food. They were brassy. I remember a couple at the next table. They were fat. And a waiter wheeled over this wagon of *hors d'oeuvres* and the woman kept telling them to put more and more of each thing on her plate, and finally she cackled, 'More beets, more beets, I just *luhv* pickled beets!' "

Now they changed again as they mimed the gluttons. They seemed to bloat before one's eyes. Lynn and Alfred weren't there. Two other persons were at the table.

They were practising five-finger exercises of illusion.

Though the Lunts have performed in serious plays, such as *The Sea Gull* and *The Visit,* my generation will always think of them most of all as the graceful, witty, sparkling, sexually charming, and terribly sophisticated protagonist and antagonist of the high comedies of the 1920's. The polished comedies of George Kelly, Robert Sherwood, Philip Barry, S. N. Behrman, Noel Coward, Marc Connelly, Sidney Howard, and George S. Kaufman came out of a special milieu (and achieved success by both expressing the milieu and catering to its taste), the milieu of the international set, if you like, a small group of persons in New York and London and Paris who lived to play and played to live, who were extremely wealthy or extremely talented or extremely charming—or sometimes all three. They savored the pleasures of the flesh—yet without any of the putrescence that characterizes the contemporary *dolce vita* of the leisure class. They were people of refinement, with cultivated palates. They enjoyed ideas and conversation as much as they enjoyed new sensations. They were a wonderful generation of men and women. They were a small group, but all of us felt we knew these rare human beings, and participated in their lives, through the make-believe of Alfred Lunt and Lynn Fontanne.

TWO

THE COMPONENT PARTS:

LYNN FONTANNE

*L*YNN FONTANNE was born on December 6, at Station Terrace, Snakes Lane, Woodford, in Essex, ten miles northeast of London. She was, or was not, christened Lillie Louise Fontanne. The exact year of her nativity is debatable. The usual authorities in such matters— *Theatre Handbook, Who's Who in America, Who's Who in the Theatre, The World Almanac, The Information Please Almanac, The Best Plays* series—have contradicted each other. *The New Yorker* once collated a dozen references to Lynn's birthday—no two of which agreed. And no wonder—with her ageless beauty ("Fontanne of youth" a wit once called it), it doesn't seem possible she could be as old as she must be.

Her father, Jules Pierre Antoine Fontanne, was French. Her mother, Ellen Thornley, was Irish. Five daughters were born of the union. The oldest was Mai Ellen Lucie (1882). The others were Antoinette Marie (1883), Frances Emma (1886), Lillie Louise (1887) and Lynn (?). In 1935, *Who's Who in the Theatre* said Lynn was born in 1882. Lynn denied it. She said the true date was not available at Somerset House. The New York *Herald Tribune* sent a man delving into its archives. He concluded that Lillie Louise and Lynn were the same person. Confronted with the birthdates of the four Fontanne daughters, Lynn smiled archly. Ah, but she was not one of *those* four. There had been a fifth daughter, don't you see?

Jules Fontanne was a designer of printing type. He owned a typefounding business which he had inherited from his father. He was a poor business man. He didn't like business. He liked experimenting with machinery and working on inventions. He liked to read and talk. He read Dickens and Shakespeare aloud to his daughters. His true profession was to be a member of the leisure class. He had an appreciation of fine wines, good cigars, and choice brandy. He dressed in elegant taste and spoke like an aristocrat. "He'd tip his hat to a cockney washerwoman," Lynn recalls, "as politely as if she were a duchess." He didn't have the money to be a member of the leisure class. He saw more washerwomen than duchesses. He was declared a bankrupt in 1895. Most of the time Lynn was growing up, the family lived in poor neighborhoods in London. Mr. Fontanne's dreamy ways of life and his impractical sense of affairs drove his wife wild. She had a violent temper and a sharp tongue. She abused her husband. They had long, loud quarrels, from which Papa would retire to his room to tinker with an invention. It was not a happy family circle. Mrs. Fontanne found fault with her daughters. She criticized them no matter what they did. "As soon as we were old enough to leave home, we went away," Lynn says.

Lynn, even as a child, identified with Papa's grandiloquent notions. When she was three, her mother asked her, "What will you be when you are a grown woman?"

"I will be a mother and have four children and twelve nursemaids for each one."

Lynn informed strangers her family was of the nobility. She made up stories about all the servants they had and how they dined off gold plate. Naturally, the other children ridiculed her. Once she complained to her father of their persecution.

"Never mind them," he said. "Remember—your ancestors walked the courts of Versailles and spoke with kings."

"But Father, if we are of noble blood, where is our title?"

"We gave it up during the French Revolution," he explained.

One morning, Lynn asked if she could bring home a friend for tea. "She's a fairy," Lynn explained. Lynn brought home a "dirty little cockney girl." Lynn imagined she was a fairy because she wore a torn, dirty ballet skirt. To Lynn's fancy that made her an authentic fairy.

When Lynn was five, the family went to Brighton for a week. Lynn got lost on the beach. They found her hours later at the police station, perched on a table, surrounded by an audience of policemen. She was reciting a poem she had composed:

> I'm making a dress for dolly.
> A beautiful dress of blue.
> For she's going away to the seaside,
> And must have something new.

Lynn memorized Shakespearean monologues. Her father would frequently summon her to recite them for his friends. Even in childhood, Lynn had a magnificent voice. "It could ring out like a bell in a room full of people when she was little," recalls her sister 'Toineau, now Mrs. H. S. Wilson, of Lavender Cottage, Chichester, Sussex, England.

Papa once took her to the Lyceum Theatre to see *The Merchant of Venice*, with Henry Irving and Ellen Terry. Miss Terry was famous for her Portia, which she once played 250 consecutive times. When Miss Terry began the "quality of mercy" speech, Lynn, in the gallery, stood up and declaimed the speech right along with Miss Terry, until "Papa forcibly sat me down and made me be quiet. I was a very noisy, happy, and exuberant child until I was eight and it was then my mother scolded me for being clumsy and I got to be self-conscious and lost all confidence in myself. It got in the way of my being a success in acting when I started out, you see. Mama was high-strung and nervous and terribly wretched about the sordid life we had to live, not having any money and all, and Papa not being able to keep any jobs he got. She had beautiful black hair, Mama, and she was a beautiful woman. There was a dramatic streak of white in her hair."

Later, Papa inherited a little money from a French relative, and he moved the family out of London's East End and into a cottage in the country. He worked on his inventions in a toolshed behind the house. He never made any money, so the daughters all had to go to work as stenographers and salesgirls. Except Lynn. She had to be an actress—and only an actress. "I was thought by my family to be a talented actress from the moment I was born," she says, "and nobody thought of any other destiny for me." A friend of Mama's knew Ellen Terry and arranged an appointment for Lynn.

Lynn called on Miss Terry one morning in September, 1905, at her Georgian house at 215 King's Road, Chelsea. Now that she was old, Miss Terry diverted herself by guiding young ladies who wanted to act. She said she liked being an "encourager." She had a real daughter, Edith Craig, an illegitimate child whom she had had by the architect Edward William Godwin. Miss Terry's marriages and love affairs had long been the scandalous delight of London society. She loved widely, if not well. It was Miss Terry's fantasy to picture herself as a noble mother. But she was wary about whom she took on. Those without talent or beauty, she discouraged—though gently. She once auditioned a plain-looking lady without the slightest sign of talent. Miss Terry said, ambiguously, that one couldn't do well in acting unless one had great talent or great beauty. The lady wrote to thank Miss Terry for the advice. She was relieved to know how valuable beauty and talent were in the theatre. "I feel more encouraged," she wrote. "I have both!"

Miss Terry was lying in bed when Lynn arrived. Lynn stood in the doorway. Ellen Terry beckoned, and Lynn approached. Suddenly Miss Terry stretched out her arms and embraced her. Lynn still remembers the delicious fragrance of Ellen Terry's perfume. Then the maid brought breakfast on a tray. Miss Terry told Lynn to "do something" while she had breakfast. Lynn at once murmured, "The quality of mercy is not strained. It droppeth as the gentle rain from heaven." Miss Terry laughed at the girl's audacity, but she listened. And she was impressed.

"I will give you lessons," she said. "I don't know exactly when, or what hours, or how often, but mind, when I call for you, you must come at once. You must make no other engagements, not even in the evenings, for I may want you to work in the evenings."

Miss Terry believed that a student learned the art of acting by going at a "big" role. She at once put Lynn to studying Cordelia in *King Lear*. She loaned her the play-script she herself had used, with her notes and her underlinings. "I remember a lovely reading she gave me," Lynn says. "I had to say, 'Oh, my dear father,' and I said it, and Miss Terry said, 'No, don't say it like that. You love him. You must say, 'Oh, my deeeere father.' And then she said she would give me no more instructions for Cordelia, because from this one reading of one line she expected me to get the sense of the whole part. During another lesson she said something that gave me the key to acting: 'Think of the meaning of what you are saying and let the words pour out of your mouth.'"

Not only were the lessons free, but Ellen Terry, knowing how hard up Lynn was, gave her 10 shillings a week. She worried about Lynn all the time. After Ellen Terry's death, Miss Craig found this entry in her mother's journals: "Must get Lynn more money. It's wicked. . . . She is so intelligent."

She got Lynn acting assignments, beginning with her debut as a chorus girl on December 26, 1905, in a Christmas pantomime, *Cinderella*, at the Drury Lane Theatre. When *Cinderella* closed in 1906, she got Lynn a walk-on in *Monsieur Beaucaire*. Then on the first day's rehearsal of *Captain Brassbound's Conversion*, Miss Terry fell head over heels in love with her leading man, a handsome American actor, James Carew, twenty-four years old. She was sixty-four. She was addicted to falling madly in love with handsome young men. She sailed to America to tour with Shaw's comedy. She said goodbye to Lynn. There were to be no more lessons now. "That's all I'm going to be able to do for you," she said. "If I helped you any more, it wouldn't be good for your character, for each one runs his own race."

Lynn was not good at racing about the West End and speaking up boldly to theatrical booking agents and producers. She was afraid. She was afraid of strangers. She was afraid even to walk into a restaurant or go to a party. She kept working on her timidity. *I must be brazen*, she'd repeat. *I must be a hussy like other girls or I'll fail.* She applied to H. Beerbohm Tree, who was auditioning girls for *Edwin Drood.* He was looking for youthful types to appear as part of a *crocodile,* a line of children guided by a teacher. He asked her some questions. She said she had played in a pantomime and done walk-ons. He said, "I don't care to hire girls who lack experience."

Lynn replied: "But how will you find girls this young with experience? And how will I get experience if you don't give me work? Am I to go from one agent's office to another and always be told I lack experience and not be able to get it because everybody is as indifferent as you, and does not give me work?"

He was charmed by her outburst and hired her. She was living with two actresses in an inexpensive flat on Victoria Street, in Pimlico. Pimlico borders on the fashionable quarter of Belgravia. When Mr. Tree asked her address, and she said she lived in Pimlico, he told her, "My dear, that's a very unimpressive address. Remember—when anybody asks you where you live, you must say Belgravia!"

So she was an actress now, which is to say that she got trivial parts in trivial plays and was out of work more often than not. There was no progress in the race she had entered and the plays—*Billy's Bargain, Mr. Preedy and the Countess, Lady Frederick*—are now forgotten, as plays written to please the ephemeral taste of an audience are always forgotten when the fashion in theatre alters like the fashion in hats or dresses, for such theatre is created to satisfy a seasonal taste, not to express the personal vision of an author.

But Lynn was an actress and life was blissful, though she would have starved if she hadn't discovered she could make money as an artist's model. In those days, modeling was considered a disreputable profession for a girl, much more disreputable than going on the stage. Lynn posed for magazine and book illustrators at 7 shillings a day. She became the favorite model of Wilfred de Glehn, R.A., and his wife, Jane de Glehn, R.A. Lynn is the girl in *The Blue Coat* by Mrs. de Glehn, and the señorita in *The Spanish Mantilla* by Wilfred de Glehn. Both were hung in the Royal Academy.

At this time there came a serious romantic digression named Edmund Byrne. He was a lawyer. Lynn met him when she went out on a blind-date with Antoinette. There were three men on the date and Antoinette was the prize for whom the men were contending. Because she claimed that Lynn was always falling for "showy" sort of men, she wanted her to meet specimens of the educated class, who also were richer and had prestige. Questions of prestige and money never concerned Lynn, who was a gypsy. Lynn was in one of her capriciously gay moods that evening and was doing impersonations of people she knew and telling wild stories about backstage life. Byrne took her home in a hansom cab. He at once tried to kiss her. She kicked him in the shins. He then wrote a poem about her and gave it to his friend Cyril Lloyd, to give to Antoinette, who gave it to Lynn. Lynn had never had a poem written to her before and she was at once infatuated with Byrne. She considered herself a romantic girl. She wanted to be taken seriously and wondered why people were only amused at her. Now at last, somebody was taking her seriously. They began to see each other often and much later they fell in love and got engaged. "We were planning to get married, but we delayed it because of the war," she says. "I can still see Teddy Byrne in my mind now. He'd be waiting for me to finish modeling in some Chelsea studio. He was tall and quite slim and he had a raincoat draped over his shoulders and he'd be leaning on the Battersea bridge, waiting, looking into the river. Then I'd come out and he'd take me home. I was living in Down Street, in Mayfair. One room. No telephone and no bath, but it had a lovely authentic Adam fireplace. And then I'd change into my one evening gown and we'd go rattling away for the evening. He took me to dinner and dancing at the best places. We'd often go to the Cafe Royale, in Piccadilly Circus—it was fashionable before the first war—and the Savoy Grill, and the Carlton, and a lot to Scott's, and Rules, and to a place called Hatchett's. Hatchett's was such a dear little restaurant—beautiful food, and a band playing, and all the best actresses in town, and society women at their tables with their escorts. Oh, I felt very much a part of the great world."

Byrne wanted her to forsake the theatre. He did not tell his family about her. They would be against his marrying an actress. She could not consider leaving the stage. One morning in October, 1913, the sisters awakened and realized there was no food in the kitchen and that they didn't have any money. They ransacked the apartment and finally Lynn found a threepenny piece under a powder box. A thruppence is good luck. They now discussed what they could buy. Brown bread? A little sugar for their tea? They were getting extremely hungry. 'Toineau had exhausted her credit everywhere, and Lynn's friends were all poor—except for Teddy Byrne. Toineau said, "Why don't you ring up Teddy Byrne and ask him to take us to lunch?" Lynn said suppose he isn't there. They decided to toss a coin. Heads they would buy sugar. Tails she would ring Byrne. It came out tails, and Byrne took them to the Savoy and treated them to an enormous meal. Then, though he disliked having her act, Byrne said he would introduce Lynn to Mrs. Higson, a leading hostess of the period, whose receptions frequently attracted eminent theatrical personalities. She was "at home" on "first Thursdays." Byrne wrote to Mrs. Higson and described Miss Fontanne; then Lynn paid her a formal Thursday call and was invited to the next reception. Here she met Denis Eadie and J. H. Vedrenne, the former an actor of note (he had played Falder in the original production of Galsworthy's *Justice*), the latter one of London's most daring and most successful producers. Eadie and Vedrenne were the producers of London's biggest hit, *Milestones*, by Arnold Bennett and Edward Knoblock. There were already two companies touring the provinces in *Milestones*, and Eadie and Vedrenne were casting a third company. They asked Lynn to read for the part of Gertrude Rhead, a spinster, who is twenty-one in Act I, forty-nine in Act II, and very old in the last act.

Lynn's road company—the White—was the least important. "We played the most obscure theatres in little villages not even on the map," Lynn recalls. "Oh, places with only one train a day and you lived in cheap theatrical digs and ate awful food and it was all one-night stands, and I loved it, I loved it, I loved every moment of it, for experience was what I needed. I was on the road in *Milestones* for six months, and I began to love the road, with all its disagreeable aspects, because I was beginning to do the real work of an actress and making an audience believe in my character. We finished the tour in May and then I knew I had become an actress. Once, we were playing a small town in the Midlands, and Teddy Byrne came up to see me, and then he came back and said, 'But you were good.' You see, he hadn't really believed I had any talent up till then."

Laurette Taylor, who saw Lynn in *Milestones* later, said, "She captured each age so completely I didn't know whether she was in real life a slender thing of eighteen or a skinny woman of eighty."

As soon as the tour ended, Eadie and Vedrenne put her into a new play, *My Lady's Dress,* which opened on April 23, 1914. Then *Milestones* was revived, with Lynn now playing Gertrude Rhead on the West End for the first time. Her performance, quick and bright and flashing with sudden displays of emotion, had a great impact on the little world of Shaftesbury Avenue and the Haymarket. Everybody in the profession now knew the measure of her talent. She became one of those young women who are seen everywhere and about whom one talks with interest and of whom great futures are predicted. But she wasn't thought beautiful; she was too slender for that. It was an age of plumpness. She was 5 feet 6 and weighed only 102 pounds. During this period of intense social whirling in the London of the eve of the war and the blood bath of 1914, Lynn became acquainted with a boy actor with wicked eyes and a wicked sense of humor: Noel Coward. Coward remembers Lynn as a "scraggly, friendly girl with intelligent brown eyes and a raucous laugh." Her eyes are described by other observers of that period as being very large, of a reddish brown color, and beautiful. She was said to be "intelligent," "sensitive," and "full of gaiety."

People watching Lynn Fontanne scintillate at parties never suspected how much of an emotional strain it was for her to mingle with the *haut monde.* She had contrived a trick that helped her: she would brace herself before sweeping into a restaurant or a party, and repeat to herself, *I won't worry about what they think about me and I will only concentrate upon what I think about them. I will look about me and enjoy the others and amuse them by being charming and eccentric and then they will put up with me or even love me.* She was remembering her formula in the late afternoon of an autumn day in 1914, as she and Mrs. Higson stood in the salon of the Marchioness of Townsend. They had come to a tea party—admission five pounds, for the benefit of war relief. There was a crush of hundreds of men and women, and the droning and laughter of a hundred conversations taking place all at once. Many of the guests were queuing up to be introduced to the guest of honor and the main attraction, the American stage star, Laurette Taylor. Miss Taylor had recently opened at the Globe Theatre in her New York hit, *Peg o' My Heart.* It was now London's most spectacular stage success and Miss Taylor was the talk of the town. A society magazine reported: "She is the first American actress to make a complete social conquest of London society. There is no function of importance now given at which she is not one of the most prominent guests."

From a distance, Lynn examined Miss Taylor, who was perched on a divan at the opposite end of the long room. She was not tall or graceful and she was got up in a garish flowered pink satin dress and an enormous black hat with ostrich plumes.

Mrs. Higson linked her arm with Lynn's and pressed toward Miss Taylor. Lynn said she would wait outside. Mrs. Higson insisted Lynn must not be so shy. She must come and meet the glorious lady from New York. Lynn protested that it was not a good moment, now, with all the people swarming around her. Mrs. Higson merged into the crowd and Lynn remained alone, receding into the background and yet unable to take her eyes off Miss Taylor. She thought Miss Taylor seemed unhappy, uneasy—*perhaps she is, underneath, a shy person, and the party is an ordeal for her too.*

A woman sitting beside Miss Taylor vacated her place.

Suddenly, Lynn crossed the room, weaving in and out of the crowd. Miss Taylor's first impression of her was of an alarmingly skinny creature in a little straw hat with two long velvet streamers. Lynn sat down. She spoke nervously:

"It's so hard meeting so many strangers, and all at once like this."

Miss Taylor looked at her again. "How did you know?" she asked, gratefully.

"I'm an actress," she said, "and you can lean on me, for I am very shy as well."

"You are sweet," Miss Taylor said. "What is your name and what have you played in?"

Lynn said she was only a "little actress," and the only important roles she had done were in *Milestones* and——

"Oh, but I saw that," Miss Taylor said. "And who were you?"

Lynn told her.

"But you were marvelous. I'd never have known you were so young." She took Lynn's hand, and asked her: "I've decided to form my own permanent acting company in America. Would you like to come to America and play with me?"

Lynn, assuming it was tea-party badinage, said, "Of course, Miss Taylor, I should love it."

"It's agreed, then," she said airily, and abruptly arose and started to leave. When Lynn didn't follow, she beckoned to her. "Come," she commanded. Lynn followed her. Lynn fetched Miss Taylor's summer ermine coat from the cloakroom. She was dazzled by Miss Taylor's furs, by her limousine waiting outside, and by her air of running the world. As they parted, Miss Taylor said she was giving a supper and dance for some friends at the Grafton Club the day after tomorrow, and would expect Lynn to be there, of course, and to be fashionably dressed. Lynn accepted. She fell at once into the relationship of protégée and master, as she had with Ellen Terry; but Ellen Terry had been soft and considerate, and Laurette Taylor, during the decade of her relationship with Lynn Fontanne, was often to be selfish and cruel and tyrannical, these moods alternating with moods of warmth and kindness. Her implied criticism of Lynn's clothes, for example, was not only cruel and uncalled-for, it was ridiculous, because Miss Taylor—probably the most sensitive actress in American stage history —was, offstage, a woman of awful taste in almost everything, in clothes, in husbands, in her choice of plays. Lynn, on the other hand, always looked elegant, even when she had no money for good clothes. Yet for a long time, Lynn would accept her inferior role in this strange friendship, perhaps because the years with her mother had trained her to play the protégée with an older woman. Laurette Taylor would protect her and promote her—and in return Lynn would swallow disparagement disguised as friendly counsel or good-natured teasing. But Lynn was one of those human beings who grow very slowly in mind and in body; nature seems to slow up the rhythms of such persons, and though she was now older she had the look, the skin, the health, the buoyancy, and the innocence of a girl of sixteen.

But what would she wear to Laurette's party at the Grafton Club? She hadn't a thing to wear. Women are always saying they haven't anything to wear when they have a closet full of clothes, and Lynn did have a closet full of clothes but nothing good enough for Laurette Taylor's ball. For already she idolized Laurette, as she always had to have an actress to worship and serve; she had not had such a goddess since Ellen Terry had fallen in love and gone to America to play in *Captain Brassbound's Conversion*. Ellen Terry had married her young leading man in Pittsburgh. When this shocked London society, Lynn defended her, claiming that even if she *was* three times the groom's age it was still wonderful for him to know such a woman as Ellen Terry.

Lynn had only three pounds in the treasury. She went to shop after shop on Regent Street and Oxford Street and couldn't find the long dress she must have. Then she heard about a shop near Cambridge Circus that sold costumes of musical comedy productions, after the shows closed. She went to the place and bared her heart. She had only three pounds and must, must, must have a beautful gown, because there was a great ball tomorrow night. She got a soiled but lovely old gown, took it home and cleaned it, and wore it to the party.

"I was a great success at the ball," Lynn says. "It's my own Cinderella story, isn't it?"

Lynn became Miss Taylor's constant companion, the satellite to the planet, the confidante of Miss Taylor's problems and pleasures, the eternal protégée. She was backstage at the Globe every matinee and evening. She lived in Laurette's dressing room and dined regularly at Laurette's house in Regent Park. She joined Laurette's ménage (or menagerie), the hurricane of people and excitement in which Laurette moved—the husband and the two children and all the servants and guests and eccentric friends. There were suppers and teas and week-ends at Laurette's country place in Maidenhead, up the Thames. Lynn often wondered about the strange, quiet, thoughtful gentleman who was Laurette's husband, the playwright J. Hartley Manners.

When the Germans began bombing London by zeppelin in 1915, Laurette became a nervous wreck. She couldn't eat or sleep or give her performances. At the end of the year she suddenly closed the show, said goodbye to Lynn at the boat-train, and returned to New York.

Lynn worked a bit here and there in vaudeville but was getting hard up again. Teddy Byrne was fighting in France. She was very lonely and very poor, and her career on the stage was dragging, when Sir Louis Mendl offered her a job as his chauffeur. He was a captain, serving in an army service corps stationed in the west of England. He was the brother-in-law of Elsie de Wolfe, a leader of the international set and the lady who founded the profession of interior decorating before the First World War. Lynn said she couldn't drive a car; Captain Mendl sent her to a school to learn to operate his Studebaker touring car. She learned how to do it all right, except that she never figured out reverse. She always had to have the car backed out and faced in the direction she was going. Lynn found chauffeuring a terrible bore but she didn't go back to London, for there was nothing to do in London. Then a cable came:

WILL YOU COME TO AMERICA? STARTING REHEARSALS NEW PLAY.

COME IMMEDIATELY. SALARY 100 DOLLARS WEEK. CABLE REPLY. FARE
WILL BE SENT YOU. LOVE. LAURETTE TAYLOR.

Captain Mendl was stunned. "But that's 20 pounds a week! Are you
worth such an enormous sum of money?"

Lynn giggled in her throaty manner. "Oh, I imagine they're getting
rather a bargain at that."

What she didn't know was that George C. Tyler, America's leading
impresario, who was producing *The Wooing of Eve*, had refused to
pay her passage. There were hundreds of ingénues in New York
who could play Winifred, he said. But Laurette, determined to have
Lynn with her, insisted that her husband had written the part just for
Miss Fontanne, and that they had to have her, as she was "a very rare
bird." Tyler still wouldn't put up the passage money; so J. Hartley
Manners cabled her the 50 pounds out of his own pocket.

Lynn had already been to America. In 1910, when she played the
maid in *Mr. Preedy and the Countess*, with Weedon Grossmith, a
fat farceur who was a great box-office attraction, a lengthy tour of
Canada and the states was planned. They played two weeks in Canada
and then opened at Nazimova's 39th Street Theatre on November 7.
The reviews were condescending. Lynn's subtle comedic touches were
unhonored and unsung by the drama critics, except for the New York
Dramatic Mirror, which rewarded her with a small pat on the back:
"A capital bit was done by Miss Fontaine* as the maid who demands
40 pounds wages instead of 30 when she learns that Preedy's guest is
neither his wife nor his sister."

The closing notice went up in three weeks. Lynn returned to London with no pleasant memories of New York, for the weather had been
miserable, and no attractive and interesting men with money had
squired her to the elegant cafés and restaurants of the town. Lynn, in
the eyes of that period, was lacking in sex appeal, so there were none
of those champagne-and-caviar suppers at Shanley's and Reisenweber's
with which the rakes of the time indulged actresses and showgirls.
She hardly saw any more of the city, either by day or by night, than
what lay between the theatre and her furnished room near Madison
Square Park. It is the unhappy fate of actors and actresses to travel
all over the world and yet see hardly any more of London, Paris, Rome,
New York, and the cities of the United States, than what lies between the railroad station or the airport and their hotel, and between
the hotel and theatre.

* She was called Lynn "Fontaine" on and off for years in the press.

Getting an American visa and a passport in war time was hard. The Germans, opening their campaign of submarine warfare, had declared the waters around England a military zone and were sinking all ships on sight, including neutral ships. England permitted traveling only on urgent business, and the British Foreign Office did not consider the Klaw & Erlanger production of *The Wooing of Eve* a vital part of the war effort. Lynn's application for a passport was rejected.

"I got it finally," Lynn says, "by falling to my knees and crying and putting on a marvelous scene before a nice old gentleman in some office in Whitehall. Oh, it was the best piece of acting I'd done since *Milestones*. I pleaded and cajoled and ellen-terryed him to the limit of my ability, and to get rid of me he gave me the passport. I got the visa by doing another hysterical scene. Hysteria is so easy to act. A week later I was on a boat to New York. I had $40 when I arrived. I went to a cheap hotel. I didn't have time to change my clothes. I had one suitcase. I put on a heavy sweater over my dress. It was very cold, so I put on an old coat as well. I guess I looked a horror. I got on a trolley car and went uptown to where they were rehearsing. They had rented a rehearsal hall because no theatre was available. They'd been working for a few days."

She made a lamentable entrance. J. Hartley Manners and the cast were seated around a long table. Manners was "holding the book." A short heavy-set man overflowed his folding chair by the table. The door slammed behind Lynn and the fat man brandished a dead cigar at her and told her to get out—there was a rehearsal going on. The gentleman who had extended her this warm welcome wore custom-made clothes but they couldn't hide his big stomach. A broad-brimmed black hat was pulled down over his head. He must be the producer, Lynn thought, the famous George Tyler. *He's little and fat, smokes cigars, keeps his hat on before ladies, and is rude and pompous.*

When Laurette Taylor rapturously embraced Lynn and told Tyler her name, he said that she was a "human scarecrow" and was pigeon-toed. Lynn had been seasick during the whole voyage and had lost a lot of weight. She was even more skin-and-bones than usual.

Laurette assured Mr. Tyler that her protégée was a talent and introduced her to the company, which included Philip Merivale, who was a handsome juvenile, also beginning his career. Lynn sat down immediately and found her place in the script. When she spoke her first lines in a high thin voice, Tyler snarled, "They won't be able to hear her beyond the tenth row of the orchestra." He made one of his muttered speeches about girls fit only for cooking and raising babies who wanted to go on the stage, but Laurette whispered to Lynn to pay no attention.

When Lynn returned to her shabby room and studied the script she felt a sensation of absurdity and horror. She had traveled 3,000 miles through submarine-infested waters to play a stupid role, lacking body and cleverness, in a confused play, a mélange of sentimental light comedy and melodramatic intrigue (though the dialogue was good). She was an ocean away from her lover and her country. She read the play over and over and attempted to analyze it. She was playing Winifred, a girl whose parents are forcing her to marry an older man, Sir Philip Grafton, because he has money and position. Winifred is in love with a young and poor man. Every time Winifred hears Sir Philip's name or a reference to the approaching marriage, she breaks down. In her first scene, the stage directions called for her to burst into tears no less than 19 times! To Lynn it seemed impossible to play this idiotic character straight, but Manners was directing her to play her seriously and she would have to do it.

To anticipate the drama critics—who invariably scorned his plays—Manners subtitled *The Wooing of Eve* "a thoroughly artificial and sentimental comedy in three acts." It opened in Philadelphia on April 10, and closed almost at once, because the Philadelphia critics agreed that it was artificial and sentimental and called it a crashing bore besides, saying that Laurette Taylor as the worldly-wise Eve Alverstone, who rescues Winifred from Sir Philip's tentacles by trapping him in a "compromising situation," came across as an unsympathetic bitch. Manners could do what he liked with the other roles, but it wouldn't do for Laurette to look like a bitch. The play was postponed. Hartley Manners then wrote a less sentimental but equally artificial drama, *The Harp of Life*. It went into rehearsal in July.

There was something about Lynn Fontanne that aroused in outsiders the same desire to improve her that an underdeveloped country inspires in American liberals. Her friends said she must improve her posture and her gait and enlarge her voice. And she should learn ballroom dancing. So she went to a dancing school every day and mastered a waltz, a tango, and a foxtrot. She didn't think she really walked pigeon-toed, but everybody said so, so she concentrated intently on splaying her feet out when she strolled around town. In her room, she would strike a pose before a full-length pier glass, and practice standing, turning, gesturing. She made lists of various postures. She decided one day that there were twelve different ways of standing and she learned all twelve. She invented exercises to make her neck graceful. One of them was to lie on a bed and allow her head to hang downward, then slowly turn her neck from side to side and up and down. She eventually acquired, by these and other exercises, a feline sinuousness of movement in her neck and body.

In discussing the metamorphosis of Lynn Fontanne between 1916 and 1921, Howard Lindsay said that people around Broadway thought of the Lynn of that period as skinny, big-footed, and awkward in motion. Theresa Helburn remembered her as "lacking grace. Her tummy stuck out. We all thought of her as *gauche* and not beautiful, but my goodness she learned how to do it, didn't she? She made herself into one of the most beautiful women of her time and certainly the most beautiful woman in the theatre."

When it came to putting on weight, though, it was hopeless. Laurette Taylor picked on Lynn constantly, calling her a "bag of bones" with "arms as thin as rails." One of her favorite jibes was: "In me, dressmakers lose the pins—on Lynn they bend them."

Laurette believed Lynn could become beautiful only by becoming plumper. Years later, in 1942, she remarked, "Lynn is the only woman I ever knew that twenty pounds turned into a real beauty." Laurette stuffed her with cream sauces and potatoes and sweets but Lynn remained slender. And yet was Lynn really as plain as they all say? We look at the photographs of the Lynn Fontanne of 1917, 1918, and 1919, and to us she appears lovely, with the cool, serene, aristocratic beauty embodied, in recent times, by Grace Kelly. I believe Broadway came to regard Lynn as beautiful in 1921 not because her body had become voluptuous or her neck moved sinuously and her toes no longer turned in, but because a revolution in the feminine ideal had taken place and, suddenly, the slender woman became fashionable, along with bobbed hair, the dropped waistline, and the short skirt. Lynn Fontanne was, so to speak, in the *avant-garde* of this trend. Young American actresses, at least, knew this and admired Lynn's appearance. Ruth Gordon, for instance, who was a young actress at the time, didn't think Lynn gauche or bony. She and her young acting friends regarded Lynn as the epitome of chic and sophistication. They thought her way of dressing and her bearing were *"soignées"* in the best sense of the word. And, mind you, this was all before 1921. "Why, in those years," Miss Gordon once told me, "Lynn was the envy of every young actress. There wasn't one of us who didn't want to look like her and be able to wear clothes like her and be as wonderful on a stage as she was wonderful."

That summer of 1916, Lynn was rehearsing in *The Harp of Life* and becoming more closely intertwined with Laurette in the relationship of disciple and master. She was in complete subjection to Laurette. On weekends she would go up to the summer home of Laurette and Hartley in Tokeneke, Connecticut, on Long Island Sound. Laurette thought that Lynn's constancy to her war lover, fighting in France, was idiotic. Laurette was a compulsive flirt, and had open liaisons with lovers under the eyes of her husband. Laurette criticized Lynn for her "shyness" and her "fidelity" and said that one could not blossom into a great actress without periodic bouts of great passion to vitalize one's erotic energies, which were the source of the vitality one emanated on the stage. She shared with Ellen Terry the theory that one converted—or, in Stanislavsky jargon, one *used*—the emotions stirred up by a new love affair into the artificial situations of the theatre. Lynn was thrown into the arms of various eligible lovers by Laurette, but she was unresponsive. Sometimes Laurette felt it was impossible to make something of this girl who was so hopelessly naive. How surprised she was—and all the others who had observed Lynn during these years—when Lynn became the acme of sophistication in the next decade.

One weekend in August, Lynn remained in town instead of going to Laurette's summer place. She didn't know why she wanted to be in New York by herself; she was filled with fears and anxieties. On Saturday came a cable that Edmund Byrne had been killed in action. He had left her all his money and possessions. Through a lawyer, she transferred the bequest to Byrne's family. She remained anonymous. They never knew how they got the inheritance. They never knew he had been about to marry an actress—he had never spoken about Lynn to his family. She mourned his death in solitary sadness. She did not want any consolation from anybody, not even from Laurette. On Monday she went, as usual, to rehearsal. Something inside her was changed, however, though it took her years to realize consciously what it was. The truth was that Teddy Byrne had been her last chance to live what is known as a normal life, a family life with a husband and children and a home, in which a woman expresses her emotions in the relationship with her family and satisfies her artistic urge by creating a lovely home. Now her only reality was to be in the make-believe imitation of life that is theatre. She became a dedicated actress during her period of mourning, accepting a pattern of life in which everything that happens is either a preparation for a dramatic role or an aftermath of the hours on the stage. *The Harp of Life* opened at the Globe Theatre on Monday, November 27, 1916. Lynn Fontanne was unknown to the theatregoer on Monday. On Tuesday she was a celebrity. She had scored one of those rare overnight sensations, though she played a minor role and was overshadowed by a great actress playing the starring role. She played Olive Hood, a young girl brought up in ignorance of sex. She falls in love with a man having an affair with what Hartley Manners called a "demimondaine," a sophisticated divorcée with her own flat in London, so depraved that she goes to bed with any man she adores. (It is extraordinary that Lynn was able to look like and feel like an ingénue, for a stage direction describes Olive as a "slight spirituelle graceful girl of eighteen." Yet some miraculous gift of nature subtracted years from her chronological age. Lynn didn't look thirty until she was fifty. And then she looked thirty-five until she was seventy. And she says she will go no further. I can't explain it, because there are other women, especially other actresses, who care for their skins and their muscles and conserve their energies as fanatically as Lynn Fontanne does. I can't explain it. I can only record the miracle.) Lynn had two big scenes in *The Harp of Life*. In Act I, Olive Hood has to face up to reality when the man she likes (and who her mother has led her to believe is going to marry her) tells her he has never loved her and doesn't want to marry her. Lynn's reaction of disillusionment veiled by a brisk resignation, all played by this slender creature in a dark, intense, low-keyed style, in contrast to Laurette's ebullient playing, focused the attention of the audience completely. In Act II, she confronts her mother in a long speech that begins, "You make me ashamed of being your daughter" and concludes, "I hate the very word 'mother.' "

Guthrie McClintic, a young actor then, never forgot that night. He recalled Lynn "as a young woman, tall, dark, very thin and angular. She was also English, and she riveted your attention from the moment of her first entrance. Somewhere in the middle of the second act she had a brief emotional scene and so true was she—so touching and so vivid—that on her exit she brought the house down. During the entr'acte her name was on everybody's lips. The following day all the critics echoed the verdict of the opening nighters. A new star was in the firmament."

Persons who have studied Greek in college may forget lines from

Homer and Sappho, but they always remember the often repeated phrase in Xenophon's *Anabasis:* εντευθεν εχελαυνεαι—"from there they marched." The armies were always marching from here to there. A similar phrase recurs in the biographies of actors. "And then she played." "And then he played." "And then they played."

So then she played *Out There* with Laurette. And then she played *The Wooing of Eve* in a new version. And then she played *Happiness* with Laurette. And then she played *A Pair of Petticoats.* And then she played *Someone in the House.*

And each time she cut a new facet and polished it brighter. In *Out There,* she played a crude, vulgar, cockney character. *Out There* was a militaristic play written in white hate by Hartley Manners. He wrote it in two weeks. It was put into rehearsal after he had written Act I. It was a call to the colors, an appeal to American youth to fight Germany. Lynn played an unsympathetic character who thought the war was silly. She fed her mother quantities of gin. She ridiculed her sister's patriotism. She coquetted outrageously with her lover and in one scene she engaged in an amorous wrestling match. It was Lynn's first go at erotic sadism in the theatre and, to everyone's surprise, it "went over" with audiences. Lynn and Alfred were to mingle love and hate many times in many sorts of plays, perhaps most athletically in their version of *The Taming of the Shrew.*

And then she played Winifred all over again in *The Wooing of Eve.* Now she asked the playwright-director if he would permit her to interpret the role differently. She wanted to play the unhappy bride comically. She said Winifred would be "more real" so. "And I am sure I can get good laughs if you will let me do it," she said. She burst into tears only once—the first time the undesirable bridegroom was mentioned. "After that I didn't cry," she remembers. "I'd bite my lip and look wretched as if I were going to—but I didn't. The audience would be waiting for me to cry. They were so on edge. But I held them on edge. And it was so, so funny. And my last entrance, decked out as I was in a bridal costume, wedding veil, orange blossoms, and carrying this prop bouquet with the longest white ribbon trailing miles after me, and you heard me crying long before I came on . . . well it was one of the biggest laughs of my career when the audience saw me as a bride."

And then she played *Happiness,* in which she was a high-strung, gossiping, excitable young society girl who is mad about clothes. She wore many costumes during the play—cocktail dresses and evening gowns and even a leather duster and bonnet (she drove a jazzy sports car, of course) in the last act. And she delivered her speeches—many of which were long block speeches—in short, clipped sentences, which she uttered very fast, very brightly, giving an impression of a glass of sparkling champagne whose bubbles are bursting. In twelve months she had run a remarkable gamut—cockney hoyden, comical virgin, dazzling society belle—and the common opinion, among critics, among actors, among theatregoers, was that she was becoming one of the great technicians of the stage. Laurette wasn't at all jealous of her protégée's success. She enjoyed it. She made her take every curtain call she could get. Laurette could be cruel and malicious in her personal relations with Lynn, but artistically she was sure of herself. Lynn found her amusing and lovable, sometimes, even in their private lives, but usually she was "maddening." On stage, however, Laurette was a dedicated artist. She showed Lynn how to relax on a stage, how never to be afraid if one forget one's lines—one could simply improvise dialogue as long as one felt the character and was relaxed. "We would often ad lib whole scenes during rehearsal," Lynn says, "and sometimes our lines were so good that Hartley Manners would make notes on what we said and put the speeches, word for word, in the script. This is true especially of *Out There* and *Happiness*." Laurette wrote: "While acting with Lynn I forgot we were actresses. We lost our identities completely and became the people of the play."

And Lynn says: "You see, Laurette had played so many years with stock companies in the west and she was accustomed to handling quickly every unexpected situation that might occur during a performance. She showed me how to exploit my resources and how to work spontaneously and not be all tensed up inside. You see, what there was about her was she could be absolutely free about expressing her emotions on stage. She hadn't any fear of doing anything she wanted to do and saying anything she wanted to say. So I saw how you must come to feel completely at home on stage and then you would forget it was a stage."

Among the men experiencing pangs of unrequited love for Lynn was Cyril Harcourt, the British actor. He was to play in *A Pair of Petticoats* and wanted Lynn to play the lead—it would be her first starring role. His motivation was probably as much sentimental as artistic—he would be able to pay court more assiduously during rehearsals. He would also be able to get Lynn away from what he considered the deleterious influence of Laurette and Hartley. But Hartley said *A Pair of Petticoats* wasn't a good play and he strongly advised Lynn to reject Harcourt's proposition—in every sense of the word. So Laura Hope Crews played it in New York, but Harcourt finally got Lynn to play the three-week engagement in Chicago.

Rumors began seeping back to New York that Harcourt had finally broken down Lynn's resistance and that she was going to marry him. George Tyler, who deluded himself into believing that he had "discovered" Lynn, nurtured her talent, and cured her of walking pigeon-toed, was horrified at the thought of Lynn ruining her career by this misalliance. Booth Tarkington, whose plays were produced by Tyler, once described him as "a nearly absolute ruler over the destinies of those who worked for him." The idea of any of his performers getting married without his permission was revolutionary. He at once dispatched a telegram to Lynn ordering her to cease and desist from Cyril Harcourt. Lynn replied:

"When I do get married, trust me to pick either a nice millionaire to back my plays or a nice little playwright—but not Cyril Harcourt! *Don't* you think you could find a good one for me—husband also playwright? You must have several blowing into your office—say you won't accept his play unless he marries me!"

And then she played *Someone in the House*. She played Mrs. Glendenning, a character based on Hermione, who was the subject of short rambling pieces in Don Marquis' column, *The Sun Dial*. The humor of Marquis was gentle. Hermione was the leader of a "group of serious thinkers," lady intellectuals who discussed imagist poetry, Bolshevism, the emancipation of women, Greenwich Village, mystical religions, vegetarianism, and other topics of the day. Using her character as a springboard, three unknown young playwrights concocted a comedy. Two of the three remained unknown. The third was a tall, thin, morose-looking gentleman. He rarely spoke, but when he did, he gave vent to brutally devastating witticisms that would be quoted around Broadway for days. He was the drama news reporter of the New York *Times:* George S. Kaufman. Most of the play concerned the rehearsal of a play—it was a play within a play, for Mrs. Glendenning is staging a play written by her husband, a wealthy industrialist. Hassard Short played the husband. He later became a famous musical comedy director. Lynn said that she and "Bobby" Short learned their lines at once and then began building up their parts, giving themselves pieces of business that were so outrageous and so riotously funny that "we knocked the play sideways. I didn't know enough to hold back. I gave it everything I had and so did Bobby. We ruined the play but we were funny." Kaufman, studying Lynn in his thoughtful, melancholy manner, began to dream of an entire play written about a similar character—a woman who is sweet and generous but a blithering idiot about reality.

John Corbin, drama critic of the New York *Times,* summed up the general feeling about Lynn Fontanne in an article that appeared on September 17, 1918:

Lynn Fontanne's performance as the society hostess in *Someone in the House* marks a step forward in the career of a notable young actress. That she has extraordinary powers of personality has been obvious from the start. It would be a brilliant scene indeed that her entrance did not lift and inspire. But such power tends to bring with it the reputation of being a one part actor; and in Miss Fontanne's case the tendency is increased by her stature and angularity which renders impossible the more obvious physical tricks of impersonation. But the truer art of character interpretation is a thing of the mind; and with each succeeding part it is more evident that Miss Fontanne possesses it in an unusual measure. Her present character is totally different from anything she has done hitherto. The *Sun* has claimed her as the incarnation of Hermione in *The Sun Dial.* She is this and more. With all her smiling impromptu platitudes of culture and uplift, she is a real person, and nowhere more amusing than in the passages where she acts with her equally ridiculous husband—and defends him from the aspersions of others. It is a sound and true impersonation avoiding all temptations to caricature.

In May, 1919, Lynn went to the Hudson Theatre, where George Tyler was holding readings with a group of actors whom he had formed into the George C. Tyler Stock Company. One member of the company was Sidney Toler, then a slender gentleman who played villains; his reputation was made when he became fat and played Charlie Chan in the movies. Lynn was in the wings chatting with Toler. Suddenly, she heard a beautiful voice coming from the stage. She looked toward the stage. She beheld a tall young man, large of face. She listened as he finished what he was reading. His voice had extraordinary resonance and range. She turned to Toler. "Who is that?"

"That," replied Toler, "is a man who is no ordinary actor. He is going far."

"What's he called?"

"Alfred Lunt," was the answer.

THREE

THE COMPONENT PARTS:

ALFRED LUNT

ALFRED DAVID LUNT, a native of Orono, Maine, was a lumber merchant. He moved to northern Wisconsin in 1850, when the pine forests of New England were depleted and the rich Wisconsin woodlands promised money. He made a lot of it, and married the sister of his timber-estimator. Harriet Washburn Briggs came from Hortonville, Wisconsin. She was a beautiful woman and, for her time, quite an intellectual. She had been graduated from Lawrence College, a highly esteemed Wisconsin institution of higher learning. She was a schoolteacher when she married Lunt in 1882. The groom was sixty years old; the bride was twenty-eight. Her first child, Inez, died in 1888. Her second child, Alfred David Lunt, Jr., was born in Milwaukee on August 19, 1892. Mr. Lunt died of a stroke in 1894. Inez had been a lovely infant and her unexpected death from pneumonia had shocked Mrs. Lunt. She went to pieces, suffering a nervous breakdown that lasted almost a year. As a result, she treated Alfred like a fragile piece of antique porcelain. She was terrified Alfred would die, and she never got over Inez's death. She always had photographs of Inez near her. She built a little world of intimacy composed entirely of herself and Alfred. She coddled him. She spoiled him. Once, when Alfred was five, he was playing in the flour barrel. The cook complained to Mrs. Lunt. But she only said, "Why shouldn't he play in the flour barrel? If Alfred wants to play in the flour barrel he probably has a very good reason for playing in the flour barrel, and I approve of it."

Those who knew Mrs. Lunt in the flower of her womanhood say Alfred is like her in his looks—in his height and air of grandeur, in his strong features, in his large brown eyes, in his picaresque temperament, in his imagination, his humor, and his general *joie de vivre*. He can, however, be quite severe in disciplining himself and the actors whom he directs or with whom he plays, and he is a well-organized person with a sense of the value of a dollar and the importance of a budget. This is perhaps a vestigial remnant of his New England heredity.

Mrs. Lunt was a striking and talkative woman who impressed everybody who met her by her elegance and her love of beautiful things. Alexander Woollcott once described her as "looking like a *marquise*. She is the kind of woman who, when she goes into the garden to gather her vegetables, attends to that humdrum duty with silk parasol, high heeled French slippers, and a dash of lip rouge."

Mrs. Lunt's philosophy was summed up in one of Oscar Wilde's aphorisms, which she frequently quoted: "I can do without the necessities of life—but I must have the luxuries."

Among the luxuries she enjoyed was a palatial stone mansion which her husband had built for her at 1701 Grand Avenue in Milwaukee. Grand Avenue was then one of the prettiest residential boulevards in America, and it compared favorably with such noteworthy streets as Commonwealth Avenue in Boston and Lake Shore Drive in Chicago. The enormous Victorian Gothic stone houses were set far back from the sidewalks. Wide expanses of closely cropped lawns stretched before each house in summer. No fences separated the lawns and for three miles "it gave one the idea that he is making his way through a park rather than along a public street." *

Alfred Lunt gave his first public performance in the house on Grand Avenue. He had seen a picture of Cupid in a magazine. This inspired him to undress himself completely. Somewhere he had found a bow and an arrow. Entirely naked, he strode into the front parlor where his mother was entertaining friends at tea. He fitted the arrow to the bow and struck a pose as Eros. Though he was only a child of three or four and showed unusual mimetic ability, the ladies were not amused.

"Unfortunately, I hadn't bothered about wearing a sash and my mother's friends thought I was a badly brought up child, but Mama laughed," Alfred says.

Mrs. Lunt loved entertainment in every form, whether it was Shakespearean tragedy at the Davidson Theatre or the twelve-act bills of vaudeville at the Alhambra. She was unusual, for Milwaukee was "the poorest theatrical city in the United States." Even Sarah Bernhardt

* An anonymous writer in *Harper's New Monthly Magazine,* 1881.

couldn't pack a theatre when she played Milwaukee, a provincial city oriented to family life. (There were more single dwellings in proportion to the population than in any other American city at that time.) The town was dominated by its German-speaking population. The Germans made up three fourths of the population and the Milwaukee River was known as the Rhine. Schools, theatres, and fire companies carried on their business in German and the baseball teams abused the umpires in German. A local journalist boasted in an article in *Cosmopolitan Magazine*, in 1891, that there were no tenement slums in the city, "no thronging rookeries of misery and vice . . . We have more saloons and less drunkenness . . . Nine-tenths of our people drink good wholesome homemade beer and let whiskey severely alone." When he wasn't drinking his home brew, the Milwaukee bourgeois was out with the family in one of the beer parks—the Schlitz Beer Garden was a favorite rendezvous—drinking beer and listening to Viennese waltzes. In spirit, it was always "more a village than a city." In such an unlikely seedbed was germinated the greatest American actor since Edwin Booth.

Mrs. Lunt began taking Alfred to the theatre when he was able to walk. He saw his first show, at the Davidson Theatre, at the age of three. It was *The Golden Horseshoe,* a musical fairy tale, sung and danced and played by a troupe of German-speaking midgets. After this, his mother encouraged his interest in theatre by buying him those colored sheets—sold in England as "penny plain and tuppence colored" —which a child could piece together to make a miniature stage and costumed actors for a currently popular play like *The Corsican Brothers* or *Mazeppa.* A condensed script was provided so that children could lisp out the dialogue as they moved the little toy actors on the toy stage. Alfred's toy theatres were so durably constructed that they survive, after 60 years, and are exhibited at the Museum of the City of New York. At six, he began keeping a scrapbook of his favorite actors and actresses. There are more pictures of Ellen Terry than of anybody else—Miss Terry as Portia, as Beatrice, as Ophelia, as Imogen. Now there is an eerie resemblance between Lynn Fontanne's beauty and Miss Terry's. I remember when I first saw Sargent's portrait of Ellen Terry as Lady Macbeth at the Tate Gallery. I had the feeling I was seeing someone I already knew and knew quite well. It was only after I had been staring at the portrait for a long time that I knew of whom the subject reminded me. It was Lynn.

In one of his early scrapbooks there is a record of his own production of *Rip Van Winkle,* given by the "Lunt Stock Company" at "Lunt's Wisconsin Theatre" in 1901! Alfred was the scenic designer, the director, the "general manager," and, of course, the star. The "theatre" was in the attic across the street at the Alexander home. Louis Alexander was the owner of a paper mill, and had had business connections with Alfred's father. Mrs. Alexander allowed Alfred to do anything he wanted in the way of theatrical effects. Once, in a production of *The Count of Monte Cristo,* he decided, being a realist, to use real earth and grass; he dug up squares of sod, and, dripping lumps of earth, brought them upstairs. The Alexanders' daughter, Pauline, was a slender girl with long naturally golden hair. She adored Alfred, and they continued to be romantic about each other for many years. When she was sixteen, she was riding in a motorboat on Lake Oconomowoc, when the engine burst into flames. She jumped into the water and was drowned.

Alfred almost died when he was twelve. He came down with acute appendicitis, and when peritonitis set in, the doctor sent him home from the hospital. Mama asked, "Dr. Levings, is Alfred going to die?" The doctor said that his condition was serious.

"If Alfred dies, you die," she said menacingly.

Dr. Levings changed his mind about sending Alfred home. He operated, removing the appendix and one kidney. Neither the doctor nor the patient died.

Like Lynn's father, Mrs. Lunt admired Dickens. She read to Alfred— *Oliver Twist, David Copperfield,* and *Great Expectations*—until he was seven. Then he read alone and went to theatres alone. It is likely that Alfred sharpened his congenital sense of farcical exaggeration by mimicking the dialect and exaggerations of Dickens' characters. By contrast with his life at home, Alfred's schooling—mainly at the Milwaukee Academy, a private school—was dull. He was bad in all subjects, especially Latin and mathematics. Though he worked hard at elocution it was many years before he finally won the annual declamation prize reciting Wolsey's monologue from *Henry VIII.* The *Milwaukee Journal* reported: "The John C. Davis medal was awarded to Master Alfred Lunt at the 27th annual prize declamation contest of the Milwaukee Academy last night at Plymouth Church. The contest was attended by a large audience."

When Alfred was seven, his mother married Carl Sederholm. He was a tall, dark, suave man of the world, and an excellent physician. He was cultured and witty; he spoke fluent Finnish, Swedish, and

German. He loved the theatre and opera, and when the Metropolitan Opera played Chicago he took Alfred to hear *Faust*. He played the piano well, and sang in a rich baritone voice. He drove a pair of fine matched black horses. He was a warm, affectionate person, and Alfred admired and loved him and wanted to be like him. Dr. Sederholm had the American passion for stock speculation, and put a lot of money into Michigan copper stocks. Mrs. Sederholm encouraged the speculations, but eventually all the money left by the elder Lunt was lost in mining stocks. The Grand Avenue mansion was sold. In 1905, Dr. Sederholm became very ill. He suffered great pain and had to walk with a cane. He thought that the sauna baths and cold clean air in Finland would benefit him, and he hoped also to make a fresh start in life there. So he went on a Scandinavian trip and took Alfred with him—he had taught him to speak Swedish and Finnish. While in Helsingfors, Alfred played Ibsen with an amateur dramatic group in the original Norwegian! In 1909, he and his stepfather were staying at the Hotel Kemp in Helsingfors. The doctor went to bed early. About 4 A.M., Alfred was awakened by the noise of heavy snoring from his stepfather's bed. The sounds ceased. He went back to sleep. On awakening at 7:30, he called his stepfather. There was no answer. He called again. No answer. He shook him, and then he realized the man had died during the night, and that the noises he had heard must have been the death rattle. Alfred rang for the clerk. He came in and Alfred pointed to his stepfather, but could not speak a word of Finnish. His Swedish and Finnish did not return for many years. The shock had driven them clean out of his mind.

Though now a poor widow with three small children—"my three Finns," she called them—Mrs. Sederholm refused to let Alfred work in a Milwaukee factory. He must go to college. She proposed that he enter Carroll College in Waukesha, Wisconsin. Carroll College in 1911 was a small school with a faculty of 14 and a student body of 110. She would make ends meet by operating a boarding house in Waukesha, then a famous watering place of the middle west. Its mineral springs drew tourists from a dozen states; White Rock Mineral Water came from Waukesha; Fox Head 400 Beer, whose unusual piquancy appealed to connoisseurs, was brewed with Waukesha water. Mrs. Sederholm rented a large frame house at 101 N. Hartwell Street and College Avenue, three blocks from Carroll. Her boarding house project was handicapped because she knew absolutely nothing about cooking. She had never prepared a meal in her life or done housekeeping, so she went about asking relatives and friends for recipes. Even when she got recipes, however, she found cooking difficult. Finally she took in a young Japanese student, Yosi, who was to cook in return for his room and board. The first day he began working he prepared a tureen of Indian pudding—enough to make dessert for twenty people. He put it outside to cool on the back porch. Then he absently stepped right into the tureen when he went out to hang up some wet laundry. After that, Mrs. Sederholm would always say, "I don't think Yosi's much use really. All he can do is step into the pudding." Mrs. Sederholm did not know very much about making beds and about washing and ironing. She was never able to learn how to iron sheets and pillowcases, let alone shirts. She had had three children by the doctor—Karin, Louise, and Carl, Jr. Karin and Louise, who were eight and ten years old, had to learn how to iron and they did all the ironing, just as Alfred had to learn the art of cooking, which eventually became his favorite sport.

Mrs. Sederholm had strange ideas about housekeeping. Once, when a neighbor complained of being worn out by the Monday washing, she smiled and shrugged her shoulders. "I don't know why people talk about being worn out by laundry," she said gaily. "I find it so pleasant and easy. I go outside and wash a bit and then I come in and sit down and play the piano a bit, and then go out and wash some more and then I come in and read a little while, and the time passes so pleasantly."

Alfred did the shopping and the cooking and operated the business of checking the guests in, making them comfortable, and seeing that they paid their bills. He also reared his two half-sisters and his half-brother. Mrs. Sederholm was bored by discipline and child care. She had no patience. And she could not stand diseases. She regarded even the common cold as an insult. She would make long, rambling, philosophical speeches to the children when something went wrong, leaving it to Alfred to discipline them, get them to bed, and give them their medicines. Once, all three came down with whooping cough at one time. Alfred was up for two nights nursing them through the crisis. He trudged wearily into the kitchen one morning to make a pot of coffee. Mrs. Sederholm bustled in and began singing merrily. Alfred looked up at her. "In God's name," he said, sighing, "please don't have any more children!"

To Mrs. Sederholm, life was a comedy. She loved fun and games.

For instance, she had saved, from the debacle of her second marriage, a set of beautiful Dresden china. When guests came out on a weekend and she served dinner, it would amuse her to ask one of the guests to help wash the dishes. In the kitchen she had an old set of cheap dishes. She would hand the guest several of the old cracked plates and tell him to hurl them on the floor. Then she would go back into the dining room and wait for the crash of dishes and enjoy the looks of horror as the visitors thought the good Dresden china was breaking.

Not that she minded if the good china was broken. Carl, Jr., loved shooting. She let him set up a sort of shooting gallery in the house. The dining room and kitchen were in a straight line and if the back door was open you could pin a target to the woodshed outside and have an excellent shooting range. Carl frequently missed and bullets would go flying into the china press. Once he smashed a rare piece of Dresden— a soup bowl. Mother laughed uproariously. She said, "You can't shoot any more in the house—unless you aim perfectly." She wrote a humorous poem about the incident. She often wrote humorous poetry and prose, but she never succeeded in publishing any of her works. Considering the burdens he had to shoulder, it is amazing that, in his freshman year, Alfred got 85 in English, 82 in History, 81 in Mathematics, 95 in Bible, and 95 in Oratory.

The term "oratory" at Carroll meant the courses given by May Nickell Rankin, who had the title "Professor of Literary Interpretation and Dramatic Literature." She was a tall, bony spinster with eyeglasses and an insane passion for the theatre. She regarded the drama as "the most universal of the arts." And she taught her students to revere the Greek and Elizabethan playwrights and to make contact with those writers, like Ibsen and Strindberg and Shaw, who were breaking new ground. She imbued Alfred with a conviction of the grandeur of the theatre. She seized upon his inborn genius for dramatic art and encouraged him to believe that he was a man with a mission. Small as Carroll College was, she staged six productions every year. Alfred was the leading man in all her plays. He designed, built, and painted the scenery. At a time when the plays of Shaw and Ibsen were still considered scandalous, Miss Rankin was putting them on in Waukesha with Lunt playing leads. In class she gave Alfred the freedom to improvise. He would take a few lines of comic verse and then see if he could draw it out by pantomime so it would play for ten minutes. He remembers once reciting

> Sittin' on a log and fishin',
> Sittin' all day and fishin',
> Sittin' all day and wishin',
> Comin' home and lyin'.

He made this into a long dumb-show in which he created a charade of a man digging for worms, threading a line, putting a worm on a hook, casting out, retrieving, casting again, looking wretched and continuing to fish. Alfred remembers that Miss Rankin never bawled him out or found fault with him, perhaps because he always played so perfectly. She gave him free rein when he was designing a production. In one play there was a snow scene and he coated the upstage windows with a hundred pounds of rock salt to make it look authentic. He always used period chairs and tables and authentic props for every scene, and he and his cohorts would pillage the best houses in town when it was necessary to furnish a parlor for a Victorian domestic drama. In *Cricket on the Hearth*, a character has to enter, carrying an infant. "Think we used a doll?" Alfred says. "Oh, no. I went out and borrowed a six-month-old baby. I tell you we were realists, we were. You know, the word 'inspiring' is so often used about a teacher but that is what May Rankin was, inspiring. And you have to know this was no college like Yale or Harvard, that had intellectual students. Most of the students were farm boys, from around the county. Well, inside of a month, May Rankin would have these big shy farmers reciting speeches from Shakespeare and loving it. And by God she'd make them do it with gestures and put feeling into the lines. I'll never forget once in class she was trying to show us how an actor has to relax and she said, 'Now I want you all to do your hands like a handkerchief.' Can you imagine a room full of rough, tough sons of bitches doing their hands like handkerchiefs? Well, they did. She was a great woman."

Alfred's best friend was Ray Bennett Weaver, later an English professor at the University of Michigan. Professor Weaver remembers the youthful Alfred as an idealist with a sense of a mission in the theatre. The theatre was to take the place of a religion in the world of the future. The theatre was to be the new church in which men worshiped. Ray and his older brother Andrew (later head of the Speech Department at the University of Wisconsin) lived at Mrs. Sederholm's boarding house. Like Alfred they played in the campus productions. Alfred was, from the beginning, obsessed with the smallest detail of any character he was playing, and, recalls Ray Weaver, he would often take as long as three hours to make up his face. "He painted a character on his face as if he were a Rembrandt painting a portrait." Yet, though he dreamed of pursuing a serious career in the theatre, Alfred found that it was his comical scenes that went over with the students. When he gave a reading of Poe's "Telltale Heart," for instance, the class roared with laughter. By his second year at college, Alfred had worked up a program of impersonations and comedy characters and he was giving concerts all over Wisconsin. He went out with one unit that included the Beloit College Glee Club and played a three week tour in towns along the route of the Atchison, Topeka and Sante Fe line, which kept its celebrated Harvey girls entertained with clean and up-lifting diversions. He also was being booked as a single. His circular read:

ALFRED DAVID LUNT
Character Artist

Mr. Lunt has for several years been one of the most successful impersonators on the platform. He has appeared with both the Carroll College and the Beloit College Glee Clubs and his work has always met with unstinted praise wherever he has gone. Now for the first time he announces himself in complete programs which will satisfy the demand for high-class amuse-ment. He will please any audience who is fortunate enough to hear him. Those who enjoy real rollicking fun of the most wholesome kind will find their demand satisfied. . . . Mr. Lunt is without a peer in his representa-tions of the songs and dances that give Harry Lauder such high place among artists of our time.

Besides doing a take-off on Lauder—in kilts, silver-buckled brogue shoes, a knobby cane, and a thick Scottish accent—he also created sev-eral original characters. There was Miss Tiny Daley, costumed in a long green dress and an absurd red wig adorned with a flowered straw hat. Another character was a Swede, a lonely Swede, done with a fine Swedish accent. The Swede played a harmonica, which Alfred at once set himself to master so he could be perfect in the character. His *tour de farce,* however, was the Mother Goose Sermon. He came out in clerical costume. He struck a hellfire evangelist's pose and preached a sermon, using as his text a Mother Goose jingle, for example, Humpty Dumpty.

"Brothers and sisters," he would cry, "let us consider that miserable sinner, I mean Dumpty, yes, Humpty Dumpty, and let us look into the black heart of Dumpty, evil Dumpty. 'Humpty Dumpty Fell off a Wall.' Now what does this mean? I repeat—what does that signify for us? How did he fall? Was he pushed? And who pushed him off that wall? I say it was Satan himself pushed him off that wall. What was Humpty Dumpty doing sitting on that wall, when he should have been in church praying for his soul's salvation? I'll tell you what miserable Dumpty was doing on that wall. He was doing the devil's work. He was boozing up there and gambling and playing around with scarlet wimmen and the wages of sin was death and Humpty Dumpty collected his wages, brothers and sisters, when the devil gave him that shove."

In his third year of college, Alfred transferred to the Emerson College of Oratory in Boston. It was May Rankin's alma mater. Alfred attended classes for two days. Then he walked in cold to see George Henry Trader on Saturday. Trader directed plays at the Castle Square Theatre on Washington Street and Castle Square in Boston, and had once put on shows for the Pabst Stock Company at the Pabst Theatre in Milwaukee. Trader said, "Yes?" Alfred said, "I want to go on the stage."

"Can you start rehearsing Tuesday?"

The Castle Square Theatre, headed by the actor-producer John Craig and his wife, Mary Young, then boasted one of the finest stock companies in the United States. Though it was situated under the elevated tracks and in an unwholesome quarter of cheap saloons and bordellos, the Castle Square was a favorite family theatre. It put on first-class productions at popular prices. Ruth Jones, an aspiring actress from Wollaston, Massachusetts, remembers going there during this period and paying only fifty cents for the best seats in the orchestra at matinees. Miss Jones later became Ruth Gordon, star and playwright.

Doris Olsson, the leading lady of the 1912-1913 season, remembers the first day of rehearsal of that season. The rehearsal took place in the balcony lobby. On a staircase sat a young man, holding the script and prompting the actors when they forgot lines. He spoke in a peculiar way, with a distinctive Swedish twang, and Miss Olsson, herself a Swede, was sure Alfred was of Swedish descent.

Alfred made his debut in *The Aviator* on October 7, 1912, in the part of Joe Hurley, a sheriff. On the program, his name was misspelled as "Mr. Alfred Hunt." He had devoted a whole afternoon to bronzing his face, fixing up an authentic goatee, penciling in wrinkles, pouching his eyes. In three hours in a dressing room he added forty years to his appearance, and he had the shuffling gait and cracked voice to go with it. John Craig now put him in character parts exclusively, in elderly character parts as often as possible. In the three years he was a member of the Castle Square stock company he rarely played any character less than fifty years old. He usually played doddering grandfathers and kindly uncles or ancient rascally bankers who held mortgages on farmhouses. (The mainstay of the Castle Square repertoire was the blood-and-thunder melodrama, *Blue Jeans, Secret Service, The Great Ruby, Under Two Flags, A Trip to Chinatown, The Girl of the Golden West, The Ninety and Nine, Madame X.* There were frequently productions of Shakespeare to raise the artistic level and occasionally one of the works of Clyde Fitch or Sir Arthur Pinero was produced.) Sometimes, when Alfred was lucky, he was able to play a middle-aged character. The stars always played the hero even if the star was several decades older. And Alfred was never cast as a juvenile second lead because in those days muscular, curly-haired men—usually with dimpled chins—were considered the juvenile type. Alfred was too tall, too thin, and too "eccentric" in his movements. "Oh, I saw that I must be a very ugly young man," Alfred says, "but I decided not to let this stand in my way and I became an expert in theatrical senility. I could give you any age from forty-five upwards and come to the exact year you wanted. I spent much time studying the use of wigs. I could do wonders with crepe hair. I got a raise the fifth week—from $5 to $20 a week, and that was all I ever received, but the training and the discipline were priceless to me."

In those days, stock company actors were worked like common laborers. Alfred played a matinee and evening show six days a week. And while he was playing this week's production, he was rehearsing next week's. Rehearsals took place in the morning and then again after the evening performance. He customarily put in a sixteen hour day. Once he was playing a telegraph operator—a very old telegraph operator, of course—in *Secret Service.* He was also rehearsing Ludovico in *Othello.* He'd get home in a state of exhaustion at two in the morning, and in order to keep himself awake while learning his lines, he would sit in a bathtub filled with ice-cold water. Through chattering teeth, he would roar out the iambic pentameters, trying alternate readings of certain lines. At the time, Alfred lived in a furnished room in the home of Kenneth Conant, a Harvard College art professor. When Lunt's nocturnal ablutions and soliloquies got on the professor's nerves, Alfred rented a room in the ménage of Al Roberts, one of the Castle Square directors. Here he could rehearse in cold water as often as he wanted. He could also keep a gas-burner in his room. (He was living as meagerly as possible so he could send Mama five dollars a week.)

A sister of Al Roberts, an actress in the stock company (she later married Charles Bickford), became concerned about Alfred's ascetic diet, and tried to get him to spend more money on food or to eat with the family, but Alfred was too proud. She couldn't understand why he would starve himself and then do something wild like buying a fur-lined overcoat and a fur hat just because he was playing a Russian role and wanted to look right in the part. He was also going through a sort of Slavic phase, at that time, in which he was melancholic and seized with a sense of the futility of life. He pondered on the apparently hopeless abyss between his idealistic vision of the stage as a poetic uplifter of the human soul and the everyday reality of the vulgar melodramas in which he was usually playing.

But he was secretly saving himself for a glorious future which would eventually come, and the Slavic melancholy was a part of his resistance to the commercial theatre in which he had to exist—temporarily, of course. He even bought, at a Salvation Army boutique, a relic of old Russia—a cracked four-poster bed decorated with gaudy peasant designs. He was obsessed with the theatre and went to see every New York company that played in Boston. He saw all the stars of the time —George Arliss, Henry Miller, Ruth Chatterton, Ina Claire, Rose Stahl, Wilton Lackaye (as Fagin in *Oliver Twist*), William Faversham as Antony, William Hodge (playing the title role in *The Man from Home*, the Booth Tarkington-Harry Leon Wilson comedy which was the most successful American play of this period and ran five years). He also saw a production of *Milestones* in Boston, at about the time Lynn was touring with it in the English provinces. He often went to the movies. The movies were new then and consequently exciting. During the dinner break, Alfred and several of the younger members of the troupe would pile into an open Oldsmobile roadster, owned by Carney Christy, an actor, and roar through Boston and then go to see a movie. Watching a play or a movie, Alfred always made mental notes on technique. Mabel Colcord, who was a leading lady at the Castle Square, was struck by the way Alfred would hover in the wings and stare out at the audience when he wasn't in a scene. When the audience reacted—either with a sudden burst of laughter or with that intake of breath that the actor knows means rapt attention—he would try to figure out what had taken place on the stage that had stimulated this response. He thought of his métier, his art, as a communication between the actor and the audience, and he therefore studied not only the tactics and the strategy of the actor, but also the responses of the audience.

And he became a maniacal perfectionist about rehearsing. Once, he played the rich villain in *Maggie Pepper,* a drama of social realism by Charles Klein. Miss Olsson was Maggie, the virtuous heroine. He always wanted to go over their big scene "just one more time." He gave her no rest. If she tried to sequester herself in her dressing room, his timid knock would be heard and then "we'd have to do it again. I remember one piece of business where he was out to 'get' me and he had this cigar jammed in his mouth and he had to snarl, *I'll be waiting for you, Maggie,* then he had to exit and slam the door behind him. He literally counted his steps to match his words. We did his exit so many times with Alfred slamming the door so many times that finally Mr. Craig, whose office was below my dressing room, told us to go and rehearse someplace else as we were driving him out of his mind. I never knew any actor, let alone one so young as Alfred, who planned every step, every gesture, every syllable, every motion, and repeated it until it was perfect."

During Christmas week he played a dragon in *The Gingerbread Man.* He wasn't satisfied just playing a dragon in a dragon costume. He had to breathe smoke. He lit a smudge pot inside the dragon and belched clouds of smoke. At one performance the dragon caught fire and Alfred almost died of suffocation.

In another show, a piece of pastry called *Merely Married,* he played the husband of Mabel Colcord. They operated a hotel. Business was bad so they scattered broken glass on the highway to cause flat tires and bring tourists into the hotel. Every time there was an offstage blowout, Alfred would grab Miss Colcord in a bearhug and then shriek insanely and whirl her around the stage. Audiences loved the improvisation, and Alfred and Mabel kept building it up; the audience roared so loudly that the other actors stood in the wings to watch this wild piece of acting. It was the sort of frenzy Alfred and Lynn were to play many times.

In 1914, Alfred came into an inheritance of $30,000 from his father, which had been held in trust. Mama at once wanted to splurge on a grand tour of Europe. Alfred said that they must hold on to the money for the sake of the children, but he finally took her on a Scandinavian cruise. The war broke out and they had to come back as steerage passengers on a tramp liner. It was at this time that he bought some property in Genesee Depot, a peaceful hamlet six miles from Waukesha. On three acres of timbered land and rolling hills, Alfred built a four bedroom house to his own design. It was like country houses he had seen in Finland and Sweden. The entire family moved in in February, 1915. The house built, Alfred planned all the color schemes and bought antique furniture. He now felt that no matter what happened, at least Mama and the three children would have a place to live. He was already sending Karin to Lawrence College. In his mind, he was the father of the three children. He had assumed the family responsibility. He was in Genesee Depot when he got a call from his agent telling him to go to Chicago and read for the leading role opposite Margaret Anglin, who was touring in *Beverly's Balance*. Miss Anglin was a wonderful romantic actress of this period. She played Shakespearean roles and the Greek classics, and had first done Ruth in *The Great Divide*. She was touring the middle west and would play a six week season of Greek tragedy at the outdoor amphitheatre in Berkeley, California. Her leading man had suddenly quit in Chicago, and the scenic designer recommended Alfred Lunt. Alfred came up to Chicago and read for the part. He read for Miss Anglin's stage manager, a young gentleman named Howard Lindsay. Lindsay thought Alfred was terrible, an opinion which Lindsay now admits was one of the most colossal misjudgments in the history of Broadway. He thought Alfred's voice was hollow and that it broke badly; that his movements were awkward and that his hips jutted out asymmetrically. His shoulders were stooped. Altogether a "most awkward, ungainly, ugly chap." Hopeless to imagine him ever becoming a professional actor. Lindsay wanted to send him packing straight back to Wisconsin. Miss Anglin insisted on hearing the young man read herself. She at once hired him for $50 a week.

"I think this boy has quality," she told Lindsay. "He will go far. True, he is ugly, but it is a handsome ugliness, rather like that of the Vanderbilts!" (The sons and grandsons of Cornelius Vanderbilt were notorious for large faces with bad features and unusually enormous and repulsive noses. However, their hundreds of millions of dollars gave them an aura of masculine beauty in the eyes of many women.)

Now, at last, Alfred felt that he was really an actor, playing important roles opposite an important star and touring in one-nighters in St. Louis, Cedar Rapids, Fort Dodge, Sioux City, Cheyenne, Denver, Winnemuca. . . . By the time they got to San Francisco, even Howard Lindsay was beguiled by Alfred's "natural sense" for comical mimetics.

Attempting, once, to define Alfred's comic genius, Lindsay told me: "Well, it's just that he *thinks* funny. I remember once casting a show, and Billy Gilbert, who was not established at that time, applied for a part, and I asked him what he did and he cocked his head at me and said, 'I scare funny.' Now with Alfred—he thinks funny. It's not anything that can be taught to a young actor. You are either born with the ability to think funny or it is hopeless and you can never acquire the knack of it."

In Berkeley, at the Greek Theatre, Alfred played Jason to Miss Anglin's Medea, and Achilles in *Iphigenia in Aulis*. The stage was 340 feet long. As Achilles, Alfred, who was extremely skinny, was loaded down with heavy armor. Lindsay has never forgotten Alfred's grand entrance. He looked like a conquering hero "about eight feet tall, and then by the time he crossed the stage, with the armor weighing him down, he was sagging more and more, so by the time he got to the position for his first speech he resembled a midget."

In *Electra*, Miss Anglin had Alfred play the spirit of decadent Greece in a prologue. Alfred didn't know what she had in mind, so he resorted to a decadent Greek wig. At the first rehearsal, Miss Anglin cried: "No, no—that won't do. I never saw a more normal American boy. You don't look the least bit decadent."

So Alfred gilded his hair and his nipples, painted his fingernails and toenails red, and draped vineleaves in his hair. He got two members of the company to be assistant deviates. He painted *their* fingers, toes, hair, and breasts. Now he came on obviously drunk and embracing two Grecian boys.

"I am sure we shall all be arrested," Miss Anglin said, laughing. "But we will do it—though it is a bit more *fin de siècle* than I had in mind, Alfred."

Alfred returned to Genesee Depot after the Greek revivals, but he got a wire from Howard Lindsay offering him a part in *Green Stockings*. NOT FOR LESS THAN ONE HUNDRED DOLLARS A WEEK, he wired Lindsay. Miss Anglin gave him the money and then she told Laura Hope Crews about Alfred. Miss Crews was looking for somebody to play with her in a vaudeville sketch. It was a part of nineteen "sides" and he had one day to get up in it "letter perfect," she told him, as she had to open in Philadelphia "tomorrow." He assured her he could do it. Like Miss Anglin, she was at once taken with Alfred's looks and charm. At this phase of his life, he was irresistible to aging actresses. Miss Anglin was twenty years older than he; Miss Crews was twenty-four years older; and Lily Langtry, to whom Miss Crews tenderly bequeathed her vaudeville partner, was forty-four years older than Alfred. Miss Langtry wanted a young actor to play with her in a thirty minute dramatic sketch in vaudeville. Miss Langtry, who had been the greatest beauty of her time in England during the 1880's, was now in her sere and yellow. Oscar Wilde had once called her the reincarnation of Helen of Troy, and declared, "I would rather have discovered Lily Langtry than America." Sarony, a Fifth Avenue society photographer, once paid *her* $500 for the privilege of taking her picture. She was enraged when he showed her the proofs: "You have made me pretty," she cried. "I am beautiful."

She had had so many love affairs with royalty that she was called "the sport of kings." She was a terrible actress but whenever she was in want of money—usually between royal protectors—she played a season on the stage or in vaudeville. But now it was 1916 and she was a fat, shapeless female; and yet her face was still beautiful, for all her sixty-three years, and her blue eyes were the bluest Alfred had ever seen. "She used to bead them with blue wax for the stage," he recalled. She took it for granted—as had Margaret Anglin and Laura Hope Crews—that Alfred would be her lover as well as her leading man. The legitimate theatre really was a far more immoral place in those days, though the plays themselves were more innocent than contemporary plays. Despite her advanced years, Lily Langtry was still an arrogant and emotionally imperious woman. It was difficult enough for Alfred to be her lover, but she also expected him to dance with her for hours before they made love. She had a phonograph in her hotel suite and she played tangoes and held Alfred in her arms and breathed heavily as they danced, stroking his hair and kissing him. She could have danced all night—and often did. Playing four shows a day in vaudeville was far less exhausting than satisfying Miss Langtry. But he did his best. The sketch, *Ashes,* was about an unscrupulous lover who blackmails a rich married woman with some "compromising" letters she had once written him. The critics jeered at the obvious age disparity between the woman and her lover. One critic wrote, "When did she give him the letters—when he was in the cradle?"

They opened at the Orpheum Theatre in San Francisco on September 7, 1916; also on the bill was a husband and wife team, Harry and Emma Sharrocks. They had an act called "Behind the Grandstand," in which they played two mind-readers. Alfred was fascinated by their act and tried to figure out how they "coded" information to each other by means of simple questions and answers.

It was not until October 17, 1917, when he was twenty-five years old, that Alfred finally made his Broadway debut, opening at the Harris Theatre in *Romance and Arabella,* an episodic comedy about a Westchester widow who engages in a series of amatory escapades. Alfred appeared in one scene, playing Claude Estabrook, a Greenwich Village bohemian, poet, and exponent of what used to be called "free love." He made love to Laura Hope Crews (who played the merry widow) on a divan, while her aunt was concealed underneath. It would be nice to report that the astute New York drama critics hailed the birth of a great new American acting talent. The fact is that Lunt was ignored by many of the reviewers while the others contented themselves with a few words toward the end of their notices, giving him such faint praise as "did capital work" and "notably good." The New York *Sun*'s anonymous reviewer wrote: "Mr. Lunt has given us the most amusing character acting of the season." This, alas, was not very much of a compliment. The season was five weeks old. Lunt says:

"I did an interesting piece of business in *Romance and Arabella.* I remembered something Mrs. Fiske did when she played *Tess of the d'Urbervilles.* After she kills her lover, she calmly goes and combs her hair. So after I did all this lovemaking with Miss Crews, I went and combed my hair. I kept on combing it and combing it like a machine. Well, it was terribly funny to the audience. I didn't say a word. Just combing, combing, combing."

At a matinee of the show, Alexandra Carlisle was in the audience. She was playing the lead in *The Country Cousin,* a comedy by Booth Tarkington and Julian Street, and was looking for a leading man to go with her on tour. She was taken with Alfred and recommended him to the producer, George C. Tyler. Tyler thought it was a ridiculous suggestion, as Lunt was known around Broadway strictly as a man for eccentric, offbeat parts. After a long argument, Tyler consented to audition Alfred. But Alfred was back in Genesee Depot. Why not ask Margaret Anglin if he was qualified, suggested Miss Carlisle. Miss Anglin was out on the road. Tyler dashed off a wire asking her opinion. Miss Anglin dictated a reply to Howard Lindsay. She carefully ticked off, one by one, all of Alfred's sterling qualities. Reading over her message, she sighed, "It's like recommending a servant."

Tyler then got off a wire asking Alfred to name his terms. The station-master, who was also the telegraph operator, telephoned Alfred and read him the good news. Lunt, on the phone, dictated the collect reply: WILL BE GLAD TO COME. SALARY TWO HUNDRED A WEEK. The next day came a reply: REPORT FOR REHEARSALS JUNE 17. ONE HUNDRED AND FIFTY DOLLARS ENTIRELY SATISFACTORY. GEORGE TYLER.

"But I asked for two hundred," Lunt said to the telegrapher.

"Now, see here, young feller," the telegrapher snorted, "I didn't send him that crazy price. I wired him asking for one hundred and fifty dollars."

"But why?"

"I felt you were pricing yourself awful high. Last time you sent a wire you only asked a hundred. Didn't want you to lose the job."

Alfred at once set to studying the script. He was playing George Tewkesbury Reynolds III, an Eastern fop. Accompanied by Ray Weaver, Alfred went to Chicago, and, a realist in even small details, ordered engraved calling cards for George Tewkesbury Reynolds III. He bought four suits of clothes at Marshall Field. He then went shopping for a cigarette case, since the character lighted a cigarette in one scene; he found a handsome golden case and had it engraved G T R III.

Weaver was shocked by this insane prodigality. "You could go into any five-and-dime store and buy a cigarette case made of tin, and who'd know the difference?"

"I would," Alfred said, smiling.

The Country Cousin had an involved and melodramatic plot and was one of those social comedies in which Tarkington played off the sophisticated and enfeebled New Yorkers against the sturdy and simple good-hearted people, the real Americans, from the middle west, but for audiences the appeal of the play lay in the battle of wits between Miss Carlisle, the representative of the homely virtues (though she was stunningly beautiful), and Lunt, who represented decadence —not Greek but Manhattan decadence, as Tarkington conceived it. Tarkington had great misgivings about an "inexperienced youngster" being able to play many of the difficult scenes. (Curiously enough, Tarkington's "inexperienced youngster" was now twenty-five years old and had been a professional actor for six years. Nowadays, many young actors are at the end of their professional tether by the age of twenty-five.)

The Country Cousin played Boston in July. Mr. and Mrs. Tarkington, who were en route to Kennebunkport, Maine, for the summer, came to the theatre intending to see one act only. It was a hot and stifling afternoon. The audience was listless. Alfred made his entrance about twenty minutes after the start of Act I, and with this entrance he galvanized the whole audience and walked into theatrical history. Tarkington was tremendously impressed by his looks and his personality and by the scintillating thrust-and-parry of his dialogue with Miss Carlisle. He and his wife Susannah stayed for the entire play, and then, in November, when *The Country Cousin* played Indianapolis, he had Alfred to lunch. After lunch, Tarkington and Alfred went upstairs and stayed in the author's study for several hours; Mrs. Tarkington was downstairs. She was suddenly chilled by a scream from above. She ran out into the foyer, and there was Alfred Lunt sliding down the bannister and roaring: "He's going to write a play for me! I'm made. I'm made."

Tarkington always wrote his plays with a specific actor and actress in mind for every major role. He was the first playwright to see Alfred's genius; he also claimed that Alfred had "extraordinary good looks" and a "full limit of manly beauty." Tyler was shocked out of his wits when Tarkington broke the news that he was writing a play for this unknown and eccentric minor actor. Tarkington beseeched his producer to keep his hands off the play. He wrote Tyler:

You've tried to work my material your way—let me try it my way. . . . LUNT . . . Let me write a play for Lunt of my own kind without telling me anything at all. You don't have to take it but you got to let it go on my way if you do take it—only keep a holt on Lunt so we can get him. . . . Lunt's got his own style; it's a gorgeous one and can be capitalized as high as Bill Hodge's was. Don't even talk it over with me—I want months to brood over it from time to time.

He brooded and composed and then he sent Tyler the playscript of *Clarence*. To "keep a holt on Lunt," Tyler, who kept a stable of stars and supporting players whom he paid by contract and kept working all year round, offered Alfred a two year contract, with $150 weekly the first year and $200 the second year. He informed Alfred that he had organized the George C. Tyler Stock Company and had scheduled four weeks in Atlantic City and four weeks in Washington, D.C. He was going to try out several new plays, including *Clarence*.

Alfred was still touring in *The Country Cousin* and was playing a split week in Buffalo when he got the proposition. Alfred had some misgivings about the deal. He replied to Tyler:

The situation as I see it is this—I am going to Washington for 4 weeks to get up in 4 plays of which you will put me in one next year, if it is successful, as we hope it will be—in other words I shall have to buy clothes for three plays which I shall not use in order to look presentable in your productions in Washington. Add to this the extreme high cost of living in Washington and I feel that I am justified in asking you for $200 a week. . . . As far as next season is concerned, I feel I should get $300 a week—after all, while I don't wish to use it as a means of raising my salary, Mr. Tarkington has taken the trouble to write a play for me so my services should be of equal value to that of most leading men. . . .

Grudgingly, Tyler conceded. After the tour ended, Alfred came to New York and read a scene from *Clarence* at the New Amsterdam Theatre. Lynn asked to be introduced to him. Alfred, who was nervously poised on the iron staircase backstage, took a few steps forward to take her hand. He stumbled and tripped and fell on his face before her.

Upon hearing of this, George S. Kaufman remarked: "Well, he certainly fell for her."

FOUR

THE WOOING OF LYNN

AND THE CONQUEST OF BROADWAY

ARKINGTON HAD been dispatching bulletins to Alfred once or twice a week. As the plot and the characters of his new play became more clearly defined on paper, he informed Alfred that he would be playing an entomologist, would wear eyeglasses, and be an army veteran. He thought that Clarence, yes, he had decided that was a good name for the character, that Clarence, a young man of many talents, could play the piano and the saxophone. Of course, he did not imagine that Alfred played the saxophone, although it would be wonderful if he did, but otherwise it would be played offstage; and it would not be hard for him to pretend to play the piano while somebody else struck a keyboard in the wings. Alfred was still touring in *The Country Cousin.* The company was playing in Denver, Colorado, when Alfred received the first two acts of the new play. Alfred wouldn't consider faking the music. He assured Tarkington that he had been taught the piano by his mother when he was a child and that while he had never mastered the saxophone as well as he had the piano and certainly was no Rudy Wiedoft, Tarkington could trust him to do a bit of practising so that he would give a good account of himself. "I could not really have played Clarence so it would be real to me," Alfred explains, "unless I played the sax myself. I nearly died when I first read Mr. Tarkington's manuscript and saw Clarence had to be a genius on the saxophone. I think I almost withdrew from the play. Why, I didn't even know how to hold a saxophone in my hands. I thought it over for two days and then I went shopping for a saxophone but, can you believe it, I couldn't find a saxophone in all Denver? Finally, somebody heard of one in Greeley, Colorado. It was a broken-down instrument with a lot of loose keys. It was in a pawnshop there. Then I got the name of an old German who taught wind instruments in Denver and I went to him for lessons. I told him I wanted to play a bit of the *William Tell* overture—because a stage direction called for this. Well, I couldn't even play a scale on the saxophone, and this man was disgusted. He got hysterical and told me that in the first place, the saxophone was a terrible instrument, and in the second place, the *William Tell* overture is not scored for saxophone parts, and also I don't know how to play and it should be better I forget the whole damn thing. I tried to explain to him it was for a stage play. He thought I was a lunatic. However, he consented to show me the fingering and tone production. I began practising as often as I could, in the dressing room or in hotels. Naturally guests complained to the desk about the noise I was making and I used to pray for thunderstorms. During a thunderstorm I could practise without any trouble."

By the time Alfred checked into the Washington Hotel in Washington, D.C., he could play six bars of the *William Tell* overture, but "I am afraid I still sounded like cats during the mating season."

On June 2, 1919, the Tyler Stock Company opened its first summer season at the National Theatre in Washington, D.C., with *On the Hiring Line*, a comedy about a suburban family with servant problems. Alfred played an unfaithful husband. The weather was excessively hot and humid, even for Washington. They played to empty houses. Washington was crowded that summer: the war was over; Congress and the Supreme Court remained in session. Though the President and Mrs. Wilson were still in Europe, a lively social season was being planned for June and July. Speculators were buying up war surpluses and making deals during the conversion of industry. Many conventions were held in Washington that summer. The first week in June, the Anti-Saloon League convened. The Eighteenth Amendment had been passed and the prohibitionists were flushed with victory. Their president's speech denounced beer as "pro-German" and whisky as "going hand in hand with anarchism." The drunken anarchists were setting bombs off all over the country. Neither the anarchists nor the prohibitionists were theatre lovers, apparently, because during the next week people shunned the National Theatre as if it were a plague-stricken area. Only a few hundred persons came the whole week, though an event of some importance took place. The second play was *Made of Money*, by Richard Washburn Child, later our ambassador to Italy during Mussolini's regime. It was in this play that, for the first time, Alfred Lunt and Lynn Fontanne played together. Alfred played Daniel Hardy, an eccentric millionaire (better known as Henry Higgins in a previous play on the same theme). He has bet $100,000 that he can take the first girl he meets and transform her into a social success in 90 days. Lynn played Mary Blake, a shy and poorly dressed rural maiden. Alfred was a lecherous roué. Almost from the beginning of his career, he played the amiable satyr. He had been a blackmailer of Lily Langtry, a dissolute bohemian seducing Laura Hope Crews, an Eastern rake toying with Alexandra Carlisle's virtue. The "real" Alfred Lunt was sweet and shy and rather innocent. In *Made of Money*, Lynn reformed Alfred and he proposed honorable marriage to her, but not before Alfred had played a magnificent scene in a salon of *haute couture* where he has taken his Galatea to buy some gowns. A dozen beautiful showgirls had been hired to play fashion models, and Alfred played the gallant rake with all the models. The play had a big cast, twenty-seven, including the models. At the Saturday matinee there were more people on the stage than there were in the theatre.

The third play was *A Young Man's Fancy*, by a new writer, John T. McIntyre. It was a delicately-wrought fantasy about a rich young man who is sexually inhibited. He lives in his imagination. He writes romantic poetry. He falls in love with a mannequin in a shop window. He buys her. He then collects a group of other life-sized waxen ladies and gentlemen to keep her company. The "wax" models were played by live actors who "froze" into position in Act I. Later, the models all come to life. The young man experiences a flesh-and-blood love and is able to relate to a real woman for the first time in his life. Lynn was praised for the "delicacy and feeling" she imparted to her role and for her ability to express a "captivating lightness and ethereal quality." Alfred gave "one of the most effective impersonations of a fantastic role a Washington audience has ever enjoyed."

But was it "impersonation"? Perhaps the theme of *A Young Man's Fancy* was a paradigm of the difficulties Alfred had had in coming to terms with existence on the plane of actuality? The world of the stage is a make-believe one and its characters, while lifelike, are essentially fabrications. Lynn was at first a dreamlike fantasy to him, an actress whom he met as an actor and with whom he played; but then she came to life, and she broke through his shell.

They had been rehearsing the dialogue of this play after performances of *Made of Money*. Sometimes they rehearsed in the empty theatre and sometimes they rehearsed in a horse-drawn carriage going around Rock Creek Park. They had a flashlight so they could look up a line if they had to. Sometimes they didn't study the script. Sometimes they made love until it was dawn. Were they acting the play or were they really falling in love? They themselves didn't really know, and perhaps they never have really found out definitely. The members of Tyler's stock company sensed that they were more than acting when they played the love scenes in *A Young Man's Fancy*. On June 21, a Saturday, the theatre was empty at both the matinee and evening performances. Tyler, enraged at the weather and at the stupidity of the Washington citizens, suddenly canceled the season. That night the troupe returned to New York. Lynn was sent out on the road to tour in *Made of Money* with another actor and Alfred was ordered to start rehearsing *Clarence*. Tyler later produced *A Young Man's Fancy* on Broadway with Jeanne Eagels and Philip Merivale. It failed. McIntyre never wrote another play, but he began to write fiction and became a distinguished novelist. To Alfred and Lynn, this play is still one of the loveliest they have ever done; Tyler believed afterward that if they had played it on Broadway it would have been a success.

For many weeks, Booth Tarkington and George Tyler had been worried about *Clarence*. Tyler was worried that Alfred was too "eccentric" an actor to play a hero. Tarkington was worried about the New York drama critics. In his own mind, he had written *Clarence* without much plot to prove to the critics who scorned him—especially Heywood Broun, George Jean Nathan, and Alexander Woollcott—that he could compose a Chekhovian comedy "whose whole substance is character and detail." He told Tyler it was a "simple, somewhat whimsical" play. He asked Tyler to put a nom-de-plume on the program, because he thought Booth Tarkington was poison to the sophisticated New York critics. Tyler was not crazy about the script, but he had committed himself to it and he produced it exactly as Tarkington had written it, under Tarkington's name. Tyler believed that a play whose principal character played saxophone to beetles to see if they had auditory powers was a play that would not inspire audience identification. It was an eccentric play and Lunt was an eccentric player and he feared the outcome. Furthermore, Lunt had begun to direct himself and Lynn. In *A Young Man's Fancy*, he first made suggestions with the permission of the director, Frederick Stanhope.

Tarkington told the producer to "let Lunt work out *his* part his own way— No stress on points—just simple 'natural' ways." Stanhope was the nominal director of *Clarence*. Its real director was Lunt. From now on, Lunt was generally the unbilled co-director of any play in which he appeared. I once asked Noel Coward, who directed the Lunts in several of his plays, what problems he had had directing Lynn and Alfred.

Coward squinted at me. "You can't be serious," he replied. "Direct the Lunts? My dear boy, when you do a play with the Lunts, nobody directs them. Oh, they have a delusion that they listen to a director, but they don't, y'know. Pay no attention to what you see on the marquee. 'Directed by Peter Brook.' 'Directed by Noel Coward.' *Quadrille*, it said, was directed by Noel Coward. Noel Coward refused this honor. I insisted the posters must read, 'Directed by the author with the grateful assistance of the Lunts.' They tried fighting me down. Wouldn't have their names up. But I insisted. Had my way. That's how the posters read. It was the truth. Of course, directors get furious at actors who want to butt into our little game, and I've gotten as mad as anybody else, but you don't mind it terribly when Lynn and Alfred take over the direction of a play you're supposed to be directing. Why not? Well, they simply know more about the theatre than anybody else living, dear boy, including even me, I'm afraid."

As Lunt grappled with the creation of Clarence Smith, the whimsical entomologist, he posed his problems to himself in terms of physical moves, rather than psychology. The main physical problem was playing the piano and saxophone. He was helped on the piano by Susanne Westford, a sister of Lillian Russell, who was playing the role of secretary in *Clarence*.

"I couldn't read music," Lunt recalls. "I couldn't memorize a tune. There was a scene, in Act II, when this girl I'm in love with, Elsie Mackay played her, has got a suitor, Herbert Stem, a grass widower as Mr. Tarkington called him, and he's pestering the girl. I'm tuning up the piano meanwhile. I was doing everything around the house. I'm a veteran looking for work after the war and I can't go back to this laboratory where I'd been researching insects before the war—and this rich man with two adolescent children, oh they were so charmingly played by Glenn Hunter and Helen Hayes, he gives me a job around the house as his assistant but actually to help discipline his unruly children. I'm an admirable Crichton. I fix the plumbing and all that sort of business. Well, in Act II, it opens with my tuning their piano.

I have to play loud purposely and Miss Westford finally figured out a way for me to play it. She wrote a number on each white key. Then she put these numbers on a piece of paper which I stuck on the music stand. She'd say now you hit note 1, now hit note 6, and I learned to play some of the Rachmaninoff *Prelude*, a little of *Afternoon of a Faun*, and bits and pieces of other tunes, but the saxophone was hard because I really had to play it, I had to breathe into it and get music out of it."

During rehearsals in New York and the two week tryout in Atlantic City—*Clarence* opened there on July 7—Alfred practised the saxophone incessantly backstage. (In Act III, he played the *William Tell* overture in "B flat—same old B flat." Whenever Alfred delivered this line with a shrug of resignation he brought down the house.) Alfred blew relentlessly in his dressing room. The other actors, even when they were working on stage, would keep an ear out for the moanings. There came a place in the music when Alfred had to reach a high note, a note he rarely hit properly. Instead, he blew an unearthly squeal, and all the actors thought this was very funny. Alfred explained the coloratura wail, saying it was the spirit of Adelina Patti returning for another "farewell performance." Whenever the high note came out, Alfred sighed, "Patti's in again."

Audiences loved the show in Atlantic City and Tyler decided to play it there through August 7 and tour until September before opening on Broadway.

Suddenly, everything went dead on Broadway. Actors Equity, chartered by the American Federation of Labor, demanded recognition from the Managers' Association. The "managers" (producers) refused. Equity called a general strike. Every theatre except the Garrick, where the Theatre Guild was presenting St. John Ervine's *John Ferguson,* went dark. The Theatre Guild was the only management that signed with Equity. The revolt of the actors was a long time fermenting. Producers had always exploited the actor's love of acting. In those days, there was no pay during rehearsals, no time limit on rehearsals. Actors were sometimes drilled fifteen hours a day for eight weeks—without a cent of salary. Actors could be dismissed without cause and without a settlement either during rehearsals or after a play opened.

Alfred and Lynn, sensitive about these injustices, joined the union. Actors divided into two hostile camps—Equity and Actors' Fidelity, the "company union" of which George M. Cohan was president. Marie Dressler, Ed Wynn, Ethel Barrymore, Mary Boland, and Ralph

Morgan were the leading spirits of the strike, which Heywood Broun supported in the press. Helen Hayes had promised Tyler not to join Equity, and enrolled in Actors' Fidelity. Cohan swore if Equity won he wouldn't ever act again. "I'd rather run an elevator or sell papers," he vowed. The Equity membership included a majority of the actors and almost all the stars. The "Fidos" boasted of many of the stars and most of the younger players. Violent arguments and fist fights replaced the traditional diversions of billiards, poker, and drinking in the theatrical clubs: The Players, the Lambs, and the Friars. The "Fidos" maintained that Equity strikers were debasing the actor's dignity. Ed Wynn, an Equity firebrand, swore that if the strikers lost, he would never play another show: "I'd rather sell peanuts and popcorn in the circus."

When the strike started, Alfred returned home to Wisconsin. He hadn't been back for two years. On the train, he felt oppressed by an overpowering fatigue. His body suddenly craved peace, after the exhausting tour of one-night stands in *The Country Cousin,* immediately succeeded by the arduous tasks of getting up his parts in three plays in Washington while studying his long role in *Clarence.* He was emotionally and physically drained. Mentally, he was a prey to fears and confusions, especially about his relationship with Lynn. She was to come to the farm next week and meet Karin, Carl, Louise, and Mother. Mother would be mad about Lynn. And Lynn about her. Lynn would become part of the family.

All through the suffocating night, his thoughts went round and round in a depressing circle. Suppose the strike lasted six months, a year? Mary Boland, who played the stepmother of the adolescent brats in *Clarence* so humorously that she opened up a new career for herself as a comedienne, was an Equity leader. She had told Alfred his fears were "stuff and nonsense." The union had pulled the actors out in August because that was the time when the producers were preparing their shows for the 1919-1920 season. It was the time to hit them hard. Miss Boland said that by Labor Day the producers would give up. Why, they'd have to, damn 'em all, " 'cause they can't put on Broadway shows without actors." So if the actors just hung together for three weeks, four weeks, they had to win. But, worried Alfred, what if *Clarence* was ditched for good and all on account of the strike? *Clarence* was his big chance. Not as a springboard to a career of commercial play acting. No, not that. But as the way to make a reputation so big that he could achieve the actor's destiny: to re-interpret for his own time the great classical roles and to introduce new plays by American and European writers. Lynn admired Alfred's idealism; she believed in his dream of a rich American theatre.

Alfred felt hot and sick on the train; his stomach kept him in great pain. He had never been right since the appendicitis operation when he had lost a kidney. Physical pain—usually mild but flaring up into unbearable agonies when he had overstrained himself—was always with him. But neither audiences nor actors suspected this. On stage, he projected tremendous *joie de vivre*. It was the great thing he gave to audiences and that was why they had such a good time when they saw him in *Clarence*.

Chicago, Union Station . . . He breakfasted in the depot coffee shop. His skin was burning. He must be running a fever. He couldn't eat anything. . . . The Chicago and Northwestern to Milwaukee, the Milwaukee and St. Paul to Genesee Depot . . . It was stiflingly hot in Genesee Depot. Summers in Wisconsin can be unendurably hot. At home, he caved in. He languished in bed all day and his mother brought him eggnogs made of fresh milk. Soon he roused himself. When the clouds of despondency lifted, he got out the script of *Clarence* and unpacked the saxophone. He tried on the soldier's costume he wore for *Clarence*; the strengthening diet had been too successful. Alfred wrote Tarkington: "That uniform has grown too tight again—Mabel, our maid, comforts me by saying, 'Clothes generally always does get tighter after a vacation, but you won't have to let out more seams after some weeks in New York.'"

Alfred was working out Clarence's shambling gait in Act I. He borrowed the shuffling gait from Bert Williams, whom he had seen in the Ziegfeld Follies. Alfred wondered whether he hadn't been overdoing his effects in Atlantic City. Too much shuffling? Too much "poaching" of his eyes? Too many falsetto breaks in the voice? (Alfred first employed his now famous falsetto "crack" in *Clarence*.) After supper, the family got together and listened to Alfred experimenting with various ways of doing Clarence. He had to "simplify the whole thing," he felt. Yet he hated to lose a laugh; that "nearly killed me." He thought he did too much "eye wig wagging," playing for these laughs. He decided to cut out two breaks in his voice in Act I, but keep the breaks in Act III. And he went to Milwaukee to have a tailor let out the uniform. How about his hair? Was he plastering it down too much? Should he use less pomade? Clarence wouldn't be *that* vain about his hair. He reported to Tarkington that the piano was progressing smoothly and he wondered what the author thought of his playing the Toreador song from *Carmen* "with one finger . . . for Stem's entrance? Sounds kind of funny." He had confessed he wasn't much of a musician. "The saxophone remains something of a mystery, but it's lots of fun and my sister and brother and I jazz considerably." Karin was on piano and Carl played ukulele as Alfred blew alto saxophone.

The circus came to Milwaukee. Karin, Alfred, and Mother went to the matinee on opening day. Alfred and his mother loved circuses. They were like children. They boarded the local train for home. They were singing loudly. Alfred, tie loosened, had rolled up his sleeves. His stiff straw hat was perched at a crazy angle on Mother's head. Karin was blowing up balloons. They were all laughing maniacally when all at once Mrs. Sederholm became aware of a tall, slender lady in the aisle. She was staring down at them. How dared this elegant creature stare at them so haughtily? She was gotten up in a smartly tailored gray gabardine suit, the skirt of which was fashionably, daringly, two inches above the ankle. Her long reddish hair was done up in a chignon on which hung a tiny plumed leghorn hat. She resembled a society woman who had wandered into a room of badly brought up children. Mrs. Sederholm poked Alfred in the ribs. He looked up.

"My gawd," he groaned, "it can't be Lynnie." He nervously tried to tie a knot in his tie. He failed. He arose, swaying with the train. "We —Lynn—I didn't expect you until tomorrow." Somebody had gotten the date wrong. "We've been to the circus in Milwaukee, what a coincidence being on the same train, when did you get in, I didn't expect you till tomorrow, do you like circuses, we do, we never miss them, circuses . . ."

She smiled. "And was it fun, Alfred?"

"I think so," he said. "Hattie, this is Lynn Fontanne, Lynn, this is my mother, Hattie, and this is Karin."

Hattie threw Lynn a dissecting head-to-toe glare. Only a potential mother-in-law knows how to do it properly. Lynn stayed two weeks. It was a bad time for everybody. Hattie's hostility was open. She rattled off jibes at Lynn whenever she could. Karin, Louise, and Carl tried to be sociable. Lynn, rather desperate, forced herself to take part in the giddy indoor and outdoor sports of this eccentric tribe. Alfred, a lost soul, wondered why there was no rapport between Lynn and Hattie. Lynn was startled by the family's camaraderie. Karin says, "I suppose it must have been a shock for her to suddenly come into this family of happy lunatics, where the mother was like a sister and just as wild as the other children and all of us doing crazy things just for the sheer fun of it."

When Lynn and Alfred were alone, out walking in the dusk among the trees, Alfred tried to explain his mother's ways, but Lynn felt Hattie was being deliberately rude to her. She wasn't wanted. She didn't want to make demands of Alfred. They had known each other such a short time. How sure could she be of his love?

Returning to New York, Lynn pondered over it all. She hadn't done anything to offend Alfred's mother. She thought of mothers and sons, of mothers she had known in England, of her own mother. Perhaps Hattie's shafts weren't aimed at Lynn. Perhaps she didn't want Alfred to marry anybody at all. She wanted her son to herself. Maybe that was why Alfred had never married. No mother, she thought, really wants her son to get married and no sisters want their brother to marry. Is a new member of a family ever welcome? No, she thought, the outsider must work her way in slowly. She has to make good, prove herself, especially when she tries to win a place in such a happy family, all of them so closely tied to each other, not wanting an outsider spoiling the fun. "I think I quite understand that," she said to herself.

A telegram from Tyler resolved Alfred's conflict between mother and sweetheart.

STRIKE OVER. RETURN SOONEST POSSIBLE. REHEARSALS AT ONCE HUDSON THEATRE.

The producers had surrendered. They had signed the agreement with Equity. On the morning of September 6, the cast of *Clarence* reunited. They rehearsed during the next weeks in a mood of exhilaration that carried through to the opening night. That night, that Saturday, September 20, 1919, all of them were bursting like roman candles, especially Helen Hayes, Glenn Hunter, Mary Boland, and Alfred himself. It was to be one of the great evenings in Broadway history. It made Helen Hayes a star. Overnight, Alfred Lunt—known vaguely to the Broadway crowd as an oddball comedy type—was recognized as a virtuoso of the comic spirit. The play was a triumph for Booth Tarkington, and it made $500,000 for Tyler.

The play began rather quietly in Mr. Wheeler's office downtown. Outside, a discharged soldier in uniform is waiting to see him about a job. The members of the family burst in one by one. The young son (Glenn Hunter) has been expelled from his seventh boarding school. He's in love with his sister's governess, Violet. Violet doesn't like him. Cora, Violet's charge, is in love with a "grass widower." Mr. Wheeler is getting frantic. At this point, Clarence enters in uniform. Tarkington shrewdly planned to cover up Lunt's charm and good looks by making him appear as miserable-looking as possible in Act I. When Tyler objected, Tarkington said he wanted to spring Lunt's "extraordinary good looks" as a surprise on the audience, by "disguising them for a time . . . by leading UP to them." Tarkington thought Lunt had the "full limit of manly beauty; my idea [is] to take full comedy value of this endowment and not sell it for a nickel at first sight."

At first sight to that first night audience, Alfred looked a wreck. He shambled in, timorously holding his army hat by its brim. His hair was disarrayed. His khaki uniform was several sizes too large. He stooped at the shoulders and the waist. He sagged from one side to the other. The final misery of this miserable veteran was a large pair of eyeglasses behind which his huge eyes blinked mournfully. Out of Tarkington's few stage directions, Alfred composed a fantastic creation. To us, knowing it only through still photographs and reminiscences of those who saw it on Broadway, it seems exaggerated. The audience of 1919 found it true to life.

At the end of Act I, the papers reported, the audience began shouting, *Lunt, Lunt, Lunt,* and demanding a curtain speech! At the end of Act II—during which Alfred discarded his eyeglasses, uniform, and bertwilliams gait and became a well-dressed handsome man—the audience again screamed his name and pleaded for a speech. Alfred had deliberately underplayed his speeches and slowed his delivery early in the play and then worked with faster speed and sharper brightness. In Act III he made a spectacular entrance, brandishing the alto sax and bleating out Rossini's wild measures as the butler did a snake-dance and banged a huge spatula against a silver tray while Helen Hayes clanged two silver tureen covers together like cymbals. The audience went mad. Alfred was belting out his lines harder and faster and by the end of the play was able to hold everybody spellbound even when he launched into an incredibly long and serious and funny oration on the importance of entomology and the challenge of insects. He was making love to Violet as he made this speech. In the last act, Lunt did something new. He played a crucial moment with his back to the audience. An important letter he has been expecting has failed to arrive. He walks upstage. His back sags in defeat. Then another letter is discovered with the good news. Back still to the audience, Alfred straightened himself and projected bliss. The play ended with Clarence and Violet leaving to get married and Cora (Helen Hayes) resigning herself to the situation and saying a "sweet tremulous" goodbye and good luck. Then she came "downstage, not weeping but swallowing. She sits again. Swallowing gently." Then Miss Hayes murmured the last line, "Oh, Clarence!"

The house was hushed for a split second. Then—pandemonium. The curtain rose. The actors took their places in a row, bowing and smiling and perspiring. Suddenly, the entire house—everybody in the orchestra, the dress circle, the balcony—everybody arose, yelling and stamping their feet and beating their palms together. The curtain came down. Went up. Time after time. Twenty-five curtain calls! Nobody wanted to go home. Programs were shredded and thrown into the air like confetti. Men threw hats. Women flung handkerchiefs. The mother of Helen Hayes remembers that night as being "as wildly exciting as Armistice Day."

The town had to wait till Monday for the reviews. And what reviews they were. Even "rave" doesn't describe them. Only one or two productions in a decade bring out such notices. For Tarkington himself, there was sweet revenge. His two arch-enemies Broun and Woollcott publicly ate crow. They had been dead wrong in maintaining Tarkington was a novelist and not a theatre writer. Broun in the New York *Tribune:*

> *Clarence* is the best light comedy which has been written by an American . . . he has written this play as all plays should be written but as only one or two a generation are . . . it seems to us that *Clarence* is the great American drama . . . it is just about the best fun in the world.

Except Broun—who doted on Miss Hayes' ravishing performances —the critics saw that it was Lunt's sleight-of-heart which conjured an amusing comedy of middle-class manners into stage magic. Burns Mantle's review was entirely devoted to Lunt's performance. Alan Dale said that "*Clarence* depended very largely upon the acting of young Mr. Alfred Lunt . . . [he] is extraordinary . . . he was perfectly flawless . . . he was irresistible . . . Mr. Lunt has made *Clarence* and *Clarence* in retaliation has made Mr. Lunt and there you are."

Alexander Woollcott, then writing in the New York *Times,* began his lifelong love affair with the Lunts by composing a panegyric to Alfred's technique. Returned from the wars himself in July, 1919, ex-sergeant Woollcott was empathic with ex-private Clarence Smith. The lead of his critique was the first review he wrote in the warm-the-heart-cockles style he made his own. He wrote:

Write it on the walls of the city, let the town crier proclaim it in the commons, shout it from the housetops that *Clarence* is a thoroughly delightful American comedy, which the world, his wife and their children will enjoy. It is as American as Huckleberry Finn or pumpkin pie. It is as delightful as any native comedy which has tried to lure the laughter of this community in the last 10 seasons."

Lunt eschewed the exaggerated gestures and elocutionary vocal effects of the time. He played comedy on a realistic, conversational level. He did "natural" things on the stage. His performance broke with old-fashioned Broadway acting techniques of comedy. He became a model to every young actor. By 1925, he was the most imitated actor in the theatre. Ruth Gordon, who was keenly aware of Lunt's wide influence, says, "I don't know how true it is to say that Alfred founded a new style of American acting. In *Clarence,* it's true, he was playing with a simple elegance, let's say, like nobody had ever done before. But, you see, he was so perfect no other actor could imitate him, or follow him, or learn from him. All they could do was copy his mannerisms, and that was never the essence of Alfred's acting style. Usually, an actor who has worked in a play with the Lunts, well, it takes him years to get over their effect on him."

From this time on, the best young talents in our theatre used the technical devices of Lunt. They separated them from his surface mannerisms. They sought to copy his method, which was a search for human reality. The simplification, the conversational mode of speaking—these established a permanent style which is followed to this day, even up to such men as Marlon Brando. Lee Strasberg, a minor player in the Theatre Guild, was greatly influenced in many of his ideas by the work of Lunt during the 1920's. And Strasberg was the transmission belt between the 1920's and the acting of the 1950's and 1960's. Alfred Lunt was steering in a new direction—seeking out and conveying the psychological truth in a play, rather than seducing an audience by stage trickery. All good actors since then have followed his lead.

FIVE

DULCY CONQUERS CLARENCE

*I*N *Clarence,* the five female characters loved the hero. Backstage, the five actresses who played them were in love with Alfred. They yearned, hoped, sighed, coquetted. As Tarkington might have put it, Helen Hayes had the worst "case" on him. Her mother tells us that in 1919, Miss Hayes "was carrying a secret passion in her heart for Alfred." But Alfred didn't love them back—not any of them. He was fascinated by a "sophisticated hussy." Helen Hayes was "certain this bony, brazen woman was not for him." When would Alfred come to his senses and requite her deep love? When would Alfred extricate himself from the "hussy's" web?

Each night, at 11, Lynn Fontanne swept in. She marched to Alfred's dressing room. She remained there until he was dressed. Then, arm in arm, they sauntered out. Mary Boland considered it "most unseemly for a single female to be going to Alfred's dressing room." To the nineteen-year-old lovelorn Miss Hayes, Lynn seemed so unappealing, an "Eliza Doolittle come to life . . . Seldom have I seen a more awkward, skinny creature. For some reason, she always wore a hat with dangling, bedraggled plumes. . . . I squirmed with jealousy and resented her fiercely. I derived some satisfaction from knowing the cast felt she tried to impress us as she paraded in front of our hostile eyes." How false was this impression! Lynn was aware of them. She was dying inside. She hated to run "the gauntlet" of their sneering eyes. She felt their looks boring through her back. Her feet got bigger and uglier as she passed them and "my plumes grew limper."

Elsie Mackay was the first to get over Alfred. She fell in love with Lionel Atwill and married him. The others found other substitutes. Only Helen Hayes was inconsolable. For years she "carried a torch" for Alfred, until she found the romantic lover of her romantic dreams in a young playwright, Charles MacArthur. At a party, MacArthur, who did not know her, walked across a room and handed her a bowl of salted peanuts. "I wish these were emeralds," he murmured. . . .

But Lynn was as unhappy as her rivals. For Mrs. Sederholm had come to town—to bask in her son's glory. She and Karin came to New York for a long visit. Hattie made no bones about her enmity toward Lynn. She was not going to allow *this* silver cord to be loosed. At family gatherings, she was so sarcastic to Lynn that Lynn said "the dislike became mutual."

Lynn said Alfred must choose between his mother and her. He said he loved them both in different ways. Let her wait until Hattie returned home. Then he'd figure out a delicate solution. Hattie would come around to it eventually.

"Time, a little more time, is all I ask," he said one evening. "I'll find a way to break it without hurting her. She's got to know you better. She'll love you as much as I do."

"I'm terribly sorry, darling," Lynn replied, shaking her head. "I don't think she wants it to happen. She won't let it happen. She wants her son. She won't let you be any girl's husband. You've got to decide who you want to be—her son—my husband."

"Why not both?"

"She won't let you. She won't let you go. It isn't that she hates me. I see that clearly now. She won't let you belong to any other woman. She wants you for herself."

After these quarrels, Lynn would seek out Laurette Taylor. Laurette understood the agonies of unrequited love. She and Lynn would talk until the middle of the night—and many times Lynn slept in a guest room of the bizarre Gothic building on Riverside Drive in which Laurette and Hartley Manners lived. She wanted really to talk about Alfred as if, not being able to have him in her arms, she could keep him in front of her by talking about him. Laurette heard her out. She counseled her. She comforted her. Once, after a violent quarrel, Alfred had to get away from New York. He took a train to Philadelphia. It was Saturday night. Laurette said, "Why don't *you* take the train to Philadelphia and have it out? It's only a two hour ride."

Lynn was shocked. "I couldn't do *that!*" Nice girls didn't follow their lovers to hotels in Philadelphia, and besides Lynn didn't know what hotel he was registered in.

"Lynn," Laurette said, "I wouldn't suffer in my soul the way you do—for any reason—without trying to end it. The longer you let this, whatever it is, stand between you and Alfred, the more powerful it will become. There are only four or five good hotels in Philadelphia. Go down there. Keep telephoning all the hotels until you get his. Go there. Say, 'Hello, Alfred.' If he says, 'Hello, Lynn,' then the world is whole. If he turns away and looks out the window, well you're just where you are now. What have you got to lose?"

Lynn went to Philadelphia.

He did say, "Hello, Lynn," after all.

But the reconciliation lasted a week and then Lynn, broken-hearted, was back with Laurette. Laurette—who really was jealous of Alfred's hold over Lynn, for she wanted Lynn all to herself—now took another line. Alfred was hopeless. Lynn ought not to waste her heart's blood on him. He'd make a terrible lover and a worse husband. There were many fine fish in the sea. And she cozened Lynn into meeting eligible bachelors. After Alfred, Lynn found them all bloody bores. This quarrel—it was the big one in January, 1920—lasted a long time. By February, Lynn was convinced all was over. Alfred hadn't written her. He hadn't sent word to her by any of their friends. He hadn't even gone to Philadelphia to get away from it all.

One night the phone rang.

"Hello," she said hoarsely.

"Lynn," said *his* voice. "It's, you know, Alfred."

"Oh," replied Lynn. She burst into tears. She couldn't say another word. Not even "oh."

"Wait," Alfred shouted, "wait right there. Don't go away. I'll be right over."

He was. They fell into each other's arms, weeping and laughing and kissing.

It was the day Hattie left New York. "What a day that was," Lynn remembers, smiling. "My, but we had a high old dinner together celebrating, and we were so happy. I didn't think I'd ever be that happy again. I didn't care if I never acted in another play again. Just having Alfred back in my arms was all I wanted."

Now George Tyler wanted her to go into rehearsal in *Chris*, by Eugene O'Neill. Originally, the role was that of an English girl, born in Sweden but educated in England after her mother's death. Anna was a nice, virtuous, well brought up young lady.

"I played Anna with a very slight cockney accent," Lynn says. "She was a good girl who falls in love with a hired hand on her father's barge. It was a most innocuous story." The rehearsals went badly. The scenes dragged. One day, during a break in rehearsals, Lynn wanted to talk to O'Neill. In the original version, there were many rhapsodic speeches about the beauty of mothers. Lynn couldn't abide these sentiments. She knew mothers made a lot of trouble in the world. O'Neill habitually sat in glum silence in the back of the theatre.

"May I speak to you?" she said. "Hear me out, please, even though I am only an actress."

He stared ahead. He picked at his moustache.

"I want to speak to you about mothers," she said. "You make mothers a symbol of everything that's good in the world. Believe me, Mr. O'Neill, all mothers are not like that. I think very, very few mothers are like that. I know writers hate actresses who give them ideas but I must tell you this idea I have. Why don't you write a play about a mother who won't let her son marry? She doesn't want her son to marry. She is possessive, d'you see? She would destroy him, rather than give him up to another woman?"

He looked toward her. "You know," he said, "I find this interesting."

Eight years later, while Lynn was rehearsing in *Strange Interlude*, O'Neill said to her, "Well, how do you like the play you suggested?"

"I don't recognize this play as anything I suggested."

"Do you remember suggesting I write a play about possessive mothers?"

She searched her memory. She dimly remembered.

"Yes?" she asked.

"Well," O'Neill said, "this is the play."

Chris opened in Philadelphia on March 1. Lynn's notices were complimentary, but the play was a literary miscarriage. Tyler wanted to withdraw it. O'Neill wanted to rewrite it. But there was a booking in Atlantic City. The company played two weeks more at the Apollo Theatre there. O'Neill disappeared to write a completely new version of *Chris*. Charm and serious girlhood were what Anna didn't need. He made her a whore now. He made her Anna Christie. Pauline Lord played her during the 1921 season. Blanche Sweet played Anna in a silent film, and Garbo played her in the talking film. Gwen Verdon played her in a musical comedy version in 1956.

In April, 1920, Laurette Taylor asked Lynn to return to her company. Lynn would play in the London production of *One Night in Rome*, a costume melodrama by Manners.

The London opening of *One Night in Rome* on April 29, 1920, stands out as the ghastliest in Lynn's career. Seated in the boxes and stalls was a scintillating audience of lords and ladies. The Garrick Theatre was jammed to capacity. The American ambassador occupied a box. The leading lights of the British theatre were on hand. Strange things begin taking place during the first act. A restiveness in the gallery. Shouts of "louder, louder" and "we can't hear a bloomin' fing." Laurette took the heckling amiably. She had the furniture moved downstage to improve the sight lines. She spoke to the audience, calming it. The plot thickened enough to command attention. The house settled down.

But Act II began with a verbose, tedious scene played by Lynn, Greta Kemble-Cooper, and Barry Baxter. The animals in the gallery stirred restlessly. Murmurings crescendoed into roars.

She played on, trying to make herself heard above the mounting uproar. The commotion turned into a riot. Mocking her, they threw coins on the stage. Lynn was struck on the face and chest by a rain of heavy English pennies—the shape and weight of our half-dollars. She was terrified. Her voice dried up. The gentry in the stalls cried out for a show of English good manners. The mob cursed. Now they were throwing stink bombs and sneezing powder into the stalls. They ripped tiles from the ceiling and flung them at the actors. Lynn covered her face, still trying to play the scene.

Finally, Charles Cochran, the British impresario, ordered the curtain rung down. There were no further demonstrations, and *One Night in Rome* ran for some months.

Lynn was humiliated by the incident, until she discovered it was the talk of London and that wherever she went she was the center of attention. Lynn had a gay social life. She went about to parties and suppers; she renewed old acquaintances with Denis Eadie, Cyril Maude, Beerbohm Tree, Jane and Wilfred de Glehn, and A. E. Matthews, who wanted to marry her.

"But I can't, can't, can't marry you," Lynn cried finally. "I'm marrying somebody else. I'm marrying Alfred."

"And who is Alfred?" he asked.

"Alfred Lunt," she replied.

"Who on earth is Alfred Lunt?"

"Just someone I know," Lynn said. "Millionaire. Made his money in meat-packing in Chicago or railroads or some such thing."

One day she lunched with Edward Knoblock. She spoke about her love and Alfred's talent and how well they had played together in *A Young Man's Fancy*. She also confided some of her worries about the frequent crises in her love life. Well, suggested Knoblock, the solution was to play *only* with Alfred. To paraphrase the church slogan: the family that plays together, stays together. Sounded marvelous, Lynn said. Well, he knew just the vehicle for them both. Lynn wrote Tyler:

"Knoblock is awfully anxious for you to revive *My Lady's Dress*. I think well acted BY ME it would be a great success & Alfred Lunt in the man's part & you have a GREAT combination."

Tyler didn't think Lunt and Fontanne were a "great combination." He had other plans for Lynn—and for Alfred. He wanted to keep them as far apart as he could, at least, professionally.

That summer *Clarence* went on vacation before going on tour in the fall. Alfred still loved Lynn. She still loved Alfred. They settled down in a theatrical boarding house at 130 West 70 Street. Lynn had a suite on the third floor. Alfred was in the basement front room. He had a complete kitchen and a small bedroom with two chairs and a bed; that was all. He could not afford luxury. He did not have a large income and out of what he earned he sent home nine-tenths, for his mother and the "three Finns." In later years, the Lunts would portray love in elegant drawing rooms, luxurious bedrooms, and fashionable hotels. And nobody except Noel Coward would ever know that the passions they improvised in so many comedies had been originally rehearsed, so to speak, in this boarding house. Everything was beautiful to them, from the flaking cabbage-rose wallpaper to the banal boarding house dinners. The weather was hot and clammy in August and they loved it. The landlady, Dr. Rounds, was a real medical doctor with a good practice. She was a woman with a nice sense of humor; it amused her to describe her goriest cases during meals. They walked in Central Park and rode the upper decks of Fifth Avenue buses and sat in Battery Park watching the freighters and the steamships sailing to Europe. They looked in the windows of the stores and attended auctions and dreamed of how they would decorate their home someday. Calendars and General Register Offices could say what they pleased, but Lynn looked a girl of nineteen in the flush and excitement of first love, and Alfred, a mere twenty-one. They felt so young and alive and romantic and the future was so exciting, wasn't it, because the American theatre, for the first time, was alive and vibrating in all directions. They sensed that they were going to be a vital part of the 1920's.

In June, Noel Coward came to our shores with $75 and a suitcase of playscripts. No Broadway producer liked the plays. Poor Noel looked up Lynn Fontanne, who would perhaps extend a bit of sympathy to a fellow Englishman. She invited him to dinner—he was going hungry most of the time—and he leaped at the invitation. He came to the brownstone on West 70th, and met Alfred Lunt. He liked Lynn's choice. When Lynn showed him around her living room, she opened the bedroom door. Noel whispered, "So this is where Alfred betrays you."

Lynn and Alfred and Noel read Noel's plays aloud. How original! How amusing! How daring! He must not be discouraged. They read dialogue and talked and drank coffee until dawn. At midnight, Alfred was sent out to a Columbus Avenue delicatessen to bring sandwiches and coffee.

Coward recalled:

From these shabby, congenial rooms, we projected ourselves into future eminence. . . . Lynn and Alfred were to be married. That was the first plan. Then they were to become definitely idols of the public. That was the second plan. Then all this being successfully accomplished, they were to act exclusively together. This was the third plan. It remained for me to supply the fourth, which was that when all three of us had become stars of sufficient magnitude to be able to count upon an individual following irrespective of each other, then, poised serenely upon that enviable plane of achievement, we would meet and act triumphantly together.

Another visitor to these "shabby, congenial rooms" was Howard Lindsay, recently returned from army service a corporal. Tyler had given him his old job of stage-managing, but Lindsay was ambitious for higher things. Couldn't he have a script to direct? Well, Tyler had optioned a play by a "couple of bright young men, Kaufman and Connelly." The authors were green; the script seemed outré. He was willing to chance Lindsay on it.

Connelly, an earnest young man tending to plumpness, had come to Broadway in 1917 from Pittsburgh. He had written the book and lyrics of *The Amber Empress*, an operetta which had flopped. He didn't want to return to journalism in Pittsburgh—he was determined to break into the New York theatre. He worked on the *Morning Telegraph*, which then devoted as much space to show business as to horse-racing. Connelly made the Broadway rounds gathering data for Rennold Wolf's column and writing paragraphs for the "Beau Broadway" column in the *Telegraph*. He was constantly running into Kaufman, who was in search of items for the New York *Times* drama section. "We always seemed to be leaning on the back rails of theatres," Connelly recalls. "We also made jokes. We laughed at each other's jokes. We thought we were both quite witty. George introduced me to Tyler. Tyler commissioned me to modernize a European musical show, *Erminie*, which had a success. Then Tyler said Lynn was ready for a big starring part. Kaufman had the idea of taking Dulcinea, who was a regular character in F.P.A.'s column in the *Tribune,* and building a play around her. George and I got to work. We planned the characters, outlined the plot, and wrote the final script in less than a month—three weeks is my best recollection—and we did very little rewriting on the road. Somehow, writing with Lynn in our mind, the play almost seemed to write itself."

So Lindsay read the script of *Dulcy* and loved it. Tyler asked Alfred his opinion of Lindsay as a director. Ah, yes, Lunt assured him, Lindsay could certainly be relied on to get a play on its feet. But did Tyler realize Howard was a damn clever actor as well?

"You've been looking for a Vincent Leach," Alfred said. "There's your Vincent Leach. Lindsay must play Leach."

Leach was one of those droll irrelevant characters whom Kaufman intruded into his comedies and who invariably stopped the show. Leach was an egotistical movie scenarist whom the script described as "slightly effeminate." At Alfred's suggestion, Lindsay says, "I played Leach to the hilt as an out and out fairy scenarist. In those days, movie writers were still a new butt for jokes, and fairies were unheard of and so the combination of the two was very funny."

During rehearsals, Lynn's nervous tension came through more openly than it usually did. She was forever fluffing and forgetting cues and getting everything "balled up." Lindsay affectionately called her "Miscue." She had reason to be high strung. This was the first time she'd had to carry a play by herself. There was no Laurette Taylor, no Alfred Lunt, no Hassard Short with whom to share the brunt. The play's success lay entirely on her shoulders. Furthermore, she'd gotten involved in a violent hassle with Tyler over her clothes. To an actress, any actress in any role, the choice of her dresses and hats is far more crucial than the same choices to a woman in everyday life. The clothes become an embodiment not just of her own personality but of the character she is playing. Tyler was so stingy he wanted her to go to

Macy's basement and buy clothes off the rack, though she was playing a fairly wealthy suburban lady who moved in chic circles.

"You won't be happy until I walk on in a tablecloth," she once cried at Tyler.

One day, she went to Bouillet Soeurs, then one of the most elegant couturiers in New York, and had them run her up three dresses for *Dulcy*. When Tyler got the bill, he turned purple with rage and fell over in a faint. The office staff thought he had had a heart attack.

Lindsay was also suffering from Tyler's parsimony. Though the setting was a Westchester salon, Tyler ordered Lindsay to employ some heavy Italian Renaissance furniture which was stored in the Tyler warehouse and had been used in some old play. Lindsay couldn't block out the action because of "this goddam Italian junk." He told Lynn he was forced to use it "to please Tyler."

She shook her head. "Howard," she said, "if you don't please yourself first, you'll please nobody else. The hell with Tyler. You use modern furniture."

He did.

Connelly remembers having a furious row with Tyler over some "miserable little" lampshades in the living room set. "Tyler hated to spend a few dollars on some decent looking lampshades," Connelly says. "I went out and bought them myself and went on the stage and put them in position and I told Tyler I was charging him for the lampshades. I don't remember whether he reimbursed me."

In order to get Booth Tarkington's reaction to this uncomfortably offbeat comedy, *Dulcy* tried out at English's Theatre, Indianapolis, opening on February 13, 1921. Tarkington came and loved it. Then they opened at the Cort, Chicago, on February 20. In the Chicago *Post*, the critic Charles Collins described Lynn as "an actress with a delicate and alert sense of the grotesque, a talent for polite caricature, and the gift, which amounts to a touch of genius, of bringing charm to the depiction of eccentricity." Percy Hammond, then of the Chicago *Tribune*, who didn't customarily flatter, heaped flattery on her: "Miss Fontanne is an impish beauty* with the gift of disguising the broadest of fun in a veil of subtlety." *Dulcy* ran four months in Chicago.

Between the Chicago closing and the Broadway opening fell a difficult six week hiatus. Lynn got more and more anxious as August 13,

---

* This, believe it or not, was the first public statement that Lynn was anything other than scrawny and bony! The winds were beginning to blow from a different direction.

1921, approached. Her moods veered "between hysterical gaiety and the most intense melancholy." * Alfred became infected with her uneasiness. Noel, as distraught as his friends, nevertheless kept up a brave front.

Saturday, August 13, finally came. Woollcott remembered it as the hottest night he had ever spent in the theatre. At seven, Alfred and Noel brought Lynn to the Frazee Theatre. She was white. After they left, she threw up several times.

An hour till curtain. Alfred groaned. He and Noel trudged up and down Broadway, trying to find solace in ice-cream parlors, where they downed "frosted chocolates and [behaved] generally like anxious fathers expecting twins." Alfred was shaking all over. He stationed himself opposite the Frazee. He trembled at the sight of the limousines disgorging the first nighters. A mob of bloodthirsty jackals, they looked. They'd tear her limb from limb. Percy Hammond—when he was still a Chicago outsider—once described a Broadway audience:

> If there was one gleam of human intelligence in all their vapid maps, my eagle eyed suburban scrutiny failed to observe it. There they sat, an empty, unthinking, overfed, overdrunk, pitiable outfit, slaking their cheap theatrical emotions at a fount of pink, theatrical piffle.

That was how they seemed to Alfred that night. But the same "overdrunk" unthinkers could also be sensitive and intelligent and enthusiastic when they saw a play of quality.

Rather numb, Alfred and Noel fell into their seats. They smiled and nodded to friends. They braced themselves for the ordeal.

About ten minutes after the curtain's rise, Lynn made her first entrance. She was costumed in a sophisticated black velvet gown "that is just a bit too much for an afternoon gathering." † Her long arms were filled with gladioli. She effervesced. Her eyes sparkled. Words tumbled out vivaciously. Save for the two paralyzed gentlemen in the last row, nobody dreamed that this self-possessed woman was verging on a nervous breakdown.

From her first speech, Lynn had the audience in the palm of her hand and she didn't let them go until the last line of the play. A scene in Act II, in which Dulcy prevails upon Leach to recite in wearying detail the plot of his latest scenario—"I am going to show Sin— throughout the ages"—devastated the audience. *Dulcy's* gossamer-thin

---

* Noel Coward, *Present Indicative.*
† Stage direction.

plot, like that of so many high, low, and medium comedies, doesn't bear critical examination. Lynn took full advantage of every opening the story gave her. A bride of three months, Dulcy is a stupid, good-hearted meddler in her husband's business affairs and in various love affairs who nearly destroys everybody with her schemings. Her trademark—both in F.P.A.'s column and in the Kaufman-Connelly play—was an addiction to cliches. In the play, Dulcy got off such observations as:

"My books are my best friends." "I always say, if a woman is good looking, no jury on earth will convict her." "Every cloud has a silver lining." "New York is a wonderful place to visit, but I wouldn't want to live there." "It doesn't take a brick wall to fall on me." "You know, sometimes I think I would lose my head if it wasn't fastened on."

Lynn uttered these sayings as if they were the aphorisms of La Rochefoucauld or Nietzsche. Heywood Broun commented, "The humor of a young woman supposed to be a deadly bore might actually become so in less skillful hands, but Miss Fontanne preserves the spirit of mockery, and the authors have been wise enough to let the bromides swirl into drifts."

Woollcott on *Dulcy*:

As Dulcinea, she is brilliant—no less. . . . It was apparent from the first that she was an actress of uncommon quality, and not even the rich role of Dulcy, which offers her her first full size opportunity, measures up to her suspected stature. She can do great things—and perhaps she will.

In 1923, he still found the play unworthy of her talent when she played Ann Jordan in *In Love with Love*:

For the second time, Miss Fontanne of London has the leading role in an essentially and ingrained American comedy. For the second time, she has been cast in a character remote from her own personality. And for the second time, her uncommon skill and resourcefulness as a player has carried her triumphantly through. Of course, the English colour to her voice does keep escaping her sedulous control until just the faint accent of 'ampstead 'eath can be heard astray in Lardnerian colloquies. She will probably be finding things 'lahvely' when she is the Mrs. Whiffen of her day. But that does not matter much. What does matter a little more is that circumstance in the American theatre seems to have seized upon a singularly intense, vital, brilliant and slightly sinister actress and hurled her into comedies as heroines who are not any too bright . . . [she is playing] a girl who is an empty babbling bit of gush who hasn't had an important thought since the spring of 1907. This, mind you, with an actress who could play Hedda Gabler and Rebecca West. It is a little as though Mrs. Fiske were cast as Lola Pratt.*

Lynn was marching to her private music, not Woollcott's. She was striving to show Broadway she mustn't be stereotyped as an eccentric comedienne. That was why, in May, 1923, she played in Laurette Taylor's revival of *Nell of Old Drury*. Alfred played Charles II. Lynn was Lady Castlemaine, a dissolute and worldly woman. Woollcott approved the result, though he couldn't discern Lynn's strategy: "Lynn Fontanne was the superb though flouted Lady Castlemaine—a part whole worlds removed from her delectable moron, Dulcy, yet as perfect in every accent lineament and gesture."

Lynn purposely wangled the lead of *In Love with Love*. It was a "straight" romantic part, a highly dressed lady with a deadly power over men. When she went to the office of Robert Milton, who was casting the play, he said the role was not in her style. Delectable morons like Dulcy and Hermione were obviously her specialty; the character, Ann Jordan, was seductive, she was glamorous, she was a "vamp." So, Lynn thought, he thought she couldn't "vamp" a man, did he? She taxied to Bouillet Soeurs and ordered the most sexually stimulating gown in the shop. The next morning, without an appointment, she surged into Milton's office, "shimmying across the room like I was Theda Bara." Milton saw a new Lynn. Though Woollcott felt Ann Jordan was unworthy of Lynn's genius, Percy Hammond, now reviewing for the New York *Tribune*, got the point, for he saw a "new" Lynn Fontanne, a "vampiric" woman. Noel Coward says Lynn was "gay and attractive in it, utterly different from Dulcy, which had been a bleating, essentially comic characterization. In *In Love with Love*, she also began to be beautiful. There was a new fullness to her figure and her movements were smoother. She wore a pale-pink dress in one scene which gave a warm glow to her skin and when I noticed how she used her eyes and hands, I suspected Alfred of rehearsing her in sex appeal."

Alfred rehearse her in sex appeal? Nobody ever had to rehearse Lynn in sex appeal. She was born with sex appeal. It was the rest of the world that was blind to it.

Yet I must admit that if there was a Lady Castlemaine and a vampiric Ann Jordan inside of Lynn, certain strains of Dulcy also existed. Not the cliches, for Lynn was a clever conversationalist. No, the affinity to

* The emptyheaded flirt in Tarkington's *Seventeen*.

Dulcy is in a vagueness about names, places, dates, historical data, and a sublime indifference to arithmetic.

When the Lunts were playing *Caprice* in London (1929) Russel Crouse met Lynn at a party. She said she and Alfred were seeking a quiet place in Europe to go for a long rest after *Caprice* closed. "Do you have any suggestions, ducky?" she asked.

Crouse did. He fancied Switzerland. There were charming little Swiss villages, far from the madding crowd. Gruyère, for instance. Crouse told her about Gruyère, the mountains, the lakes, the solitude.

"It sounds marvelous," she said. "By the way, tell me, is there ocean bathing at Gruyère?"

Alfred loves to tell about the time when they were touring *Reunion in Vienna*. "Next week," he said, "we're playing Minnesota."

"If it's in Texas, I'll love it," she said.

During the run of *Dulcy*, Tyler had a spasm of generosity, and gave Lynn a handsome raise—without her asking. He was hurt when she didn't show her gratitude. Finally, he took it up with her. "Oh dear," she said, "I should have thanked you, only I didn't know you gave me a raise. I didn't count it, you see. The only funny thing I noticed was it took a little longer to spend than usual."

She once told a reporter: "I love poultry but I can't bear to think of a chicken being killed. I've persuaded myself that the ones in the shops were always like that!"

She is terrible about remembering people's names. The Lunts once threw a big party at their home. Among the stage celebrities was a young playwright with three hit plays running at the time. Lynn had frequently met him and knew him fairly well. When Lynn's sister, 'Toineau, who was at the party, asked Lynn who that interesting man over there was, Lynn said that he looked familiar and his name was on the tip of her tongue but she couldn't remember. She finally decided he wasn't an actor. She went over to him and said, "Excuse me—but what is it you do?"

He thought she was pulling his leg. "I try to write plays," he said, "but I haven't had much luck lately."

She looked blankly at him. The name wouldn't come. She asked, "Please—what is your name?"

"I wish it were Alfred Lunt, but it happens to be Moss Hart."

Quite unfazed, Lynn turned to her sister and chortled triumphantly, "Well, I *told* you he wasn't an actor!"

She'll get hung up on certain words. Her brother-in-law, George

Bugbee, is the executive director of the American Hospital Association. She'll pronounce it "exxaccative direccative." Siobhan McKenna (pronounced Shi-vaun) comes out "Sis-boom Mechanic."

She likes to chew gum and play solitaire. She is devoutly superstitious. Seeing a pin onstage, she will stoop over and pick it up. It's good luck to find a pin in the theatre. Backstage, she won't ever pass another actor on the stairs. She retreats to the nearest landing or pops into a nearby dressing room and waits until the stair is clear. It's bad luck to pass another actor on a staircase. She considers it good luck if it rains on opening night and good luck if there's a cat in the theatre. She loathes people who whistle in her dressing room.

She is never on time for trains and planes. She forgets gloves, handkerchiefs, handbags, everywhere. Before she leaves home or the theatre, her maid has to check off every possession she must take—compact, purse, papers, handkerchief, and so on.

Yet the same woman who is an idiot about geography can "sweep you right off your feet at a game of Scrabble," as Crouse puts it. Lynn is neither stupid nor scatterbrained. Her brains are concentrated on one thing at a time. She is oblivious to everything else. "Lynn has trained her mind to run on one track at a time," says a friend, "but her mind is not a one-track mind."

SIX

MR. AND MRS. LUNT AT HOME

*A*FTER A successful tour in *Clarence*, Alfred returned to Manhattan in the summer of 1921. Gregory Kelly, who played Dulcy's husband, was leaving the cast. Tyler asked Alfred to replace Kelly. A. L. Erlanger vetoed the decision. Klaw and Erlanger operated the most powerful theatrical syndicate in the country—though it was being challenged by Lee and J. J. Shubert—and the old-line producers, including Tyler, were still tied up with the Klaw and Erlanger "trust."

One day in August Alfred was summoned to Erlanger's office. When Alex Aarons, an Erlanger deputy, brought him the royal summons and said that the emperor was putting him in a new play, Alfred protested he was going to play Gordon Smith to Lynn's Dulcinea Smith. Aarons said not at all and rushed him into the chief's office. Alfred's mind was in a whirl. Erlanger ordered him to be ready to go into rehearsal next Monday in a new play by Booth Tarkington. Alfred was "in mortal dread" of the mighty Erlanger, who could always "put the fear of God into my heart." Erlanger talked loud and fast. He brandished a script in one hand and a contract in the other. Aarons shoved a fountain pen at Lunt.

"It's a star's part, my boy," Erlanger bellowed. "Sign right here."

"But—Mr. Tyler—he said—that is—*Dulcy*—what will I say to Lynn, Miss Fontanne——"

"Made to order for you, it is. Written by Booth Tarkington for Alfred Lunt."

"I never heard of the play. Mr. Tarkington never mentioned it to me." What was its title?

"Title? Title? Just sign here. Don't worry about the title. Rehearsals Monday. Eleven. *The Intimate Strangers*, is that it, Alex? You'll love it. We signed up Billie Burke. You fall in love with her. You meet her in a railroad station up in the woods somewhere. There's a flood or a hurricane, see? Trains washed out. You miss the train. You're with Billie Burke all night in the station—alone. . . . She's a single girl. You're a bachelor. She's not a girl—more like an older woman type. She hasn't married because she's all her life looking for a classy husband like you. So then you come along but she thinks you're in love with her daughter—"

"Her niece, sir," interjected Aarons.

"Her niece."

"What niece was that?" Lunt inquired, slightly dizzy.

"What difference does it make what niece? You're a man about forty-five. Distinguished type. Banker type."

"I beg you, Mr. Erlanger, I am not suitable to play a middle-aged character part, that is, when there are so many finer character men than I to play this. I'm young."

"So we'll whiten your hair up."

Lunt's lips twitched. "Whiten my hair?"

"Tarkington specifically said he wants you."

Alfred signed the contract.

Lynn knew it was a cunning plot to keep them apart. Klaw, Erlanger, Tyler, Mrs. Sederholm, and destiny were against her. Tarkington surely never had written a play with such an insane plot. Alfred inquired of Tarkington:

All those stories about managers luring innocent young things into their offices and by lies and arch cunning inveigling them into signing contracts —drove me mad. Is the play really yours? Did you say you really wanted me?

Yes, Tarkington really had written the play. And Alfred really would have to look forty or forty-five. Alfred vowed he would wear a "bald wig and Mormon whiskers" if Tarkington required it. But Miss Burke was so eternally youthful that he would have no "difficulty in playing either up or down to it, as the case may be." He thought that if he grew a moustache, perhaps, it would age him, or "at least give me a man of the world expression." But he hated to whiten his hair. Whitened hair always looked artificial.

It's sort of painting the lily—after all, the age ought to come out in the acting—then I've gotten rather fatter too, which may help—fat but not vulgar.

Now that he definitely was to play Ames, the bachelor, Lunt's mood changed. He would be an "affable bachelor." He was "frightened to death and too happy to live. It's marvelous."

Tarkington himself took over the direction of the play. He hadn't directed a play since his Princeton years. Alfred admired Tarkington— no, he worshiped him—the father he would have liked to have had. Tarkington was tall, elegantly dressed, considerate of other persons, sensitive, sophisticated, cultured, and rich. Tarkington was generous. He was always forking out dollar tips in an era when the dime tip was standard. Alfred was awed by Tarkington's free-handed generosity, his gracious manners, his tact, his humorous easygoing attitude toward life's difficulties. Alfred always signed his letters to Tarkington, "your loving son."

Mr. Tarkington was a truly great American gentleman. Bob Sherwood was a little like him.*

The Intimate Strangers was Tarkington's most charming piece. It was too charming for its time and place. On the one hand, it lacked theatrical "sock," and, on the other, its morals were outmoded and its humor was too amiable. A new comedy school of hostile repartee and incisive social comment was coming into vogue. For 1922, a heroine like Miss Burke's Isabel, who doesn't believe in cosmetics, bobbed hair, smoking, or short skirts, was pitiable, not amusing. And Alfred's Ames, who dislikes the "young things" of the "new generation" because they "smoke and drink and wear men's clothes and short hair," was a ridiculous anachronism. Isabel was Tarkington's archetype, the "country cousin," the superior provincial. Her niece, a "wicked" flapper, was played by a "young thing" named Frances Howard, who married a young movie producer, Sam Goldwyn.

The first-act badinage between Miss Burke and Lunt delighted audiences. Percy Hammond said this was "one of the most sweetly sophisticated interludes of Mr. Tarkington's achievements as a playwright." The New York *American*'s Alan Dale, who had been worried lest his praise of Lunt in *Clarence* would ruin his future, said he was relieved to report that Lunt's performance was superb though he was "much more avoirdupoiser than in Clarence."

On December 9, 1921, in the second month of the run, Miss Lynn Fontanne and Mr. Alfred Lunt officially announced their engagement in the dramatic columns.

* Letter to the author from Alfred Lunt, April 7, 1962.

After 91 performances on Broadway, *The Intimate Strangers* began a national tour in Boston. Billie Burke, reported Lunt in a worried communication to Tarkington, was getting more and more "kittenish" and coy, slowing up her lines to suck every drop of sugar out of them. "Of course," he says, "her voice *is* so lovely when she gets 'that way' and no doubt someone has told her so, but she shoves it in where it doesn't belong now & then—but oh she's such a dear, perhaps it really doesn't matter." Alfred was refining his own role, cutting down on his gestures, whenever he sensed the audience was—in his phrase—"getting breathy." He tells Tarkington that he has "simmered down and simplified my performance and I really think you'd be pleased—I've taken out all the head shakes (or all I could, that is). . . ."

Here is the first clear intimation of that desperate pursuit of perfection which was to plague Lynn and Alfred throughout their careers. It was a divine dissatisfaction with any stage moments that fell short of an impossible ideal—namely, to be more real than reality.

From Boston, the company journeyed to Buffalo and then to Chicago. Miss Burke traveled like a queen. Two baggage cars transported her luggage and enough furniture to furnish an apartment. She rented an apartment or house wherever they played. No hotels for her. Her Rolls-Royce was shipped from city to city.

"How else, indeed, should an actress travel?" she asks in her memoirs.

Her entourage included a nurse (for her small child), a chauffeur (for her limousine), a *chef de cuisine*, two maids, and three dogs.

"All we need now," Alfred remarked, "is a calliope and a shetland pony for a morning parade!"

Billie Burke demanded *two* dressing rooms for herself in each theatre. Alfred was jealous. He asked for equal rights for leading men. In Chicago he got two dressing rooms. But, he confessed to Lynn, the extra room "only embarrassed me—my other suit hanging there all alone never looked so shabby and dejected."

As the wedding day approached—though neither Alfred nor his fiancée knew exactly when it would be—Alfred became nervous. He couldn't eat. He couldn't sleep. Miss Burke's romantic heart went out to poor Alfred, pale and wan, starving to death. She had him to dinner and offered him rarefied meals to arouse his lovelorn palate. "My kitchen," she says, "was teeming and steaming at all hours with special delicacies intended to tempt our lover to nourish himself."

On May 20, *Dulcy* closed in New Haven. *The Intimate Strangers* finished in Baltimore and there was a week until the Atlantic City engagement. Lynn and Alfred were able to reunite in New York. They were sitting in Central Park one balmy morning. Suddenly Alfred leaped up.

"Let's get married," he said.

"Today?" Lynn said.

"Now," Alfred said. "Immediately."

They didn't go back to the love nest to change clothes. They didn't telephone a soul—not even Noel Coward. They went by subway to the Municipal Building. They entered the Marriage Bureau. They filled out the forms. Two witnesses were needed for the civil ceremony. Alfred scrambled out into the corridors. He flushed out two bewildered gentlemen to witness the nuptial rites. A clerk united them in holy matrimony. It was May 26, 1922. The clerk asked for the fee of two dollars. Alfred's hand went to his inside breast pocket. It was empty!

"Good lord," he said, "I forgot my wallet." Lynn, of course, *always* forgot her purse. Between the two of them they had 95 cents. Alfred borrowed two dollars from the witnesses. The clerk gave Alfred the license. Lynn seized it. She read it. She read it again. Yes, they really were man and wife, at last. She kissed Alfred. She kissed the witnesses. She kissed the clerk. They danced out of the bureau. Where should they go for the wedding feast? They went around the block to Huyler's. They banqueted on chicken salad sandwiches and chocolate sodas.

They honeymooned in Atlantic City. But wouldn't they have to be publicly married to have a honeymoon? It was one thing to carry on a clandestine affair—but a clandestine marriage? So they were married in a religious ceremony by an Episcopalian minister and Miss Burke gave the bride and groom a wedding reception. Alfred was so unhinged by the second ceremony that he went completely dumb during the next performance. The stage manager had to hide behind the stove or under the benches of the Act I set and read Alfred's lines while Alfred synchronized his lip movements to the speeches.

Now Alfred had to break the news to his mother. He sent her the shattering intelligence by wire: HAVE MADE AN HONEST WOMAN OF LYNN.

Hattie Sederholm wired congratulations. Wouldn't Mr. and Mrs. Lunt summer in Genesee Depot? Hattie loved pleasure so much she couldn't bear holding a grudge. She accepted Lynn wholeheartedly and soon came to love her. They had a wonderful family summer in Genesee Depot—elaborate meals indoors and more elaborate picnics outdoors, hay rides, barn dances, excursions to northern Wisconsin, fishing trips for bass and pickerel, walking trips all over the hills. Great quantities of home-brewed high potency beer and Mrs. Sederholm's pungent berry wine were drunk by one and all.

As much as Lynn loved the vagabonding existence of an actress, she also yearned to have roots. Now she had found them. She had found a family and a land she loved. She shared Alfred's fondness for cultivating flowers and fruits and breeding poultry and cows. In 1922, he owned three acres of land; she encouraged him to buy more. But it was so expensive, he complained—they were asking $25 an acre! He was too conservative to put money in real estate. He liked to keep cash in the bank. But Lynn made him buy more land. Eventually, he bought forty acres, and, out of her own income, Lynn bought another sixty-five acres, across the road. Today, land in the county, if you can find any, goes for $500 an acre.

The maddest escapade of that summer resulted from Alfred's delusion that he could drive a car. Alfred was so euphoric he thought he could do anything. He bought a Model T Ford. The dealer showed him how to set the ignition spark and gas, how to crank her up, and put her in reverse. It looked easy. Alfred got behind the wheel and careened wildly back to the farm. He bumped into the property, jolting wildly from side to side, blowing his horn, terrifying the chickens. Mrs. Sederholm was aghast. Alfred was proud of himself. He invited the family to come for a ride. He said he could race as fast as thirty miles an hour. Quite a wind blew up. "I think you better put on something warm, Mother," he said.

"I guess I'll wear my ascension robes," Hattie said drily.

Lynn and Alfred started married life in New York in a four room unfurnished apartment on the second floor of 969 Lexington Avenue. They didn't feel they had enough money to furnish their place in the style they wanted. They wanted to decorate it with fine antiques. So they would buy them, one at a time. Nor would they throw away money on cheap rugs; so the floors were bare. Most of the apartment was bare. Their first purchase, at Bloomingdale's, was a large icebox. Their second purchase was a double bed. At least, it looked like a double bed. The dealer assured them it was a double bed. Years later, they found out it was a three-quarter bed. "We were so skinny in those days," Lynn remembers, "we didn't realize it was just a three-quarter bed and we slept in it for years until an interior decorator told us the awful truth. I suppose we'd have found out eventually when we put on weight. We still have the bed. It's in one of the guest rooms at Genesee Depot."

The living room was furnished with a large theatrical trunk, over which they threw a Spanish shawl. An orange crate served as a table. They had only two chairs—fine Beidermeier chairs—in the room. The second bedroom was entirely bare.

After six months, they had saved enough for carpeting. "I waited until we could afford a thickish carpet to cover every inch of the apartment," Lynn says. "I didn't want half measures. We saved for a thick carpet—oh, it must have been three inches thick pile—in a neutral shade, a sort of beige, to harmonize with whatever color scheme we'd have when we could afford color schemes. At this point, we didn't even have drapes. We ordered the carpeting. It was going to be wall-to-wall—in both bedrooms, the parlor, the hall, even the bathroom and the kitchen were to be completely covered. The night the carpet finally came—we'd been dreaming of it like little children waiting for Christmas morning—well, we were working and at the theatre and it was laid down while we were away. We came home and there it was—the whole apartment carpeted. Alfred and I were so excited. We took off our shoes. We took off our stockings. We danced around and around, we were so excited; we were twirling in the living room and then we went from one room to the other, digging our bare toes into the carpet, and we were so happy with it and each other and the world."

Though the place was still sparely furnished, they now began to invite friends over. At least, there was a carpet for them to sit on. Sitting on floors was quite fashionable during the 1920's. "We entertained a great deal," Lynn recalls. "We had wonderful theatrical parties after the theatre, and we had dinner parties too, as we now had our marvelous Louise Scott working for us. She cooked divinely." She was a tall, beautiful Negro woman, who became an essential part of the ménage.

Their first dinner guest was Noel, of course. He had gone back to England in 1922, a failure. A year later he returned to New York, still a failure, but determined to succeed as a playwright. He now lived at an imposing address—the Ritz Carlton Hotel. Nobody but the Lunts knew it was the cheapest room in the hotel, "practically a linen closet," as Lynn says. Frequently, Coward lacked the price of dinner. Lynn was never surprised when Noel, looking ever more emaciated, suddenly appeared backstage at the Frazee Theatre, waiting for her to take her curtain calls for *In Love with Love*. She knew by a certain pitiful look in his eyes that he'd been unable to wangle a dinner invitation. She'd put her arm in his and say, as if suddenly struck by an inspiration, "Would you like to have dinner with us tonight—that is if you haven't any other engagement?"

And Noel would look up dreamily, as if he were flicking over an invisible social calendar. Then he'd break out in a smile. "Why," he'd say, "as a matter of fact, I *am* free tonight."

Louise's personality soon became famous in theatrical circles. Once, at the butcher's, as she ordered a fancy cut of prime shell steak, the butcher said, "What the hell do those Lunts want anything like this for? Actors never eat anything but beef stew."

"Not these actors," Louise said proudly. "*My* actors live *high*."

Once, for Christmas dinner, the Lunts had invited eight guests and Lynn ordered an enormous turkey. The turkey was delivered while they were out. When they came home, Louise cried out, "Oh come in and see the bird. It's in the kitchen—the great, big, brazen thing."

Louise often took it upon herself to extend invitations. Once, Donald MacDonald phoned and asked if Alfred or Lynn were in.

"No," Louise replied, "they're not in—but I'm expecting them for dinner. We're having an awfully nice dinner tonight. Why don't you come too?"

He accepted.

When the playwright Sidney Howard married Claire Eames, the actress, they moved into the apartment above the Lunts. The various kitchens of the building were serviced by a dumbwaiter which conveyed the garbage to the janitor in the basement. Louise liked examining the different garbages as they were descending. She once said, "That Mr. and Mrs. Howard—they certainly do have awful nice garbage!"

Louise was especially good at cooking creamy soufflé desserts and delicious pastries. Her sister, Maud, worked for Noel Coward after Noel became affluent. Once when Noel was dining at the Lunts' and wallowing in a chocolate mousse that Louise had created, he looked up at Louise and said, "Why don't I have sweets like this? Why doesn't your sister make me desserts like you make for Mr. and Mrs. Lunt?"

Louise drew herself up. "Mr. Coward," she explained, "my sister has always worked for sportin' ladies and *they* has their desserts *sent* in."

Elaborating on this, Lynn says, "Maud was considered to be in a higher social strata than Louise, because sporting ladies were much more important than actors. Oh, Louise was respectful to Maud. The sporting ladies paid higher salaries. Indeed, it was a comedown for Maud, working for Noel Coward."

Once, Lynn happened to be slinking naked from the bathroom to the bedroom.

"My, you has lovely legs," Louise remarked.

"Do you think so?" Lynn said, quite pleased, as she kicked up her heels.

"Yes, they're like champagne bottles, they are."

Louise loved it when they threw a grand supper party. She adored celebrities and talked to them as respectfully as if they were sporting ladies. She hated to go home. Sometimes she stayed until four in the morning. The morning after one fête, Louise remarked that all the guests had been so charming, especially "that little man you could be so sort of playful with. What was his name?"

It was Efrem Zimbalist. Alfred says Louise had given in a few words a perfect description of Zimbalist and anybody who knew him would have recognized him at once.

At dinner parties, Alfred carved at the table. Once, as he was carving a chicken, Louise, standing behind him, called out, "For chrissake, Mr. Lunt, now don't give no guests no wings."

To Lynn and Alfred the difference between a successful and an unsuccessful actor was that the former could have breakfast in bed. Now that they had both arrived, they insisted on this. Louise would come in the morning and prepare a substantial breakfast while the Lunts were still sleeping. Louise would knock on the bedroom door at ten.

Alfred would open his eyes. "In the morning in bed," he says, "Lynn was the most beautiful thing I ever saw. She'd lie there and her long hair glowed all around her face. Y'know, she always looked as if she hadn't been sleeping, fresh and pretty as if she'd been at her dressing table an hour." He got out of bed first and performed his ablutions. Then Lynn roused herself and soaped her hands and face with an ordinary brand of soap. She believed plain soap and water to be a fine facial cleanser. She tied up her hair in a black ribbon. She clad herself in a pink *peignoir*. She then returned to bed.

Louise carried in two trays heaped with food. Lynn and Alfred liked big breakfasts. They began with fresh fruit, followed by eggs with ham, bacon, sweetbreads, liver, or a fish, and finally hot biscuits and tea. Since they rarely had lunch when they were playing and omitted dinner, the breakfast had to sustain them until the supper after the performance.

Ellen Thornley Fontanne and Jules Pierre Antoine Fontanne with three of their daughters, Lynn (who was twelve), Mai Ellen Lucie, and Antoinette Marie

Lynn Fontanne at fourteen

Lynn at sixteen with cherries in her mouth

Lynn's mother at
sixteen

BELOW:
Lynn's father at
forty-five

Two-year-old Alfred Lunt with his father, Alfred Lunt, Sr.

Alfred, at six, with his mother, Harriet Washburn Briggs Lunt

Alfred (*right*) as a moody Valentine in a 1911 Carroll College production of Shaw's *You Never Can Tell*. On the left is May Nickell Rankin, who kindled Alfred's artistic spark into a flame.

Alfred (*top row, left*) with the Carroll College Glee and Mandolin Club, which gave concerts all over Wisconsin

Alfred
impersonating
Harry Lauder

Alfred in his dressing room
at the Castle Square
Theatre, Boston, around
1913. He was not
considered handsome.

Lynn in 1916. She was not considered beautiful.

Laurette Taylor and Lynn in harlequin costumes for a number at a
Victory Ball at the Palmer House in Chicago, December 7, 1918

Alfred getting a saxophone lesson in 1918 in preparation for his role in *Clarence*

Lynn in 1921

Lynn on the M-G-M set of *The Guardsman*. She was sulky at posing for "cheesecake."

Wide World Photos, Inc.

The Lunts, with Elsa, Lynn's dachshund, at Ten Chimneys, Genesee Depot, Wisconsin

Robert E. Sherwood and the Lunts at the first reading of *There Shall Be No Night*

AT RIGHT:
The Lunts and Tallulah Bankhead
serving coffee to a British sailor at the Stage Door
Canteen, where Alfred was usually
on the garbage detail

Alexander Woollcott, a lifelong friend, visiting the Lunts backstage in 1940

Theresa Helburn, John C. Wilson, and Lawrence Langner welcome the
Lunts home in 1945 after their tour of army bases with *O Mistress Mine*

Noel Coward and Alfred escort Lynn to the opening of Coward's film *The Astonished Heart* in 1950

The Lunts with
Russel Crouse and
Howard Lindsay
at a party
following the
opening of *The
Great Sebastians*

The Lunts at
Balmain's salon
in Paris in 1957

Around 1927, Louise began to come in later and later. The Lunts were disturbed. One day, Alfred finally demanded, "Why were you so late this morning?"

Louise said, "Mr. Lunt, I was a ten months baby, I was born late— and, sir, I'm marked, *marked!*"

Alfred was not one to question the influence of heredity. But breakfast in bed was essential to their happiness. Couldn't she possibly come in earlier? Difficulties would arise, if she didn't. No, she said she couldn't. Wasn't she afraid of losing this well-paying position?

"I'm afraid of nothing but Jesus," she explained.

She came later and later and finally when she came at noon, Alfred told her, "I'm afraid you'd better get your things and go. We'll give you a month's salary instead of notice. Mrs. Lunt and I can't stand not having breakfast in bed."

"I'm sorry, Mr. Lunt, I surely am, as I think you and Mrs. Lunt is wonderful people to work for but I'm a ten month baby and I'm marked for life."

"It's not that we don't appreciate you," Lynn said. "We do think you're a marvelous cook, but we need somebody most of all in the mornings when we wake up. Above all, when we're in rehearsal. That's when we need you to get our breakfast most of all. D'you see?"

When they weren't in rehearsal and had all day to themselves, Lynn customarily immersed herself for an hour in a hot tub perfumed with expensive cologne. She exercised each day for thirty minutes—mainly walking. She also did stretching and bending exercises to keep her abdomen firm. Bloat and fat were enemies, and she fought them constantly. It was not easy because she loved fine food.

And the miracle of Lynn's face? She once told me:

I think it is a gift of nature. I was born with a thick skin. Either you have a thin skin or a thick skin. A thin skin shows wrinkles. I don't use pancake makeup. At night, I use a standard low priced brand of face cream. I don't think I have any secrets of beauty. Around the farm, I don't put on makeup. In town, I do, of course. I use a lotion as a powder base. I use a bit of dry rouge on my cheeks. I like to blend the rouge myself. I combine brunet rouge with a light orange powder, the orange gives the rouge an animation it doesn't get by itself. Naturally, Alfred and I have studied makeup. It's our trade, wouldn't you say? Even when we did films, we made ourselves up. I do have one theory, though, I should tell you about. I believe the line of a woman's jaw is very important to her looks. I've worked hard to keep my jaw line firm. I have an exercise I do. I raise my neck and twist it from side to side, and then around and around. About twenty minutes. I do this in the morning. I've never had my face lifted. Never had any plastic surgery.

Two dowagers were once discussing Lynn's looks during a matinee of *There Shall Be No Night*.

"Her hands," one lady remarked, "oh, what lovely hands she has."

"Ah, but are they her own?" her friend said.

Lynn once said—she was then thirty-five years old—that if a woman were determined to remain young and pretty "in some way just the determination" influences her beauty. And it was important for a woman to be beautiful. It was "an aesthetic matter."

She loved beauty for its own sake, all things lovely, the human face and form among them, but now that she was infected with Alfred's theories of the theatre, she had another motivation. Her youth, her beauty of figure and brightness of motion, were the channels by which she transmitted her feeling of a character to an audience. She had fought to be beautiful and she fought to retain her beauty. Her beauty became more eloquent as she aged. In a sense, she had "nor youth, nor age," but, as it were, a dream of whatever age of woman she had to represent in a play. Her representation of the three ages of womankind in *Milestones*, which was her first big stride forward in the theatre, convinced her that, within reasonable limits, a woman could control her own looks by her intelligence, her dedication, and her art.

Clothes, the best designed and best made, were part of the "aesthetic matter." She has been gowned by the best ones—Worth, Chanel, Vionnet, Molyneux, Valentina, and Dior, Balenciaga, Lanvin-Castillo. And she uses hats for stress and punctuation and dramatic shadings of her appearance. She can—and does sometimes—make her own dresses and her own hats. And she chooses her accessories, her shoes, gloves, hose, jewelry, as carefully as her gowns. Clothes are not merely objects to be put on and off, to be worn for a special occasion or to express the mood of an hour. They become a part of her body. There is no such idea as "artificiality" in her concept of beauty. She was shocked once when an English friend, a beautiful and wealthy woman, told her she didn't know how to put on false eyelashes. Lynn at once presented her with a set of them and told her exactly how one applied them. Like Ellen Terry, Lynn loves "benefiting people," and she has counseled many women in how to choose their clothes and accessories and how to arrange for themselves to look beautiful. There is no such thing as an ugly woman in her philosophy. There are only women who are lazy or discouraged or unimaginative about colors and styles. All women, she thinks, can be beautiful in their own sort of beauty. And she, who was for so long considered plain and bony and scrawny, should know better than anybody else that beauty is a victory of mind over matter.

Sleep is one of her fundamental doctrines of beauty. A woman can never get enough sleep. She sleeps late in the morning and retires early in the evening.

During the frenetic hedonism of the 1920's, in which the Lunts participated, many of her friends burned the candle at both ends. Lynn tempered her pursuit of pleasure. She could stay on her feet at a party as late as anybody else, if the party was a good one, but she didn't do it every night. She loved dancing and going to speakeasies and cabarets —but not night after night. She said "constant late hours and dancing in restaurants and rushing about are the worst things in the world for the woman who wants to keep her beauty and her happiness."

She has a cat's instinct for instant repose. Joyce Carey, a British actress who has played in many of the English productions with the Lunts, once remarked, apropos of her vitality, that Lynn not only looked beautiful, but somehow outshone all the other beauties around her. Once, during an English tour, when they were playing at Cambridge, George Rylands, a Cambridge don and a Shakespearean scholar, gave a supper party for Lynn and Alfred. Many beautiful women, some from the theatre, had come up from London.

"As the evening went on," Miss Carey says, "we all got fatigued and tired-looking. Our makeup seemed to get streaked and our clothes disarrayed. But Lynn got more and more beautiful. By midnight, she was the finest looking woman of the lot and I can tell you this was a lot that included some frightfully stunning girls in the flush of youth."

Except when performing, she takes an aperitif before dinner and wine with dinner. Lynn controls her drinking. Uncontrolled drinking by an actor is a quick, sure road to disaster. There is a slowing of emotional reflexes, a slippage in making contact with the role. And alcohol, she believes, bloats the face, leading to a slow physical dilapidation that destroys the acting illusion. Alfred has told me that any actor who drinks during rehearsals or performances in any of their productions is summarily dismissed. There used to be a sign posted on the bulletin board backstage of any play with the Lunts:

WE DON'T MIND GARLIC OR ONION ON THE BREATH—BUT
WE DO OBJECT TO THE SMELL OF LIQUOR

Lynn's fear of alcohol was intensified by Laurette Taylor's tragic deterioration. Even if Laurette Taylor had not become an alcoholic, she and Lynn couldn't have been friends the way they once had been. The merger of two identities into a new being, which was the kind of love Lynn and Alfred were experiencing, excluded any other fervent relationship. Theirs was a rare love, the sort of which Aristophanes speaks in Plato's *Symposium,* when he describes how in ancient times there were no men and no women. There were round creatures with four arms, four legs and two faces; Zeus sundered them. Now and then certain persons sought and found the other half of their original beings and wanted now to be in the other's company all the time and even "be melted into one." (How odd that of all the speakers in this dialogue it should be a playwright, and a comic writer at that, who presents this romantic theory of love! Did Aristophanes base it on a couple who acted in his plays in Athens? Grecian ancestors of Lynn Fontanne and Alfred Lunt?)

In Laurette's bedroom hung a full-length portrait of her mother, Mrs. Elizabeth Cooney. Marguerite Taylor Courtney, Laurette's daughter and biographer, once told me that Mrs. Cooney looked exactly like Lynn. She mentioned the resemblance to her mother. Laurette said, "Yes, it might be Lynn—except the lips. Lynn's lips welcome the imprint of pleasure and never cry 'woe is me.' "

Laurette was jealous of other women. She had only two women friends, the actress Jane Peyton, who married Samuel Hopkins Adams, and Lynn. Laurette competed with every other woman, even, at times, with these two. She wanted to be the only woman in a world of men. She didn't, at first, drink seriously. She hated alcohol, the more so because her husband was drinking heavily now. She confided to Lynn that whisky was his "liquid bride." During the tour of *Happiness,* Lynn and Laurette were at a Philadelphia country club. Lynn was dancing with one of the local gentry. Laurette imagined Lynn was flirting with "her man," although Lynn did not know Laurette had a crush on the gentleman. Laurette turned on Lynn. She accused her of making a play for him.

"I'm not," Lynn assured her, astounded at this unexpected accusation, "in the least interested in that man—and he isn't in the least interested in me."

She couldn't understand why Laurette acted as if she were an enemy.

"Another reason Mother quarrelled with Lynn was over Lynn not wanting to play games at Mother's parties or entertain," recalls Mrs. Courtney. "You couldn't sit still with Laurette and just talk peacefully. You had to 'do something.' She'd always pick on her women guests. She once savagely criticized Ethel Barrymore in front of other people and Miss Barrymore never came again to the house."

Laurette had given an elegant opening-night party honoring Lynn after the premiere of *Dulcy*. Laurette got drunk. She suddenly began ridiculing Lynn in front of everybody. Alfred was disgusted. He said he didn't see how Lynn could put up with such unprovoked nastiness. Lynn said Laurette was only teasing. Shortly afterwards, at a dinner party at Laurette's, Laurette began harping sarcastically on Lynn's naïveté and ridiculed her the whole evening.

"She's a cruel person and she's a bitch," Alfred said, when they were alone.

"Oh, Alfred, it's just her way."

"I don't want to have anything to do with her. I'm not going to her house any more."

"I can't drop her like this," Lynn said.

Alfred shrugged. "Then you go there—alone."

"Why should she be deliberately cruel to me?"

"She's jealous, that's why."

"Jealous? Of me? Oh, come off it, Alfred."

"Why don't you ask Noel?"

Noel revealed that he had wanted to do his comedy, *Fallen Angels*, with Lynn and Laurette. Laurette had refused.

"Lynn," she sniffed, "just clowns around on stage and she'll ruin every scene." Noel had never told Lynn, because she worshiped Laurette. But Laurette was undergoing a profound alteration. Formerly, she had been lightly sardonic and amusingly superior to Lynn—but there had been a foundation of genuine affection for her protégée. Now she was drunk every day, and failing in the theatre. As Lynn got recognition for her beauty and her talent and became a star, Laurette was going downhill faster and faster. Now her moods of resentment, her sudden storms of insanity and wrath, became uncontrollable.

Once, Lynn went, by herself, to a gathering at Laurette's. Laurette started discussing mental telepathy and said some people were gifted with telepathic powers. She was, for one. She began to read everybody's mind. Lynn was impressed. Then Laurette laughed. It had all been previously arranged and she and Hartley and the guests had all been in on the joke. Hadn't it been a funny game?

"I didn't know you were playing a game," Lynn said. "I thought you were really reading our minds."

"Don't you like games, dear?" Laurette sneered. "Are you too old to play games? Are you above games now that you are a star?"

At that moment, the friendship died for Lynn. It could not be revived again as it had been before, even when Laurette, during a sobering-up phase of her alcoholic cycle, came to Lynn pleading for Lynn's forgiveness and apologizing for her outbursts.

Laurette never got over losing Lynn's friendship. When Hartley Manners died and she retreated into melancholy, she wondered why Lynn didn't come to help her. "Lynn lived within five blocks of me," she wrote later, "and I had no desire to see anyone except Lynn. I expected some mental help from the friend I had helped when she was miserable from the same cause—loss of her man."

Her daughter was strictly forbidden to go to Lynn's plays or to talk to her. "Lynn Fontanne was black market to me," Mrs. Courtney says, remembering her girlhood and how she had to go secretly to the theatre to see Lynn perform.

Laurette made one of her periodic "comebacks" in *Alice-Sit-By-the-Fire.* Lynn sent her an expensive leather bag and a box of violets on opening night. Still bitter after so many years, Laurette sneered that the violets were lovely but "they were six years too late."

Their final meeting occurred during the 1943 revival of *Outward Bound,* in which Laurette Taylor was starred. Laurette had supper with Lynn after the performance. Alfred retired early. The women stayed up and talked all through the night. They reminisced about the events in their long friendship and all the plays they had done together and all the odd and beautiful and talented people they had known in London and New York and the men they had loved. When they separated, before breakfast, they had come to some sort of terms with their pasts and with each other.

Lynn did not want to flaw this understanding and she never saw Laurette again, either socially or professionally. She never witnessed Laurette's shining portrayal of Amanda Wingfield in *The Glass Menagerie.* She deliberately refrained from going to see her. She would keep the memory of Laurette Taylor as it was on that last, long evening of intimacy.

SEVEN

THE WHOLE IS GREATER THAN THE

SUM OF ITS PARTS

*I*T TOOK about eight years after Lynn and Alfred were married until they fused into a new being, until they were no longer Lunt and Fontanne, but The Lunts; yet the Lunt and the Fontanne remained, separate personalities in the one being. They retained certain temperamental differences and sometimes these differences clashed so violently it seemed as if the Lunts would be split in two.

Lynn is the more emotionally stable component. She is the gyroscope of the combination. Alfred seesaws. He is vulnerable. He goes through moods of despair. Following *Clarence* he played a variety of parts in a variety of plays. He was an old-fashioned romantic hero in Tarkington's *Intimate Strangers*. He was a cynical sophisticate in *Banco*. He was a young Confederate soldier in John Drinkwater's *Robert E. Lee*. He played a dissolute sinner in *Outward Bound*. In Sutton Vane's fantasy about life after death, which took place on a mysterious voyage, the passengers are all dead, but they do not know it and only gradually realize they are traveling to the next world. During the brief run at the Ritz Theatre in New York, Noel Coward returned to America. Two of his comedies had already been done in England and *London Calling*, a revue for which he had written words and music and sketches and in which he co-starred with Gertrude Lawrence, was the hit of the 1923 season. Noel had never seen Alfred act and he looked forward to *Outward Bound*. He was "deeply moved" by Alfred's portrayal. He went backstage, still feeling "wrought up" by the emotions of the play. He found Alfred sitting at his make-up table. Alfred was staring glumly into the mirror. Noel launched into an ode to Alfred's performance. Alfred groaned. He glanced at Noel out of "rolling tragic eyes." He said he had given the clumsiest performance of his career. He had overacted. He had played to the gallery with shabby technical devices. He had employed "every ham trick that had ever been invented." Noel argued that, on the contrary, Alfred's work had been subtle and tender. He had played "truly." He had hypnotized the audience into rapt attentiveness by the honesty of his emotions. Alfred, sighing and groaning, shook his leonine head.

Then Noel went out to supper with Lynn and Alfred. Alfred was still in despair. Lynn ignored him. She was chattering vivaciously. Noel thought she was a callous wife. Finally, as Alfred continued lamenting his bad acting, she turned to him casually, and murmured, "Never mind, darling, you gave *such* a *lovely* performance last Thursday matinee."

And she went on calmly enjoying her scrambled eggs and bacon.

Noel learned that these exhibitions of self-doubt and self-hatred were chronic with Alfred. He wrote, "It's just Alfred going through his hoops. I know those hoops so well now that I can hear the paper crackling in anticipation before he dives through the first one; but then it was a surprise to me, rather a painful surprise."

The late Theresa Helburn, who was the executive director of the Theatre Guild, described Alfred as a highstrung person, skittish as a thoroughbred racehorse. In every Guild production in which he appeared there would arrive a moment of crisis when Alfred would be seriously convinced he had lost his powers of acting.

"I think it was the tension of opening in a new play," Miss Helburn said. "The tension mounted. It became more than he could bear. So the only way he could help himself was to decide never to act again. He would leave the theatre forever. He was sincere about it every time. You must realize that. He was sincere when he said he was no good and we must close the production down at once."

Sometimes, Lynn could jerk him out of melancholia by ridicule. Once, when he was in one of his monumental funks she cried: "Oh, Alfred, do stop looking like a horse in a fire."

He paused in his ravings and looked at her. Then he burst into laughter.

When Alfred finally gets into the skin and the soul of a new character, he calls it "getting my green umbrella."

During his depressions, Alfred is convinced he is an ugly-looking monster. Once he wrote Laurence Olivier, "my hair is a nice color, brown like expensive mink, but my face reminds me of nothing quite so much as a discarded douche bag."

Jules Johnson, Alfred's dressing-room valet and his *bon à tout faire* on the farm, once discovered Alfred staring at himself in the mirror. Alfred was sunk in melancholy. He was moaning; "Oh what a terribly ugly face I do have. What a curse for an actor to have such a face. And now I'm also tired. And when I get tired my eye gets completely out of line."

"Why, Mr. Lunt," Jules interposed, "but that's one of your charms!"

Are Alfred's sufferings an affectation? Are they baited hooks to catch compliments? Does he perhaps enjoy revelling in bogus despair like a masochist? Noel Coward believes that Alfred's wretchedness is "completely genuine, a nervous reaction from having tried too hard for perfection; an actor's disease from which we all suffer from time to time, although few can plumb the depths so wholeheartedly as he does. In *Design for Living* we all three gave the 'worst' performances of our careers every night together for months, and managed to be very good indeed."

Alfred's elations are as gargantuan as his depressions. Trivial things —a peony bush in bloom, a soufflé risen perfectly—can make him absolutely euphoric. Aristotle's golden mean is not his philosophy. With the poet William Blake he cries, "Everything in excess." And of all the pleasures in Alfred's life, none is more pleasurable than the reading of a new play, especially one in which there are marvelous roles for Lynn and himself. Though they were now Broadway stars of the first magnitude, each separately drawing between $500 and $750 a week, they had not acted together since Washington. Lee Schubert was the first producer to agree that they ought to be a team but he could not find a script for them. Nor could Gilbert Miller or William Harris, Jr., since there are few plays in which the woman's role and the man's role are equally balanced. Other producers, however, thought they were unsuitable candidates for an acting partnership; they still thought of Alfred as "a shy, repressed, neurotic young man with some kind of physical deformity as though he had been wounded in the liver. Lynn was a funny gawky English girl who didn't care how ridiculous she looked as long as the laughs came regularly. It was impossible to imagine that either of them could ever become a glamorous figure or that they could ever find star parts like Clarence or Dulcy to fit their peculiar measurements." [*]

Theresa Helburn thought their "peculiar measurements" fitted the

[*] Robert E. Sherwood, writing in 1931.

leading roles of an old Ferenc Molnar comedy, *The Guardsman*. The Theatre Guild had had it under option for two years and still couldn't cast it properly. Written in 1910, it had been a success in Budapest, Vienna, Paris, and Berlin. On Broadway, where it was done in 1913, it closed in two weeks. It had been called *Where Ignorance Is Bliss*. Hans Bartsch, who was Molnar's American agent and who had translated the play with Grace I. Colbron, had faith in it and had been trying for a decade to get it on. For ten years, the script had been shown to every leading actor and actress. All spurned it. When the Theatre Guild, which had had a small success with Molnar's *Liliom*, announced it was going to produce *The Guardsman*, and in a new acting version, the established stars wouldn't even look at the script. The Guild, a young and struggling "art" theatre, was noted for miserably underpaying actors, being difficult to please, and for never putting an actor's name in marquee lights. The Guild was opposed to the "star system" on principle. Stars were in favor of the star system. Stars were in favor of high salaries. In those days the Guild was proud of not being a capitalistic profit-making organization. The Guild directorate did not care about money since they all had other sources of income—Lawrence Langner was a rich patent attorney, Maurice Wertheim was a rich Wall Street investment banker, Lee Simonson was a rich scenic designer, Miss Helburn had a rich husband, Philip Moeller had a rich papa, and the actress Helen Westley had rich lovers. Personal advantages aside, the Guild had, in six seasons, acquired a reputation as a serious group. It was putting on such daring and unprofitable plays as Shaw's *Heartbreak House*, Strindberg's *Dance of Death*, Capek's *R.U.R.*, Elmer Rice's *The Adding Machine*, Ernst Toller's *Man and Masses*, and John Howard Lawson's *Processional*. It had even dared to put on the complete uncut version of Shaw's *Back to Methuselah*, and Shaw had allowed the Guild the right to stage the world premiere of *Saint Joan*. The Theatre Guild operated without stars. It could not secure the rights to the plays written by the popular American dramatists of the time. It lacked money for lavish productions. Its plays were done in a small shabby theatre on 35th Street, the Garrick. With all this, the Guild represented a powerful force for a theatre of social significance and literary quality. It put on as many as five and six new plays every year—and it expected to lose money on them. Its expectations were rarely disappointed.

The famous actors of that period were not interested in submerging their identities for the sake of a play. They wanted to play in dramas specifically written to display their qualities. They wanted vehicles. They wanted money. They wanted star billing. They were bored by talk of "art," the new techniques of expressionism, the Stanislavski theories of ensemble acting and the projection of inner emotional states. (The Moscow Art Theatre, with Stanislavski, played in New York in 1923. It had a tremendous effect on a small number of people, among them a man then in the wig and toupee business, who gave up artificial hair for the theatre and joined the Theatre Guild's acting troupe. He got $25 a week. His name was Lee Strasberg.) In 1924, there was no prestige in working for the Guild. Broadway producers, dramatists, and actors regarded it as a group run by amateurs who fancied themselves aesthetes.

The Guild directorate had approached scores of actors to play in *The Guardsman,* but nobody thought of Lynn and Alfred until Miss Helburn had a sudden flash of inspiration in April, 1924. Her colleagues derided her brainstorm. She urged them to forget Lynn as a Dulcy and Alfred as a Clarence. Didn't they remember Alfred's elegant lecher in *Banco*? None of them had seen *Banco* except Helburn. (A young publicity man, striving to learn the art of high comedy writing, had seen *Banco* twenty times in order to study Alfred's comedy technique. He was S. N. Behrman.) But, insisted Helburn's associates, even if by some miracle Alfred could play The Actor (that was what the hero of Molnar's play was called—no proper name, just The Actor), that ridiculous gawky farceuse Lynn Fontanne could never in a million years play The Actress, the worldly, the sulky, the passionate, the oversexed heroine. Nobody on the board, not even Helburn, had seen Lynn do *In Love with Love.* Helburn swore Lynn could play Molnar because she had been trained in the English theatre and there was in her playing—even in her Dulcy—a sophisticated aloofness.

"I was desperate," Miss Helburn told me once. "Our option on *The Guardsman* was running out. Something told me the Lunts were perfect for it. They were married and in love like the hero and heroine of *The Guardsman.* I believed their chemistry would make the play." But the others wanted to forsake *The Guardsman,* with or without the Lunts. Had it not already failed a decade ago? Miss Helburn, by now, was possessed. She was a small volatile woman, with straight black hair cut in a pageboy bob. She was one of those American women who were part of the first wave of emancipation and equal rights, the ones who were defying conventions before 1914. She was intellectual. She was bright, quick, effervescent, enthusiastic. She was Bryn Mawr '08. She had been the drama critic of *The Nation*. Her column was a pulpit from which she raged against the vulgarity and banality of the Broadway commercial theatre. The theatre, she believed, was an art form. She worshiped it.

Between a matinee and evening performance of *Outward Bound*, she had tea with Alfred at the Knickerbocker Hotel. She handed him two copies in typescript of *The Guardsman*. Her eyes sparkling, her lips crinkling in a characteristic smile, she rattled on about what a tight amusing new version Philip Moeller had made of the old play and how well she believed Moeller could direct Alfred and Lynn and what a "quality" production the Theatre Guild had in mind. Had Alfred and Lynn ever thought of themselves as an acting team? She believed that they could be one and this play would be just the beginning of many plays they would do with the Guild, fine plays, artistic and challenging plays, classical masterpieces of comedy by Shaw and Shakespeare, and new comedies by new American writers because, she went on breathlessly, there was a ferment in the theatre and the old Broadway theatre with its contrived plots and star vehicles was dying. A new theatre was rising and the Theatre Guild represented the noblest spiritual values of the new age. The Guild dreamed of a permanent acting company, like the Moscow Art Theatre, and the Lunts should join them in this great adventure. Why, they would play in repertory! Yes, repertory! They would work all the season around and they would not be victims of the feast or famine life of an actor, who was either unemployed or trapped in a long and enervating run in the same play.

Miss Helburn lectured with the idealism of Alfred's old professor, May Nickell Rankin. Alfred's philosophy of the theatre as a religion and the actor as its high priest had been laid away in cold storage for years. Could he take it out again? The dream she talked about was his own dream of an American theatre. Yes, he said, rising, he and Lynn would read the play within a week or two and he would let her know about their reaction and yes, he and Lynn wanted to play together if they ever found the right play.

But, Miss Helburn cut in, she had to tell him in all frankness that if they decided to play it they would not receive star billing. With the Guild, the play was the thing, you see. And also, she said nervously, she hoped Alfred and Lynn realized the Guild was a poor and struggling society and they must not think of getting their usual pay which, she had heard, was about $300. Alfred smiled and murmured he was being paid $500 in *Outward Bound* and that several managements were offering Lynn $750.

"Oh, I'm afraid we couldn't pay you more than $250," Miss Helburn said. "Even that is going rather high for us, you see. Last season we only made money with one play out of six we did." It was the Guild's idea to put the profits of their hits—and anything that ran more than 3 weeks was a hit at the Guild because it cost them only two or three thousand dollars to produce a play—into an artistic though unpopular play. She told him how much money they had lost this season on Galsworthy's *Windows*, Lenormand's *The Failures*, von Scholz' *The Race with the Shadow*, Vadja's *Fata Morgana* and Toller's *Man and Masses*. She almost had poor Alfred crying. If she wanted to play on Alfred's sympathies, she was succeeding nicely. Of course, she had no way of knowing that unlike the run of Broadway celebrities Alfred was more romantic than she was about the theatre and thought the Theatre Guild was a heroic band of missionaries.

He said he and Lynn believed money was secondary to the quality of the play. Let them read the play. Perhaps they would not like the play. Miss Helburn, on parting from him, felt she had done a good day's work. The Theatre Guild always appreciated actors who spurned money as crass and vulgar.

After supper, Alfred repaired to the living room and opened the script. Lynn took her copy to the bedroom. Upon finishing Act I, Alfred couldn't contain himself. He was in a fever of ecstasy. He dashed down the hall and flung open the bedroom door. He cried, "Lynnie, Lynnie, we've found it—" and almost collided head on with his wife who was simultaneously racing into the living room to tell Alfred that if he did not think *The Guardsman* was a heaven-sent play she would immediately file suit for divorce.

"Isn't it divine?" she said.

"Then we'll do it?"

"We *must* do it."

"Suppose the second act is bad?" he said.

"It mustn't be," she said. "But if it is?"

"I'll kill myself," he cried.

"Not yet," she said. "Let's read the second act."

"Yes. Aloud. Together."

With mounting excitement they read all the parts of the play in different voices. It was about a leading Hungarian actor who, for six months, has been married to the leading Hungarian actress, a wicked woman who has had at least nine major love affairs. Now the husband is insanely jealous. He hasn't any reason to question his wife's marital fidelity but he's suspicious anyway. To test her, The Actor decides to disguise himself as a captain of the guards who is a military attaché of the Russian embassy. As a "guardsman" he has already begun a flirtation with The Actress. She has been reserved and yet has not entirely discouraged him. The best friend and confidant of both The Actor and The Actress is The Critic. The Actor confides to The Critic that under the pretense of having to fill an emergency engagement with an out-of-town stock company he's going to seem to leave Budapest for three days. Now, as The Guardsman, he will make love to his own wife and find out, for sure, whether she is faithful to him.

It was almost three o'clock in the morning when they finished reading. They were already seeing themselves on the stage as The Guardsman and The Actress.

"I simply must have a sensational evening dress for the second act," Lynn said. "It's much the weakest part in the play and it will need every help we can give it."

"Yes," Alfred said thoughtfully. "What color?"

"Black or red, I think."

"I rather imagine white, a long white velvet gown, would go better."

"I look better in black—stronger, Alfred."

"It would be too strong," he said firmly. "It must be white. What a chance this is. Well, we must go to Europe."

"How wonderful," Lynn said.

They were prancing around the room.

"First to Budapest. We'll see Molnar. We must. I'm not quite clear about some of the lines in the last act. I mean—do you really know it's been me all the time disguised as the Russian or have I fooled you?"

"I've never been to Budapest, darling," she said. Then he suddenly looked grave. "Lynn," he said solemnly, "I forgot to tell you—the Theatre Guild can only pay us $250, instead of our usual fee."

"That comes to $500," she said. "I'm sure we'll be able to scrape along nicely on that, don't you think? How much do you think they'll allow for my costumes? I need—let me see, two in the first act, one in the second, three in the third. I think I ought to get my dresses in Paris."

"*Da, da, da,*" he said, "and think of doing Shaw with the Guild. I am determined to do Shaw. And we'll play repertory." The next morning Alfred phoned Miss Helburn and they had a long talk. He hung up the receiver. He looked crushed.

"What is wrong?" Lynn asked.

"It is terrible," he said. "There was a misunderstanding. She says the Guild means to pay us $250 for you *and* me. The both of us. She says that was what she had in mind when she mentioned the sum of $250."

"She can't be serious," Lynn said.

"And that isn't the worst of it," he said. "She won't allow you more than $50 for each dress."

"I think she's taking advantage of us because we're artists and not too sharp about money," Lynn said. "I think this is sharp nasty business. I don't like it. I don't trust the Guild. They've got a reputation for paying actors badly."

"But they have a mission," Alfred said. "We will do Shaw and Shakespeare in repertory."

"Then let's accept it without bargaining," she said.

Lynn confessed that she'd been secretly saving money. She had $6,000 in the bank. They would spend the money on a trip to Europe and on proper clothes for the play and they would still have several thousand left to keep them going while they were playing in *The Guardsman*.

He balked at spending her savings like this.

She said it was the chance he had been dreaming of. He must seize it. Now. Who knew when they would get another chance? But, he demurred, though it was tempting to be able to act with each other and for a dedicated management, yet it seemed so childishly idealistic to think of acting as an art and to throw away all that money.

"The hell with the money," she said.

(Twenty years later, Alan Hewitt, a young actor who had played with the Lunts, was undecided whether to go to Hollywood and act in films or remain in the theatre. He wrote to Alfred for advice. "I really don't know what to advise you," Alfred replied. "It seems to me that it is up to you. What do you want—the theatre or money? You can make up your mind there is not much money in the theatre, and there will be less as the years go on and that is really all I can tell you. I went into the theatre with no idea of making any money, except on which to exist. I have been lucky, but times are changing, plays are fewer, and perhaps my luck has run out. However, I have had a hell of a good time and I don't regret one day of poverty, and God knows I was poor for a great many years.")

Well, it was a mad expedition they made to Europe in the summer of 1924. They dallied briefly in London and then pressed directly on to Hungary for the rendezvous with Molnar. But Molnar had vanished. He wasn't at home. He wasn't at any of the theatres or newspapers with which he was connected. He wasn't at his favorite café, which happened to be named the New York Café, or his favorite restaurant, Gundel's. They inquired of various Hungarians in the theatrical and journalistic worlds of Budapest. Persons acted mysteriously. Shoulders were shrugged. Faces went blank. What could be the matter? Being a race of natural-born intriguers themselves, the Hungarians naturally assumed that this handsome couple, pretending to be married, but obviously having a stupendous love affair, were likely secret agents of an American theatrical impresario who planned to bilk their compatriot out of his royalties or might even be the relatives of a certain young actress with whom Molnar was having a wild liaison. Molnar always fell madly in love with a new girl whenever he began writing a new play and he was continually writing new plays. Perhaps this tall gentleman passing himself off as an American actor was a Chicago gangster sent to kill Molnar. The truth, of course, was unbelievable. Two unknown American actors traveling all the way to Budapest to ask Molnar's advice on how to act? Nonsense. Two impostors. Who ever heard of actors taking advice from playwrights? Everybody knows that actors know better than playwrights how plays should go and were always "improving" plays by putting in their own words. Well, if they were not actors, what were they? And what did they want with Molnar?

Lynn and Alfred scoured Budapest night clubs and cafés. They were two characters in search of an author. Lynn was impressed with how fluently Alfred spoke Hungarian to the natives. Alfred shrugged and said oh, Hungarian was an easy enough language and he'd picked it up just before they went by studying a Hungarian grammar. Nothing at all, really.

In Budapest, Lynn bought her first short dress—a black cocktail model with low hipline and a hem that was an inch above her knees. Daring, it was. Her figure had been fashionable for years before it became fashionable and this was her first essay at dressing her 1924 figure in a 1924 style.

Alfred, seeing a chance to satisfy his Slavic obsession, had decided to make the guardsman a Russian. In Budapest he chanced to meet a Russian émigré, one Samsonoff, who had been a professor of philosophy and was now a cabaret doorman. Samsonoff had been a guardsman. He wore his old guard's uniform on duty. Alfred sketched the uniform and then had the costume made later in London. He planned to deliberately make the character of Samsonoff ugly. (He even changed the guardsman's name in the play to that of the Russian prototype.) He shaved his head for the guardsman. "I wanted the guardsman to have a mysteriously ugly sex emanation," Alfred explains. "And so he would contrast with The Actor, whom I played as a handsome matinee idol. The guardsman's black uniform increased the ugly quality. Well at our first meeting, Philip Moeller said flatly, 'You can't play comedy in black.' And Lynn replied, 'Mr. Moeller, you can play comedy in a burlap bag inside a piano with the cover down *if* the lines are funny and the audience can hear them.' "

They found out the truth about Molnar eventually. Another playwright, who hated Molnar and hoped Alfred would kill him, confided that Molnar was in the throes of a romantic escapade with a Lili Darvas, an eighteen-year-old actress. (Molnar was fifty-six years old at that time.) She had fled his courtship. He had pursued her. He was believed to be in Vienna, Carlsbad, Nice, or Venice. The Lunts gave up the chase. They never did meet Molnar, not even when he came to this country in 1941 and became a resident of New York. (Molnar, by the way, married Miss Darvas.) On the train to Paris, Alfred confessed to Lynn that he had been a shameless rascal pretending to speak Hungarian. He had actually been speaking a Finnish patois which he had remembered from his youth. Finnish and Hungarian are both Magyar languages.

"I think I could murder you except that we have signed a contract to play *The Guardsman*," Lynn said, lovingly.

To bob or not to bob—that was the question, in 1924. In Paris, on their way home, Lynn finally made up her mind. She had her long hair cut down into a sleek short coiffure. In Paris, also, she examined the autumn collections of the important couturiers. At Poiret's she saw a long white evening dress and she at once decided it was what The Actress must have for Act II of *The Guardsman*. It came with a matching cloak. The ensemble was embroidered by hand, of course, and it cost $1,000. Costume jewelery, known as "junk jewelry" or "fake jewelry" was all the rage that year and she bought heaps of "junk jewelry," costing hundreds of dollars. They had no money when they landed at the Cunard pier in New York. They had spent all the $6,000. There was only enough left for a taxi to their apartment. They had to touch Condé Nast for a loan to pay their rent. The next day they met with Langner, Miss Helburn, Moeller, Lee Simonson, and a young slim aesthetic chap who lurked behind Simonson. Simonson introduced him as Jo Mielziner, who was going to design the settings for *The Guardsman*. Mielziner, a fine-arts student who had worked in Paris and Vienna, wanted to be a scenic designer and had been getting experience as a bit player and assistant stage manager with the Guild. *The Guardsman*, the first Broadway play he designed, was the beginning of his brilliant career. Lynn had brought her costumes in a trunk. The committee inspected the Paris dresses. They were satisfied. Lynn then had a conference alone with Helburn. She asked, "Can't you do better than $50 a dress? My clothes have cost about $4,000."

"Impossible. The Guild can't afford to invest more than $300 in your wardrobe. Even that is steep for us, you know. My dear, we are an art theatre. We do not make any money."

Lynn suddenly found herself going shrewd. If the Guild masterminds were going to be sharp with her, she could be sharp right back.

"Suppose," inquired Lynn casually, "that our play were to run longer than ten weeks, would you then agree to reimburse me for the costumes? If not—then I will simply keep all the dresses including the white evening gown and you people can order your own dresses for me."

Miss Helburn cogitated. Guild productions usually ran about two or three weeks; if they were wildly successful they might go to five weeks. The Guild had a small list of subscribers and when the subscribers were done with and the small number of aesthetes around New York had had their fill of experimental theatre, the Guild put on another production. After a slight hesitation, she agreed to the proposal. They went into rehearsal at once and worked intensely for a month. In Moeller, the Lunts, for the first time, worked with a creative director, and one who was responsive to their improvisational method of working out the problems of a play. Moeller was a tall, shy, highly sensitive, high-strung man, somewhat of a dandy in his dress. He smoked a cigarette in a long cigarette holder. Unlike other directors, he did not carefully lay out the moves and he did not chart a careful production in advance. He worked on the inspiration of the moment and as he watched the Lunts slowly making the roles of The Actor and The Actress come to reality he would suddenly leap up from the front and climb on the stage and enthusiastically tell them to try this or try that.

On the whole, he controlled them with extremely loose reins. The only way to direct the Lunts is not to direct them, to let them direct themselves. It is to be aware of what they are working toward and to aid them in working out more perfectly what they are intuitively fashioning. They are always polite with a director but if they once sense that he is pushing them about they become—while still polite—absolutely adamant. They cannot be made to do anything they do not see the relevance of doing on a stage and they are invariably correct.

There was a run-through of *The Guardsman* the night before the premiere. After the performance, the Lunts met in a conference with the board of directors. The directors looked as if they had been attending a funeral. It was a disaster, they chorused. Alfred was absolutely wrong in his conception of the Russian guardsman. He was ugly-looking and darkly caparisoned and he lacked charm and elegance and sex appeal. Why, such a monster could not possibly excite any woman's tender emotions. Samsonoff would certainly not be convincing as Lynn's lover. And women in the audience would not be sexually aroused by this gargoyle. No, Alfred must change his costume and his make-up and his conception of the role. Oh, it was a disaster, they repeated. But it was too late to do anything about it, Alfred said over and over again. He said he believed in the rightness of his conception, for The Actor was a vain peacock—but the Guardsman was a different type. He *had* to be a different type. But the Guild directors had shattered his self-confidence.

"I left the meeting with nothing to believe in," Alfred recalls. "It was the cruellest thing anyone has ever done to me. When we went to bed that night, I cried—for the first and last time in my life, I cried, cried like a baby. I cried and cried for a long time and Lynn comforted me all night but it was very hard."

When they were rehearsing *The Second Man,* there was a delicate scene which the Lunts hadn't quite polished but the Guild directors insisted it must be cut—at once. Alfred stalked to the footlights and yelled down at them, "Playing light comedy for you is like feeding a soufflé to a horse!"

The Guardsman opened at the Garrick Theatre on Monday, October 13, 1924. Nobody, of course, with perhaps a single exception, knew what a significant event this was in the history of the Theatre Guild, in the lives of Lynn and Alfred, in the future of the American theatre. As Langner later wrote, "The curtain rose on a crackling comedy performance of a kind which had never been seen before in our theatre

. . . this performance of Alfred Lunt and Lynn Fontanne . . . was a high watermark for the young Theatre Guild and established the beginnings of an acting company which, later on, climaxed this period of our career."

Above and beyond the subtleties of their high comedy technique, Lynn and Alfred projected an animal vitality, a spirit of gaiety and intense pleasure in being alive and in being in love and in finding love in the physical grace of their bodies. Separately, they had been original and brilliant actors. Together, they were an irresistible expression of the life force, of the joy of living.

The Guardsman played at the Garrick Theatre to full houses for five weeks and then it was moved uptown to 45th Street to the Booth Theatre and it played not only the ten weeks after which Miss Helburn was to pay for the costumes but almost forty weeks. *The Guardsman,* observed S. N. Behrman, "was the first production of the Theatre Guild that made real money." It was also the first Guild production that made Broadway aware that the Guild was more than an experimental and aesthetic organization. It was a production that stirred into high activity a whole set of young and talented comedy writers, because the Lunts set an acting style that made it possible to play out their charades.

In his review in the New York *Sun,* Alexander Woollcott set down a remarkable prophecy on October 14, 1924: "They have youth and great gifts and the unmistakable attitude of ascent, and those who saw them last night bowing hand in hand for the first time, may well have been witnessing a moment in theatrical history. It is among the possibilities that we were seeing the first chapter in a partnership destined to be as distinguished as that of Henry Irving and Ellen Terry."

EIGHT

HALCYON DAYS AT THE
THEATRE GUILD

*T*HERE WERE clotheslines on the roof of 969 Lexington Avenue. One afternoon, maids and housewives hanging out the wash were be-mused to see their fellow tenant, Alfred Lunt, pinning a damp uniform to a line. It was a period uniform—blue trousers and navy-blue coat. It might have been worn by a *mittel-european* officer of the late 19th century. It was going to be Alfred's costume as Bluntschli in *Arms and the Man*. George Bernard Shaw describes Bluntschli's entrance through Raina's bedroom window, as follows: "He is a man of about 35, in a deplorable plight, bespattered with mud and blood and snow, his belt and the strap of his revolver case keeping together the torn ruins of the blue tunic of a Serbian artillery officer."

Alfred left the uniform on the line for several weeks, through rains and heat-waves. Now that the uniform was weatherbeaten, Alfred pro-vided himself with a rattan rug-beater and proceeded to flagellate the uniform into "torn ruins." It only lacked blood to look authentic. Alfred pricked his thumb and squeezed drops of hot blood on it. Now he was satisfied.

Whenever he plays anti-romantic parts like Bluntschli, Alfred seeks a moment of intensity in which he can make the audience feel sympa-thetic toward him. Alfred had selected his first entrance in *Arms and the Man* as that moment. He was going to convey such fatigue by his body, and such misery by his uniform, that the audience would feel sorry for him even though he was going to say things and do things that went against conventional ideas of patriotism and love. He succeeded. Woollcott reported his exhaustion as comparable to a spent rubber band; his "skull [seemed] somehow detached from his spinal column . . . I never saw any player so completely express exhaustion. Come to think of it, I never saw any player express anything more completely."

Arms and the Man closed the seventh season of the Theatre Guild, 1924-1925. It was almost as great a hit as *The Guardsman*. Howard Lindsay says that Alfred's Bluntschli "was cold, precise, hard, and one of the greatest performances he ever gave, and probably one of the greatest high-comedy performances any actor, American or British, has given in our time." The Lunts did not have an opportunity to discuss the production with Shaw himself until four years later when they were in London playing in *Caprice*. They were invited to lunch, along with Philip Moeller and Lawrence Langner, at Shaw's London apartment in Adelphi Terrace. They were received by Mrs. Shaw. She suggested they all sit right down to eat as nobody ever could be sure when Mr. Shaw would appear. Alfred was nervous and uneasy—he had convinced himself that Shaw thought him a wretched actor. He was pacing about, when, suddenly, Shaw strode into the dining room. He raised his white bushy eyebrows and at once crossed the room and went straight up to Alfred. Shaw cried, in a high piercing voice, "Ah, I know *you*. You're Alfred."

Alfred blushed with pleasure at being called by his first name by a great man whom he had never met before.

Shaw, ignoring the rest of the party, inquired: "Now, Alfred, tell me —did you embrace Raina when you played *Arms and the Man?*"

"Why, certainly not, Mr. Shaw," Alfred replied. "It would not have been in character. It would have been all wrong."

"Then," Shaw demanded, "what is the explanation of this cutting?" He whipped out a newspaper photograph which showed Lynn and Alfred in costume. Alfred's arms were around her. Alfred said, "I am only putting on her coat according to your direction."

Shaw scrutinized the photograph carefully. He ruffled his beard. "Ah, I see, Alfred," he said, "ah yes, that is quite all right, in that case."

Later, the Lunts did *The Doctor's Dilemma* and *Pygmalion*. Usually any deviations from the master's text or stage directions somehow leaked to Shaw. To this day, nobody knows exactly how Shaw's intelligence service operated so efficiently. The general opinion is that there was a rich New York woman, passionately devoted to Shaw's plays and determined to see that they were played exactly as written, who employed spies to watch all performances. "You could not cut a line without Shaw finding out," Lynn says. "The only actor that cut Shaw without being found out was Henry Travers. Henry played the dustman, Alfred Doolittle, in *Pygmalion*. Henry had a slight stutter and he had got into a habit of swallowing and twisting sentences and words around so he wouldn't meet his stutter, do you see? I once asked him, 'How is it that you sound so natural when you're speaking Shaw's dialogue and the rest of us don't?' Because, you see, for an actor, Shaw's dialogue is not how people really talk and it does sound like a book not stage dialogue. And Henry whispered to me, 'M-my d-dear, I gargle all those lu-lines and tu-tu-whist them about.' And so you know I went off and did the same sort of things with some of my lines, gargled them and chewed them about a bit, oh it was marvelous fun, and, you know, Shaw's spies never found me out and it was mainly because of this that many people said my Liza Doolittle was more natural than Mrs. Campbell's, for whom Shaw had written the part."

During the run of *Arms and the Man*, the Guild signed a three year contract with the Lunts. They were to receive $750 a week and a small percentage of the gross of each of their plays. Since the Guild was firmly opposed to the "star system," the Lunts were deprived of star billing. They also had to agree that if the Guild desired, they would have to appear in separate plays. Lynn and Alfred insisted, however, that even when they did separate plays they must play in the same city. With Lynn and Alfred as the star attraction, the Guild now recruited a permanent company of actors, including Dudley Digges, Margalo Gilmore, Morris Carnovsky, Ernest Cossart, Claire Eames, Edward G. Robinson, Earle Larimore, Claude Rains, Blanche Yurka, Philip Loeb, Edgar Stehli, Henry Travers, and Tom Powers. During the next three years, the Lunts appeared in a greater variety of plays, both modern and classic, in a shorter period of time, than any leading American actors before or since. By 1926, the Guild had waxed prosperous and had built a luxurious playhouse of its own on 52nd Street. Its lobby was decorated with antique tapestries. The Guild had given a benefit to raise money for these tapestries. Woollcott, who had always supported the Guild's visionary idealism, was disturbed by such extravagance. He warned them: "The Gobelins will get you if you don't watch out." But the Guild ignored him. They were riding high. They gained 10,000 new subscribers during the 1927 season and now had 24,000 members. They were doing the new plays of Eugene O'Neill, Sidney Howard, S. N. Behrman, and George Bernard Shaw. They had become the mightiest producing organization in Broadway history. Langner wrote that in these 3 years "the Guild achieved the greatest period of its entire career." It was the "golden age" of the Guild. "Those were the halcyon days of the Theatre Guild, believe me," Miss Helburn once said. "Those were our wonderful years, because every one of us was filled with the ambition to achieve high art in the theatre and we were able to carry out our vision in a way we were never able to do after 1929."

Their permanent relationship with the Guild freed the Lunts from the fear of unemployment between productions that haunts every actor —even stars. They moved to a handsome triplex apartment on East 30th Street. It had a grandiose living room which Alfred decorated in splashing reds and yellows. There were gold brocade curtains on the windows and antique tables and commodes and Louis XV *bergères*. They now began entertaining on Sundays, and Alfred, who was taking up *haute cuisine* as a serious pastime, cooked meals which Lynn often served. They would arrange small tables in the living room and seat their guests in groups of three and four. One Sunday evening, Noel Coward brought Charlie Chaplin. Alfred greeted them and placed them at a table. Lynn brought them drinks—excellent scotch whisky provided by a reliable bootlegger; Alfred dished up exquisitely scrambled eggs with chives and parsley. Noel and Chaplin remained for several hours, chatting with each other and, now and then, with Lynn and Alfred. When they got up to leave, Chaplin complimented Alfred on the food and liquor. His tone struck Alfred as oddly impersonal. At the door, Chaplin suddenly smacked his forehead.

"Good God," he said, "*you* are Lynn Fontanne and *you* are Alfred Lunt. I didn't recognize you. How could I have been so stupid! Why I saw you in the Shaw play only last week."

Coward, assuming they knew each other, had not introduced the Lunts to Chaplin.

"You must have thought me a very rude person," Chaplin said, laughing, "but all this time we've been here I thought Noel had brought me to a swell speakeasy."

Lynn and Alfred continued to fight the battle of the sexes in their next play, a serious and poetic work, Franz Werfel's *The Goat Song*. Langner had discovered the play in 1921 while on a European trip for the international patent-law firm, Langner, Parry, Card and Langner, of which he was the senior partner. The firm represented such clients as Coca-Cola, General Electric, Bethlehem Steel, International Business Machines, and General Foods. Although each of the six directors of the Guild had an equal vote and an equal—and extremely loud and argumentative—voice in its affairs, it was generally agreed that just as Terry Helburn had proved her ability to sense intuitively which actors fitted which roles, so Langner was skilled in dealing with plays and playwrights. He was the Guild's liaison with authors. Yet most of the Guild directors considered themselves authorities on dramatic construction. They were frustrated playwrights, even the financier Maurice Wertheim having studied playwriting under the famous George Pierce Baker of Harvard's 47 Workshop. It was Langner who had persuaded Shaw to give his plays to the Guild. In Vienna, Langner had attended a party where a guest raved about a young poet, playwright, and novelist—Werfel, by name. She introduced Langner to Werfel. Werfel's play *Bocksgesang* was running in Berlin and Vienna. Langner put down a small deposit out of his own pocket for an option on the American rights. He had the play translated by his sister-in-law, Ruth Langner. Then it took him about four years to argue the Guild directorate into producing *The Goat Song*.

It was an obscure, if powerfully written, drama, laid in Hungary in the 18th century, with parallel political and amatory themes. Politically, it was ahead of its time. In his portrait of the intellectual Juvan, the student who leads the landless peasantry in a revolution against the rich landowners, Werfel drew a man motivated not by idealism and love of humanity, but by neurotic hatred of both the rich and the poor. Stanja, the girl with whom he falls in love, is betrothed to the son of a big landowner, who some years before had begotten a bastard son, half-man and half-goat. The goat-man had been kept hidden for twenty years. The goat-man was a symbol—but of exactly what nobody was certain.

Periodically Langner would bring up *The Goat Song* at meetings of the board, and be shouted down on the grounds that any actor and actress who had the imagination and rhetorical powers to play Stanja and Juvan would not work for the Guild, which paid the lowest salaries on Broadway. Now that the Lunts were under contract, however, Miss Helburn proposed that they play Stanja and Juvan. Absurd, countered Miss Westley, Wertheim, Simonson, and Moeller. The Lunts were sophisticates. They were worldly. They were virtuosos of the elegant scene and the intellectual dialogue. They couldn't possibly play this deep, dark, sinister drama of love and revolution.

"The Lunts," Miss Helburn flatly affirmed, "can play anything—*anything.*"

"But will they?" Langner asked, still unwilling to believe that Lynn and Alfred could play these roles. A few years before nobody on Broadway had believed that Clarence and Dulcy could portray sophistication.

"They will," Miss Helburn assured them, "if they like the play."

Well, naturally, Alfred revelled in the Slavic bitterness of Juvan, and Lynn discovered in Stanja a role of hotblooded sensuality such as she had not yet acted in her career. It was a long and complicated and difficult play in five acts and forty-four scenes. In several of the scenes— notably a scene in Act II, in which she dexterously juggles two men, flirting with them and arousing them, and in Act V—she stunned New York audiences by her powers of projecting a tragic mood.

Impressed by European theories of the "mass" as a character, the Guild did the play with a cast of ten principals and forty bit players— soldiers, farmers, vagabonds, servants, priests, landowners, Turks. Lee Simonson designed stylized sets and Jacob Ben-Ami, then America's only prominent Russian actor and director, was hired to direct *The Goat Song*. He directed it as if it were an Eisenstein movie. He had crowds of actors dashing about the stage, shouting, threatening, menacing, struggling, drinking, carousing, shooting, killing. The mob noise was so deafening that you often couldn't hear what the leading players were saying. Sometimes when you did grasp what they were saying, you still couldn't understand the lines.

For some reason, probably sheer stupidity, many of the subscribers thought *The Goat Song* was Bolshevik propaganda, though one of its themes was that revolutions are made by warped persons who don't especially love the masses. The Guild lost several hundred subscribers, some of them on moral grounds, because Stanja has gone to bed with the mysterious goat-man, symbol perhaps of the up-and-coming worker and peasant, or maybe a symbol of Pan, the earthy sex-god. As the play ends she proudly declares that she is pregnant by the satyr. Even though 1926 was for Manhattan the era of the mad fling and sexual liberation, many sophisticates were apparently not liberated enough to look with tolerance on demi-bestiality, even symbolic demi-bestiality. Mrs. Vincent Astor addressed a stinging rebuke to the Guild, criticizing them on the grounds of taste and politics. She objected to *both* the sex *and* the politics. "Please take my name off your membership list," her letter ended. *The Goat Song* was the most controversial play of the year and everybody simply had to see it. The aesthetic and academic community went to see it and discovered the Lunts. "Alfred Lunt, who, as the dark bitter frustrated student leader of the uprising, trails clouds of the French revolution through the rich tapestry of the play . . . Lynn Fontanne, who, as the scornful stricken Iphigenia in this altar piece, enters magnificently with him at last into one of the most beautiful colloquies of the modern theatre," said Woollcott of their playing.

The Goat Song did not play to an empty seat during its run. It was Standing Room Only every evening and on matinee days. But the Guild was losing money on it every week. After seven weeks and fifty-eight performances they closed the show. Maurice Wertheim, the financial genius of the directorate, wrote a complicated essay for the *Theatre Guild Magazine,* a publication sent free to the subscribers, in which he attempted to explain the opening as well as the closing of *The Goat Song.* He said the Guild had lost $25,000 on one of the smash hits of the season and had had to close *Goat Song* because even at capacity it lost money, but the Guild was proud of having put it on in the first place because Werfel was a poet and *The Goat Song* an example of art-in-drama, of which the Guild was an exponent. Wertheim said it was Guild policy to put the profits of one play into other plays which might be experimental; this explained also why the Guild could not pay their actors a good salary. He went to great lengths to justify the salaries of the directors, which they received in addition to their fees as playreaders, stage directors, scene designers, and administrators. Actors generally, including the Lunts, always suspected financial hanky-panky going on behind the scenes, but they could not prove it. Two years later, the Guild put on five productions, in three of which the Lunts appeared—*Porgy, The Doctor's Dilemma, Marco Millions, Strange Interlude,* and *Volpone.* All five were hits, and *Strange Interlude* was a smash hit. But the Guild was still paying coolie wages to most of its actors, even principals receiving as little as $75 a week. The Lunts, at a time when the Guild was paying them $1,000 a week as a team, could have received five times as much from any other management—but under what other management could Alfred, *in one season,* have alternated playing Dubedat, Marco Polo, and Volpone? Or Lynn done Jennifer Dubedat in *The Doctor's Dilemma,* and then Nina Leeds in *Strange Interlude?*

Incidentally, the cost of a Guild subscription during the period of 1926 through 1929 was only $15, for which you got orchestra seats to six Guild plays! By 1927 there was a long waiting list of would-be subscribers.

Lynn was interviewed by a reporter for the Brooklyn *Daily News* at this time. She was asked if Stanja were not the most difficult role of her career. "Oh, no," she replied with an imperious toss of her head. "Not at all. Stanja is much easier to play than the wife in *The Guardsman.* There I had difficulties that the audience didn't realize. I had to make lines that were sometimes dull sound continuously brilliant, just as in *Dulcy* I had to make lines that were witty sound continuously silly. And in *Arms and the Man* lines that were witty but literary sound conversational. I know that audiences are confused about the meaning of *The Goat Song* and the characters. I think the confusion is caused by the noise of the mob in the mob scenes. Important lines are drowned out by this noise. Though I must say I don't see why it is particularly necessary to understand a play. It's preferable, of course. Yet do we not thrill at a mass of color that has no story? We can vibrate to music that is unintelligible."

The Abstract-Impressionist Theatre-of-the-Absurd did not exist in 1926, yet Lynn and Alfred were always open to plays of every kind of structure and form of composition, and always played in them when they had the chance. When William Saroyan began writing his improvisational plays during the 1930's, the Lunts paid him a generous subsidy to write them a play. The project never worked out, because Saroyan never completed the play. After the war, when the Lunts became identified in the minds of a new generation of playwrights as specialists in comedy, they never got a chance at any of the new plays. They resent being stereotyped as farceur and farceuse who can play only one style in one kind of play.

"Why didn't Elia Kazan," Alfred says, "give us a crack at *Death of a Salesman*? I would have loved to play Willy Loman. And wouldn't Lynn have made a heartbreaking Mrs. Loman? But nobody even showed us the script. They assumed we'd only play S. N. Behrman and Noel Coward and Terence Rattigan. How stupid, really. We'll play *anything* that's good and that we like. I'm afraid we're past the point of playing Romeo and Juliet, though. We'd love to see scripts by Arthur Miller, Tennessee Williams, and the avant-garde writers like Edward Albee and Beckett and the others. Why, Lynn and I would be as excited to play in one of these theatre-of-the-absurd plays as we were excited when we joined the Theatre Guild, only they called it 'art theatre' then. We did it for the joy of acting. We did it because we believed the theatre has a mission to perform for its audiences."

Lynn and Alfred completed their second Guild season with *At Mrs. Beam's,* a lightweight British comedy of the 1923 London season. Its author, C. S. Munro, had revised it in 1925 and expanded the roles of Laura Pasquale, a Brazilian gentlewoman-thief, and her lover, Joe Dermott, an English gentleman-thief. Lynn, who was now becoming quite a curvaceous creature, played the Brazilian beauty, and Alfred, good-looking and slim, with the bodily grace of a juvenile and the technical skill of the veteran actor he now was, played her paramour. In the original version, Miss Shoe, a spinster boarder in Mrs. Beam's lodging house, carried the play, and it was one of those comedies with a boarding-house as background for intrigue that English novelists and playwrights love. Miss Shoe was played by a great English comedienne, Jean Cadell. Miss Shoe is a suspicious lady who believes that the oddly-assorted couple who have come to stay in the boarding house are a notorious murderer and his next victim. In the new version, Laura and Joe held the center of the stage and the Lunts used Munro's written dialogue as a diving platform from which they proceeded to execute a dazzling series of triple jackknives. It was another variation of the battle of the sexes, an expression of the universal truth that there are elements of antagonism in all intense relationships, even those in which love predominates. The last scene of Act I gave them an opportunity to play their most uninhibited stage fight up till then. Unable to get him aroused in any other way, Laura loses her temper at Joe's business-like attitude—he's occupied in forging passports so they can get out of England with a trunk full of loot. She throws a book at him and a cushion and then, from a fruitbowl, she flings banana after banana after him and then hurls her shoes at him. Joe, laughing merrily at her as he dodges the ammunition, finally opens a bag of cakes and throws cakes at her. She becomes more furious and rips up her dress and tries to throttle him and punch him. He backs away. She wrestles with him. He moves to a chair. Sits down. She still wrestles with him. The chair goes over. They roll over and over on the floor kicking and screaming and swinging away at one another. The battle royal (and the act) ended with Lynn slapping Alfred "hard in the face." During rehearsal, Lynn couldn't bring herself to strike Alfred hard enough. Nothing director Philip Moeller could say would make her deliver a convincing slap. One afternoon, when the whole scene was dragging, Alfred groaned in disgust, pushed her away, and snarled, "Goddamit, Lynn, you are the rottenest actress I have ever worked with."

He turned on his heels and started trudging away.

Lynn lost control of herself. She grasped his shoulder, spun him around, and then hauled off and swatted him across his mouth so hard that his jaw rattled. Alfred waited for the vibrations to cease. Then he folded his arms. He smiled. "That's more like it," he said, smugly.

"Alfred, darling," Lynn said, "sometimes I think you are a cold-blooded son-of-a-bitch."

"Sometimes," he sighed, "I agree with you."

This scene, which lasted about twenty minutes, was played with such *brio* and perfect timing and the blows were so convincing—both parties looked as if they were really knocking each other about and really hurting each other—that even though you knew it was make-believe you forgot you were in a theatre, and knew this was a man and a woman fighting. You could hear the audience gasping with fear and embarrassment whenever the fight started. Many persons went to see the play several times just to see the fight scene. Vilhjalmur Stefansson, the Arctic explorer, saw it forty-two times!

This was the first time Lynn and Alfred engaged in physical jousting. It was also the first time they played unmarried lovers reveling in their illegal lust. On top of this, they were criminals—gay, happy, lovable criminals it's true, but criminals all the same. If anybody doubted it, one of Joe's tender little speeches was: "Oh, my dear Laura, you're a dreadful woman, an awful woman, a frightful woman, a dreg, a weed, a parasite, and a whole lot more words like that. Why, you're not even married to me! You're not fit to associate with pure angels like Miss Shoe and Mr. Durrows. It's a scandal that you should. I shall denounce you, you foul woman. Denounce you to them!"

And audiences simply adored the Lunts. They had, by means of charm and technical versatility, been able to overcome the great taboo of the American theatre. In *Materia Critica,* a collection of essays on the theatre published early in 1924, George Jean Nathan wrote, quite correctly:

The American actor, when he attempts to cavort in French farce, is a sad spectacle. Where the French actor is able to play naughty farce with the same air of blithe unconsciousness and moral unconcern that he displays in a Biblical drama, his American colleague can never quite rid his playing such farce of an air of moral consciousness and ethical superiority. He seems to say, this American actor: 'Although I am supposed to have seduced the midinette Gaby and to be making a pass at Fifi, my best friend's wife, to say nothing of carrying on secret liaisons with Heloise, the pretty parlor maid, and Margot, the laundress, you surely know that I am personally a pure gentleman who loves his wife and child and am, further, a member of the Asbury Park Methodist Episcopal Church and up in my dues to the Players Club.' This American actor—and the American actress even more so—conveys the impression that there is something *infra dig* in playing risqué farce and that if he had his way and didn't need the money, he would much prefer to go out with the Ben Greet company [a group of actors who played Shakespeare]. . . . The truth of the matter is perhaps this: that where the Frenchman is able wholeheartedly to act dirty farce in the spirit of clean entertainment, the American cannot do other than to act such farce in a spirit of half-hearted moral qualm which makes it dirtier than it otherwise would be.

Of course, offstage, as Alfred insists, he is anything but the lascivious rakehell and sophisticate that he portrays so cunningly. By an act of creative imagination, he becomes his worldly stepfather acting out Count de Lussac in *Banco,* The Actor in *The Guardsman,* Joe Dermott in *At Mrs. Beam's.* But since he is also Alfred—which means that he is gentle and generous and idealistic and sensitive and in love with only one woman—he is able also to infuse his depraved characters with an almost religious sense of the joy of living and the pleasures of the senses. The paradoxical counterpoint of these two forces in his character, brought to an extremity of art by his technique, created precisely the quality that made him so engaging in the most risqué of stage situations. As for Lynn, she had had to overcome such shyness and inferiority in her struggle to become a woman, that, in losing her inhibitions about speaking up and asking for her rights as a human being, she had also lost all her self-consciousness about the amatory experience in life. As Alfred once said, "Some recent playwrights have made sex a dreadful thing. Sex doesn't have to be ghastly. Sex can be most enjoyable. Lynn and I did the most morally outrageous things on the stage, and we enjoyed it, and the audience enjoyed it because it was gracious and lovely; and most persons have also known the happy experience of sex, in marriage usually, as Lynn and I have, but when one plays comedy, naturally, there is going to have to be a plot and this means there will be some sexual intrigue and infidelity, but it is always in a spirit of pleasure not of tragedy."

In July, the Lunts sailed to England. They were facing a strenuous Theatre Guild season in the fall because in the 1926-1927 season they would play as a team in *The Brothers Karamazov* and *The Second Man.* Separately, Alfred would do *Ned McCobb's Daughter* and *Juarez and Maximilian,* and Lynn would appear in *Pygmalion.* Why did the Theatre Guild masterminds sunder what God had joined? Its prosperity was due to a widespread craving on the part of New York audiences for the outrageously immoral actions of Lynn and Alfred on the stage. The Lunts as a team were already a powerful box-office draw. They were also instrumental in bringing the scripts of new and veteran American playwrights to the Guild, which hitherto had had to rely on European plays because American dramatists spurned them. The word was getting around that even if your plot was flimsy and your dialogue stilted, if you gave the Lunts two interesting characters to impersonate and plunged them into a noisy conflict, they were able to invent such delicious pieces of business that your success was assured. Nevertheless, in their collective wisdom, the Board of Directors split Lunt and Fontanne. The board now included an additional member from its acting company, tall, slender, sullen Claire Eames. She had no real voice in the decisions but the doges thought to mute the actors' discontent. I believe the Guild broke up the Lunts because they sensed how popular the Lunts were with playwrights, audiences, and critics. In the theatre, popularity is equated with power, and the Guild directors wanted power, all power. Alfred and Lynn didn't like being sundered, but meanwhile, they hoped to have a nice holiday. They took their scripts with them. Even if they hadn't taken their scripts, they would never have been able to enjoy a carefree holiday. Wherever they went, whatever they were doing, they were, in a sense, working, because they were studying the people around them. In building their characters, they used as raw material their memories of persons they encountered casually in the present, as well as their memories of persons in the past. But this trip was more of a holiday than they had ever had. It was a wonderful voyage. It was the most exhilarating journey of their lives. New York was behind them. Europe was still to come. They were in that limbo of an ocean crossing. The seas were calm. There were good friends and gay companions aboard. Their cabin was an outside cabin. The champagne flowed at luncheon and dinner. Yet they could not stop their habitual observations of the human species. Lynn was absorbed in examining the interesting women on the ship. How women walked and spoke and contrived to lure men at different ages in a woman's life fascinated Lynn. Their nervous unconscious gestures, a tug at a hem, a brushing back of the hair, a way of powdering a face . . . Mabel Boll, Peggy Hopkins Joyce, and Irene Castle, three beauties of the period, were on the ship.

Lynn remembers conjecturing what it was about women like Peggy Hopkins Joyce that made them "such great fascinators of men. Well, it wasn't their physical beauty, really, or the way they dressed, because there were women like Neysa McMein, for instance, who was not beautiful and didn't care about fashion and yet was a great fascinator of men. I finally decided it was because they were persons of warmth and generosity and they made men feel happy because they made everybody feel happy who was around them, d'you see? They did not make

a man feel challenged and fearful. I knew this because they were kind
to other women, these great fascinators, and I've observed many women
who are cutting, who are hard, who are bitchy with other women, and
who are pleasant only when they are with a man, and this does not
work. Such fascinators as Neysa McMein or the others, they were not
what you'd call bitches or catty persons. Now Mrs. Stella Campbell
was very beautiful, in her time, and was a splendid actress, but she
was not a great fascinator, because she was not a kindly person as Ellen
Terry was. Mrs. Campbell, poor thing, had this great need to assassinate
other women, especially if they were famous and lovely looking. She'd
find some physical deficiency or other lack and then they'd get the
sharp end of that wicked tongue. But she was nice enough to me. I met
her in London when we had that ghastly experience with *One Night
in Rome*. Nineteen-twenty it was. There was a luncheon party at Laurette's, and she had some of the leading British stars—Gerald du
Maurier, Robert Lorraine, Denis Eadie, Mrs. Campbell. And Laurette
whispered to me, 'Lynn, you're the most defenseless one here, and Mrs.
Campbell is sure to make a beeline for you and so I will sit you next to
me so you will be protected from her.' Well the first thing Mrs. Campbell
said when she sat down was, 'Who is that intelligent-looking child over
there?' And she said it sincerely in that deep voice of hers and Laurette
was surprised and answered, 'It is a young actress I took over to America
and she had great success in several parts and now I'm bringing her out
here.' And Mrs. Pat said to me, 'You are very lovely, my dear, though
your chest is rather flat. I am sure it will fill out becomingly like mine,
because I had a flat chest like yours when I was your age.' "

(Though Lynn believes sincerely in Mrs. Campbell's amiability, I
don't. I think Mrs. Campbell was giving Lynn the "sharp end of that
wicked tongue.")

Among their shipmates was a tall, skinny, nervous, fast-talking man
of twenty-six: Jed Harris. A former press agent and then editor of *The
Clipper*, a show business trade paper, Harris, in this year of 1926, had
become a producer. His first play, a bedroom farce, *Weak Sisters*, closed
in four weeks. His second, *Love 'Em and Leave 'Em*, was a big hit.
Love 'Em and Leave 'Em was written by John V. A. Weaver (husband
of Peggy Wood) and George Abbott, then a minor playwright and a
minor actor. Nobody aboard ship on that enchanted voyage would have
imagined in their wildest dreams—not even Harris himself, though he
had an extravagant opinion of his own genius—that within two years
he would become Broadway's *wunderkind*, the most talked about pro-

ducer-director in the American theatre. In 1927, Harris optioned a play by Philip Dunning that had been rattling around for years. He commissioned George Abbott to collaborate with Dunning in a revision. Abbott directed the play, now called *Broadway*, a melodrama of gangsters, gun molls, speakeasy cabarets, suckers, jazz bands. *Broadway* ran three years on Broadway. At one time or another, twenty-six road companies played it in this country and Europe. In 1928, Harris had four smash Broadway hits going for him at the same time: *Broadway, Coquette, The Front Page,* and *The Royal Family.*

But, now, en route to Europe, Harris was still an uncertain young man, though he talked a lot on every subject—politics, history, philosophy, religion and, naturally, the theatre. He remembered every important play since the Greeks. He held forth brilliantly on theories of acting. He was opinionated and clever. He fascinated Lynn and Alfred. He became part of the group that had formed itself aboard ship. But Jed's range of interests was broad. Like Alfred, he was passionate about vaudeville. He knew, like Alfred, all the great standard vaudeville acts since 1900. He and Alfred amused everybody with their impressions of Smith & Dale, Fred Allen, Frank Tinney, Eddie Lambert, Frank Fay, Willie & Eugene Howard, Lewis & Doty, Burns & Allen. Jed was a remarkable mimic. He could take off anybody—in vaudeville or the theatre—with uncanny exactness. His *pièce de résistance* was Alfred Lunt—he had gotten Alfred's unexpected comical crack in the voice. One of the things about Jed that made the Lunts fond of him was his open and unabashed admiration for the Lunts. They were, in truth, getting fed up with the nagging and nattering of the Theatre Guild pooh-bahs. They found Jed's appreciation of their gifts—and he had not only seen their work but had studied it and understood it—a delightful change. Jed was charming. He was articulate. He outlined his future plans. He wanted them to play under his management when their Guild contract was finished next year. He thought they ought to play Julie Cavendish and Anthony Cavendish in a marvelous *drame à clef* which George S. Kaufman and Edna Ferber were rewriting. It was about the Barrymore family, Julie Cavendish being modeled after Ethel Barrymore and Anthony after John Barrymore.

To pursue his long-range seduction campaign, Jed even moved into a house opposite theirs on East 35th the following year. Why, he kept asking the Lunts, did they have to work so hard for the Guild, for those slavedrivers?

Once, a friend of Jed's, knowing he was a neighbor of the Lunts, asked him, "What do the Lunts do in their spare time?"

"The Lunts don't have any spare time," Harris said; "they work for the Theatre Guild!"

The Lunts told Woollcott they were at the end of their rope. They contemplated leaving the Guild. They would go with Harris. Woollcott was against the idea. Even though he ridiculed the Theatre Guild's tapestries and pretentiously overblown productions, he respected them as the best on Broadway. His respect for the Guild went back a long way. In fact, during its first five years, Woollcott had supported it by paying for his tickets! He told Lynn and Alfred they were out of their minds to forsake the Guild. He thought it would be bad for them and bad for the theatre. But his arguments weren't strong enough. Then Woollcott said Harris was vulgar. To prove that Harris lacked taste, Woollcott went into Wadley & Smythe and selected a dozen of their gaudiest orchids. With these he combined orange gladioli and blood-red roses and had the flowers arranged in the most expensively vulgar vase in the store. He signed the card "Jed Harris" and had the posies sent to Lynn.

She was shocked. "Alfred," she said, "we cannot ever, *ever* do any plays for that Jed Harris. He's a dear man, though he looks forever in need of a shave with those dark cheeks of his, and he's ever so amusing and bright—but he's . . . he's . . . *squalid*."

On this voyage, however, he was their friend and they thought him so nice. Harris was socially insecure. He confessed it was his first trip to Europe. And he had never worn a dinner jacket before. He didn't know how to tie a black tie. Alfred showed him. Harris was so grateful that he gave the Lunts an expensive Bell & Howell movie camera. The Lunts became amateur cinematographers. They still are. They take home movies all the time, still using the same 1926 camera! Not long ago, they projected the movies they shot on the ship almost forty years ago.

"The men still looked rather well," Lynn says. "But we girls, my, we do look so dreadfully funny because of the way clothes have changed, and hair-styles are so different."

In London, Lynn and Alfred went about shopping for costumes. Alfred found a lavender double-breasted suit which he felt suited the character of Clark Storey in S. N. Behrman's new play, *The Second Man*. Lynn, ransacking second-hand shops for her costume for Act I of

Pygmalion, found a pair of "debilitated shoes, a wilted boa, and a hopelessly impaired hat," as Alexander Woollcott reported. Then they went on to Paris. Lady Mendl, the interior decorator, professionally known as Elsie de Wolfe, rang them up at the Ritz Hotel and invited them to her country home near Versailles for the day. Since they were taking a late train back to Paris, they didn't bother packing the usual weekend bags and only took the two costumes to show Lady Mendl and her friends. At Lady Mendl's chateau, the Lunts were shown to their luxurious bedroom. There were Poussins on the wall, quilted panelling, and Empire beds. They washed and went down to the terrace for the cocktail hour. Lady Mendl, going to the kitchen to discuss dinner with her chef, passed the chambermaid and valet in a corridor. She overheard them muttering about *"cette pauvre dame qui est arrivée"* and *"son mari, d'un goût incroyable."* Could they be discussing the Lunts? They were. Assuming that the Lunts were staying the night, the servants had laid out their clothes and thought Alfred was in the habit of wearing purple suits to dinner and that his poor wife had nothing more decent to wear than the shabby Liza Doolittle costume!

Back in New York in September, they plunged at once into rehearsals. One half of the Guild's permanent acting company was to do Werfel's *Juarez and Maximilian* with Alfred as Maximilian. The other half would do *Pygmalion,* with Lynn as Liza. The plays were to alternate weekly at the new Guild Theatre on 52nd Street. The Guild also leased the John Golden Theatre on 58th Street. Those actors who were not working during the alternate weeks would be playing in two other productions at the Golden Theatre. It was the season for repertory. Down on 14th Street, Eva Le Gallienne opened her Civic Repertory Theatre with true repertory—a different play every night and matinees as well. From every point of view, including quality, this year was the "peak year in New York's theatrical history, the year of the most plays, the most producers, the most theatres and the greatest theatre ticket sales." * Why, on December 26, 1927, no less than *eleven* plays opened on the same night—more plays than had ever premiered at one time, or ever would again.

Like a delicate Moselle, Werfel's play did not "travel well." In the original German, its poetic diction expressed a mood of royal dignity in the face of the revolutionary mob. Werfel, living in the Vienna of the 1920's, saw the charming life of the Hapsburgs going under from the assaults of the Fascists and the Bolsheviks. The old order was done

* Ward Morehouse, *Matinee Tomorrow: 50 Years of Our Theatre.*

with and nothing good was coming in its place. He captured this nostalgia and tragedy in the play, except that it was not a play, but more like a series of impressionistic sketches of Emperor Maximilian, the puppet of the French emperor Napoleon III, and of some of the Mexican revolutionaries. Juarez was never seen in the play. The chief Mexican character was General Porfirio Diaz, played by Edward G. Robinson. But there was not a character for Alfred to create. Maximilian was not involved in the action. He was hardly involved with his wife, Carlotta, who was played, or rather modeled, by that ivory-white creature, Claire Eames, who was so desperately, intensely, and, as it turned out, hopelessly loved by Sidney Howard. Alfred could not develop any interaction with Claire Eames, because she departed the play in Act II. Or rather Phase Two. Werfel called his play "a dramatic history in three phases and thirteen pictures." And it was produced like pictures at an exhibition. It was a pageant of costumes and scenery. There was a cast of fifty-six, including a young theatrical aspirant named Harold Clurman. He was a man of all work around the Guild. He read playscripts. He contributed scholarly essays on modern playwrights to the *Theatre Guild Magazine.* (He signed these *feuilletons* Harold Clurman, Ph.D., as he had recently received his doctorate in letters at the Sorbonne.) He was an assistant stage manager. He acted. In *Juarez and Maximilian,* he doubled as Escobedo, a revolutionary general, and Polyphemio, an Indian.

"During rehearsals," Lawrence Langner wrote, *"Juarez and Maximilian* seemed headed for a long run, the final run-through without scenery and costumes being so moving that all of us who witnessed the rehearsal were dissolved in tears. A curious thing happened however when the full dress rehearsal took place in the scenery and costumes. Whether this was due to the height of the scenery, which tended to dwarf the actors, or because the uniforms and costumes seemed to make a wall between the emotions of their wearers and the audience, I do not know, but the fact remains that the play was no longer the touching experience that it was during rehearsals and while it received considerable artistic acclaim it was written down as a distinguished failure."

The Guild, of course, would never stoop so low as to have an undistinguished failure. How sad it was that the original idealism of the Guild was giving place to snobbery and pomposity.

Yet with all their arrogance and combativeness and debating, they could, though they quarreled incessantly with one another, put up a common front. Lynn once said to me, speaking of Moeller, Helburn,

Simonson, Wertheim, Langner, and Westley, "As individuals, they were not very good as producers, but all six of them made one good producer."

In *Juarez and Maximilian*, Alfred's notices were hardly enthusiastic. Hammond shrugged him away as a "very nice archduke," implying that he was nice if you liked Austrian archdukes, a species he personally could very well do without. Gilbert Gabriel thought he was miscast. Alan Dale thought he was horribly miscast. Heywood Broun was out of town. Brooks Atkinson suggested that Lunt "might learn a good deal from Mr. Daly's clean-cut enunciation." (Arnold Daly played Marshall Bazaine.) Woollcott said, "In particular, the playing of Alfred Lunt in the long, spacious, perilously difficult role of Maximilian is a notable achievement." Taking into consideration Woollcott's usual ecstasies over Alfred, this meant he was saying, "God, how bored I was."

Apropos of the question of scenery "drowning out" actors, I once watched a runthrough of *Ondine* at the 46th Street Theatre. The actors worked on a bare stage, of course. I knew the play depended to some extent on creating a mood of the supernatural by means of lighting effects and scenic trickery. So I asked Alfred, who directed *Ondine,* to give me an idea of how the play would look on opening night.

"I won't do that," he said, "because the play will never look as good as it is going to look now, when it's going to be played without costumes or sets and only a piano for the music. It is pure now. Your imagination can work miracles. There is no audience to spoil it for you by laughing at the wrong time or snorting or coughing or rustling their damned programs. And the actors are pure because they're not distracted, not worrying about the reviews or the publicity. They can give themselves up to the illusion, feel what the playwright wanted them to feel. Oh, I promise you a performance so beautiful you'll not be likely to forget it as long as you live."

It was, and I didn't.

And yet, though he believes the emotions in a play come through more clearly without scenery and costumes, Alfred does not believe that they can "drown out" the performer. He is opposed to heavy settings and opulent costumes, and when he staged *Cosi Fan Tutte* at the Metropolitan Opera House he insisted on simplicity of decor.

"Oh, you don't need anything in the theatre but actors and the audience," he says. "And yet, you know, a performer can come through despite the most lavish scenery. You remember that great big ridiculous Viennese spectacle they put on at the old Center Theatre? *White Horse*

Inn, it was called. They had a hundred thousand dollars worth of scenery on that stage. And Kitty Carlisle looked absolutely dwarfed in that collection of lush scenery. And she sang and acted as if she were playing in a little theatre off-Broadway and well you'd think she'd have been overpowered by the scenery but, ah no, she wasn't. You couldn't take your eyes off Kitty Carlisle. You forgot the scenery. So I don't think Langner is right in blaming the scenery for the failure of *Juarez and Maximilian.* There wasn't a play there. He didn't have characters. Above all, he didn't have a plot. My God, you've got to have a plot in the theatre. It doesn't matter what sort of a plot you've got but you've got to have a plot."

To get the weekly repertory system going, the Guild alternated *Pygmalion* with *Juarez and Maximilian.* Lynn's Eliza Doolittle was one of her greatest achievements. She played the cockney guttersnipe with vulgar abandon, and her cockney dialect was pungent and true, because she had grown up among cockneys. Other actresses, even other British actresses, have had to study it. It came naturally to Lynn. She once told me there were at least five kinds of cockney, though you had to have a good ear to catch the nuances. She didn't think any American actress, even with proper coaching, could ever do a first-rate Liza Doolittle. Alfred said it was also true of Shakespeare. "I don't like Shakespeare's plays spoken with the American speech," he said. "You must have English actors. Oh, there was one, though, one American who spoke beautiful English. John Barrymore. When he played *Hamlet,* he played it with perfectly beautiful speech. His speech was so pure, so musical. He could speak poetry and act the part. He didn't make mistakes. And, you know, he played Falder in Galsworthy's *Justice;* it was one of the greatest things I've ever seen. And he had to speak cockney. And his cockney was so good. It was perfect."

"Not perfect," Lynn said. "He made one mistake. I once met him at a party and said that his cockney in *Justice* was divine and I couldn't believe he wasn't a born Englishman. 'Except you made one little mistake,' I said to him, 'a strange little mistake, but the sort an American would make. You know that line where you say, "No light comes into my cell at all," and you said it, "at all." Well, we would have run the words together, saying, "atall, atall." ' "

Charles Brackett, writing in *The New Yorker,* said, "Lynn Fontanne's vibrant young Eliza Doolittle makes one's memory of Mrs. Patrick Campbell in the part seem like a faded cigarette card." Percy Hammond found her "more lifelike . . . closer to the flower girl type than Mrs. Campbell." Miss Helburn recalled: "What Lynn did so especially well was the cockney part of Liza. She made no compromise of any sort with the vulgarity of Liza. She was the dirty snotnosed draggletail without a trace of the gloss that both Gertie Lawrence and Stella Campbell couldn't get rid of when they played Liza. I think they softened Liza. Lynn didn't. She didn't romanticize Liza Doolittle one bit."

Mrs. Campbell was in New York when *Pygmalion* opened. She lunched with Noel Coward after the opening. She was furious at the New York critics. "How dare they say she's better than I was," she shouted. "I don't believe it. I tell you I *don't believe it.*" A few weeks later, she went to a performance. Then she went back to see Lynn. "When she showed her face in my dressing room," Lynn says, "I thought, *dear God but now I'm really going to get it,* but no, she sat down, as politely as you please, and she did what a great actress should do to a younger actress. She told me several things Shaw had told her to do when he directed her in the original production. They were very valuable things for me to know, quite helpful."

Pygmalion was the Guild's big hit that season of 1926-1927. It ran 143 performances. *Juarez and Maximilian* ran six weeks, long enough to accommodate the subscribers. During the last two weeks of the run, Alfred began rehearsing in Sidney Howard's second play, *Ned McCobb's Daughter.* He played Babe Callahan, a New York bootlegger, who plots to turn a small Maine restaurant, Carrie's Spa, into a front for a liquor-smuggling operation. Carrie was played by Mrs. Sidney Howard, Claire Eames. Carrie is a noble New England lady, married to Babe's brother, George. George is a thief, a liar, and a "skirt chaser." Babe himself is no lily. He is a blackmailer and a gangster, although basically he is decent. Having recently played the decadent, poetic Maximilian, the mastery with which Alfred conjured up a hoodlum astonished the critics. He rasped out gutter dialect as nimbly as he had recited the mournful numbers of Werfel. Percy Hammond did say that he thought the "predominant delicacies of Lunt's speech and manner interfere with his illustrations of a brutal and illiterate blackguard," but Hammond's reaction was the exception. More typical was E. W. Osborn in the New York *World:* "Alfred Lunt simply revels in the role of Babe Callahan. He thrives visibly on the swaggering, the bullying, the rough jesting, and the rollicking brutality that go with the part. Let the highbrows of the Guild constituency regret the fact as they will, this, their prized star, has found mighty easy and graceful the descent from the Hungarian or British classic to a Yankee carousel."

"After we saw him do Babe Callahan," Miss Helburn told me, "we knew he could play anything." For Babe, Alfred had to master a dialect as peculiar as Liza Doolittle's Covent Garden cockney—namely, New York slang, of the "dese, dem, dose" type, the Brooklyn variety. Sidney Howard gave the character lines like, "Don't be standin' dere dat way. It gets my goat." Callahan sounded more like Jimmy Durante, then a speakeasy cabaret star, than a bigtime gangster. Alfred modified the exaggerated dialect. Then he figured Babe should have a prominent gold tooth. He had a dentist fit him with a gold cap on a side tooth, which he kept on during the run of *Ned McCobb's Daughter*. Some little detail about a character would always obsess Alfred. Here it was a problem of handshaking. How does a gangster shake hands? For Alfred it became crucial to know.

In the final scenes of the play, Carrie Callahan fights back against hopeless odds. She is trying to run a restaurant. She has two children. Her father has died of a heart attack in Act I. Her husband has stolen $2,000 from a ferry company and will be sent to prison if she doesn't make restitution. He has been having an affair with Jenny, the waitress at her restaurant, and has borrowed money from her late father for an abortion for Jenny. Babe Callahan is putting pressure on her to go into bootlegging with his syndicate. Finally, Carrie—largely due to the playwright's desperation—solves all her problems. She tricks Babe and gets money out of him without joining his schemes. Babe is a blackguard, with a heart of gold. In the last moments of the play, he expresses his appreciation of Carrie's nobility and then shakes her hand. But how to shake it? Grasp firmly? Squeeze hard? Come close up, hunch shoulders, and suddenly thrust out paws? Reach slowly, take hand, pump rapidly? Alfred consulted some speakeasy owners who knew Larry Fay, a leading rum-runner of the period. They all suggested that he extend his arm slowly, kind of suspicious like, as if he wasn't sure Carrie might not have a gun in her palm and when they were palm-in-palm he should press her hand gently and release it quickly. This and the other details of the character were convincing even to those who, like Walter Winchell, knew the Prohibition era hoodlums at first hand. Writing in the New York *Graphic*, Winchell said Alfred's was "the most unforgettable roughness that has ever barked from beyond the footlights . . . grafted from right off a Sixth Avenue corner . . . that bootlegger,

Babe, is a man for you to meet. His arrival in the room of death is magnificent."

Winchell was referring to a scene in which Alfred swaggered into the parlor where Carrie's father was laid out in his coffin. He entered loudly singing the following to the tune of *My Bonnie Lies Over the Ocean:*

> My mother sells snow to de snow boids,
> My brother sells synt'etic gin,
> My sister sells love for a livin',
> Good God how de dollars roll in!

He plunked a foot on the coffin and proceeded to go into several lengthy monologues about death and life and his experiences with the American Expeditionary Forces in World War I, and then he played a tenderly tough scene with Carrie in which he said she had a "wonderful character . . . Yeah, an dat's what counts in dis world. By God, if it don't. 'Beauty fades but character goes on forever.' You know. Huh? I don't know nothin' I admire like I do character. . . ."

Alfred uttered "character" while staring at Claire Eames as if she were a creature from another world.

Terry Helburn never forgot how Alfred spoke the word "character" and how he looked at Claire Eames. Twenty years later, the Theatre Guild was transforming Molnar's *Liliom* into the Rodgers and Hammerstein music drama *Carousel*. The original Hungarian setting was transposed into a New England setting with New England characters.

"We had Jan Clayton playing Julie in *Carousel*," Miss Helburn once reminisced. "The part had some of the quality of the Claire Eames part in *Ned McCobb's Daughter*, the inherent character of a strong woman surrounded by evil and coming through. During rehearsals, we'd sometimes lose the mood of *Carousel*. I wouldn't know what was going wrong and then I'd say *character, character*, exactly as Alfred had read it, meaning, 'strength of character,' and when things went badly and it seemed the music and lyrics were lovely but we were all wrong in changing the locale to New England and I'd come back to Alfred saying 'character' and his speech in *Ned McCobb's Daughter* and I knew it was right for us to put that Hungarian play in New England and Julie's strong character was like Carrie's in Sidney Howard's play and once I told them all—Jan Clayton, Rouben Mamoulian, who was directing *Carousel*, Dick Rodgers and Oscar—I told them about Alfred and Claire Eames and the speech about New England character and that Alfred and Claire had played Julie and Liliom, even though there wasn't a love affair between them, but there could have been. Anyway, after I made my long speech, we never had any more trouble with *Carousel* because we all knew what we were working for and why we were in New England."

During the period beten 1926 and 1929, Lynn and Alfred worked and worked and worked. Together they played in *The Brothers Karamazov* at the Guild Theatre, alternating with Sidney Howard's *The Silver Cord*. *Pygmalion* was in weekly repertory at the Golden Theatre with *Ned McCobb's Daughter*. Then in their spare time they went into rehearsal for *The Second Man*. During that time, the Guild decided to ship the *Pygmalion* company to Philadelphia for two weeks. Lynn acted in Philadelphia at night, went to New York by the midnight train, rehearsed all day, and returned to Philadelphia in the evening. *The Second Man* opened, and alternated in New York with *Pygmalion*. After Philadelphia, the Guild knew there was a road audience for their kind of theatre. They had the Lunts set up a temporary branch of the Guild in Chicago, with a repertory of *Pygmalion* (Alfred now playing Henry Higgins), *The Guardsman,* and *The Doctor's Dilemma*. After three months of hard labor in Chicago, the Lunts opened in *The Doctor's Dilemma* at the Guild Theatre on November 21, 1928, and almost at once, *Marco Millions* was put into rehearsal with Alfred as Marco Polo. Then Lynn began rehearsing as Nina Leeds in *Strange Interlude,* Eugene O'Neill's five hour play. Oh, how weary they were. Lynn was giving eight performances a week as Jennifer Dubedat in Shaw's comedy. She was rehearsing as Nina Leeds, probably the longest role ever written for an actress. It was the hardest work of her life. "Only someone young and strong could have done it," she says. Poor Alfred was so worn out that at the premiere of *Marco Millions* he almost fainted from sheer physical exhaustion. Woollcott noted that Alfred's playing of Marco was "marked by an almost hypnotic weariness, each line of the long role parting from him as if, although certain what the next must be, he had not quite decided whether to buck up and say it, or just to curl up there on the Guild stage and take a good long nap."

A few weeks later, the Guild loaded another burden on Alfred's back. He was to play Mosca in *Volpone*. Upon hearing this joyous news, Lynn told the Guild directors what she thought of them. "You call yourselves an art theatre, do you?" she said. "Art theatre, my foot. This isn't an art theatre—it's a sweatshop."

"It was Lynn who did the impossible," Alfred says. "I only did the improbable. I was stupid. She was heroic. She learned her lines for *Strange Interlude* at home, of course. Now you know I never heard one word of her lines from Lynn at home. We lived in the same house, ate together, slept in the same bed. She didn't say a word about the part." They occupied a triplex apartment. There were two bedrooms on the second floor, and a studio on the third floor. Lynn learned her lines in the studio. "In the last week, preparing for *Strange Interlude*, Margalo Gillmore was supposed to replace Lynn in *Doctor's Dilemma* so Lynn could concentrate on *Strange Interlude*. Margalo called up and said she was afraid she would not be able to be ready in time and could Lynn go on playing Mrs. Dubedat for another week? And Lynn did it. I don't know how, but she did it. And they were now doing run-throughs of *Strange Interlude*, the whole ghastly nine acts of it, every day, and then she was giving a performance of *Doctor's Dilemma* at night."

"No," Lynn says. "It was really harder on Alfred. He wasn't in good health at the time."

Only a very few people have ever known that Alfred has suffered all his life from the operation that saved his life when he was a boy. He had lost a kidney and much of the muscular wall that supports the abdomen and the lower back, leaving only a layer of skin before and behind. He had to wear a support. Yet you would never know this, meeting him at a party, or watching him swagger on a stage. "You could say literally that Alfred had to have guts to do what he has done all his life," his boyhood friend, Bennett Weaver, once said to me. During periods of stress, Alfred's remaining kidney and his intestinal system naturally got inflamed, and he was in excruciating pain. Yet he rarely missed a performance and he never used his bad health as an excuse to get out of his responsibilities to the audience.

Like Mary Baker Eddy, Alfred refused to believe in the existence of pain and disease. Once, during the run of *Design for Living*, Noel got a severe cold which became laryngitis. His doctor said that if he did not play Friday night and Saturday matinee and evening and if he rested in bed all day Sunday and Monday, he would be able to play Monday evening. Noel broke the news to Alfred. Alfred was outraged at the idea of missing a performance merely because one had a congestion in the chest, a raw throat, and a diseased larynx. Nonsense. Just coddling oneself. Acting was a "sovereign balm" for a sore throat.

Good for the lungs too. And the stomach. Coward, now feverish and losing strength rapidly, had to prove he was sick. He took his temperature and showed the mercury reading to Alfred. It was 103°. Coward moaned that he could scarcely move about, that they had an understudy whom they had been paying $250 weekly for five weeks, and that it was high time the man earned some of this money. He would only miss four performances; the world would not come to an end if Noel Coward didn't play in *Design for Living* four times, and it wouldn't hurt business, because people wanted to see Lynn and Alfred.

"He wouldn't hear of it," Noel remembers. "He argued, implored, coaxed, cajoled me into going on with a high fever and such hoarseness I couldn't be heard three feet away. On Friday night, wouldn't you know it, Alfred got so upset by my condition that he dried up completely. He forgot all his lines, and the performance was one enormous shambles. What's so delightfully, appallingly immoral about Alfred is that he felt not a twinge of guilt about badgering me into acting when I was deathly sick. He thought my appearance was required for a good show. He only cares about the theatre. The theatre comes first. He's willing to jeopardize his own health for it, so one can't very well cavil when he insists on ruining your health, can one?"

At one point, during the sweatshop phase of their work in the Guild, Lynn was playing in *Strange Interlude,* which never played matinees, and Alfred was doing *Volpone,* which did. Lynn awakened Alfred one night and said she was burning up with fever and she thought they ought to call a doctor. Alfred glared at her. How dared she disturb him? He had a matinee tomorrow. He must have his sleep. He seized his pillow and got a quilt out of the linen closet. Then he descended to the living room and bedded down for the night on a couch. As far as he was concerned, Lynn's fever did not exist.

Lynn can be as fanatical as Alfred. When Noel saw *Strange Interlude,* he went back to pay his respects to Lynn. "Naturally," Noel remembers with a shudder, "she asked me what I thought of her performance. You know, Lynn and Alfred will grill you like Scotland Yard about their plays. And they want specific details. Well, I made the mistake of saying, 'In the seventh act, Lynn, I think you overacted. You groaned too much.' I could have bitten off my tongue as soon as the words were out of my mouth. Two weeks later, she rang me and said I must come and see *Strange Interlude* again as she thought

131

she had improved the scene I criticized. And she wouldn't let me come and see just the seventh act. Oh, no. I had to sit through the whole bloody nine acts of that bore—from the beginning to the end."

During a brief vacation in England in the summer of 1927, the Lunts visited Noel Coward at his country place in Kent. They began telling him what a wonderful comedy *The Second Man* was, how the role of Clark Storey was made for his acting style, and that he must, he simply must, do a London production of it. Noel, having read the play, said he thought it was rather literary, though extremely witty, and would not play well. Lynn and Alfred were dismayed at his reaction, and to prove how well it played, they put on an impromptu performance of *The Second Man* in Noel's drawing room, playing all four parts. They threw themselves into the performance so intensely that, during one scene—and all this for an audience of one—Lynn began criticizing something Alfred was doing and he began bickering with her. They continued playing it and Alfred got a severe attack of nerves and forgot "one of the most important scenes and burst into tears, but I gathered enough inspiration from their performance to set about getting hold of the rights of the play at once."

I once expressed amazement that at such short notice Lynn and Alfred could have done an entire play all by themselves. Noel said he hadn't been surprised. "I assure you," he said, "that if the subject had come up, they could have taken all the parts in *War and Peace* and done them quite nicely, too. They love to act so much, to act for the sake of acting, especially for someone whom they love and who loves them."

When they were about to open in *Amphitryon 38* in Cleveland, ten years later, they learned, to their dismay, that Archie Bell, the drama critic of the Cleveland *Plain Dealer,* was quite sick and would not be able to review the show. They went to Archie Bell's house and put on the complete play, every word, every scene, playing, between them, all the twelve parts.

During the run of a play, the gears of their private life are inextricably meshed with the gears of the play. Never invite them for dinner during the run of a play unless it is for a Sunday dinner. Supper, yes, after the performance, but never dinner, from Monday to Saturday. Once, a gentleman who did not know the Lunts and their rigid schedule insisted that they come to his home for dinner on a Friday night. Politely, they tried to get out of it, but he would not take no for an answer. They rather liked the old gentleman and did not want to be rude or to seem lah-de-dah. He would not give up. Finally he said, "You can make it any time you choose."

"All right," Alfred said, "we'll be there at four P.M.!"

Even their best friends and their old friends, even their friends in and of the theatre, who are as mad about the theatre as they are, sometimes think that the Lunts carry their passion for theatre to the verge of monomania. Miss Claire, who has been living in San Francisco for many years and is married to a wealthy industrialist, once arranged an intimate dinner party in honor of the Lunts at one of the finest restaurants in San Francisco, The Blue Fox. Whenever the conversation was in danger of veering into the areas of politics and current history, Miss Claire recalls, either Lynn or Alfred would at once manage to get the conversation back to the theatre and especially to *O Mistress Mine,* which they were playing at the time. "You sometimes get the feeling," reports Miss Claire, "that nothing outside the theatre really exists for them."

Once, when *Idiot's Delight* was trying out in Boston, Alfred was backstage, hovering over the chief electrician, who was operating the dimmer-board. Alfred was concerned about several of the light changes. Woollcott, who happened to be in Boston, dropped backstage and looked about until he found Alfred.

"Hello, Alfred," he said.

Absorbed in the lighting problems, Alfred didn't turn around and didn't acknowledge the greeting.

"Listen, you faun's behind," Woollcott said sweetly, "how are you?"

Alfred mumbled.

"And how's your wife?" Woollcott inquired, in a louder voice.

"Who?" Alfred murmured dreamily, "Lynn Fontanne?"

After the war, Noel Coward moved to Jamaica, and the Lunts came to visit him. Lynn had never been to Jamaica before. One afternoon, Noel took her around to show her some of the sights. There was a certain view of which he was very proud. You had to climb up a mountain to see it. So he took Lynn up to the top of this mountain. "Oh, the view's breath-taking when you finally get there. But you've got to climb up and up, there's one nasty crag after another, you know like in that French movie, *The Wages of Fear,* those sheer drops, and it's rather like a series of terraced cliffs." They were out of breath when they arrived at the summit. Noel displayed the vista as if he had personally built it. The mountain and its precipitous terraces, one below the other, and then the jungle terrain in the valley below, and further out, the sands of the beach and then the turquoise waters of the Carribbean. . . .

"Isn't it lovely?" Noel asked, pointing to the view.

Lynn looked down. "It looks like rows and rows of empty seats," she said.

In truth, however, Lynn and Alfred have a diversity of interests. They love nature and they love to cultivate flowers and vegetables. They love animals, especially dogs. They love to listen to clever people say clever things. They love to travel. They love to eat good food and drink fine wines. They love to go to parties. And they have nonacting skills, too. Lynn is a marvelous seamstress. She designs and sews some of her own clothes, and she loves to sew clothes for her friends. She also likes to wash and iron dresses and skirts and blouses. She once went through a period of fabricating nightgowns. She made two for Vivien Leigh. One was a "simple blue silk with a white wool jacket and the other was a flowered thin wool with long sleeves and lace ruffles." She explained to Miss Leigh that "I am concentrating at the moment on night-dresses." And Alfred's cookery is his *violon d'Ingres*. He pursues delectability in his kitchen as seriously as he pursues the truth of a character in a play.

NINE

ALEXANDER WOOLLCOTT'S
FAVORITE CHEF

*A*LEXANDER WOOLLCOTT was a gourmet and a gourmand. He liked good food and in large portions. He frequently got indigestion. (His remedy, on one occasion, was to eat four welsh rarebits, which gave his intestinal tract "something to think about.") He traveled widely and dined widely and well in the best private homes, restaurants, and clubs. He had partaken of Alfred's cuisine since 1927. In 1939, not long after he had enjoyed a sumptuous repast cooked by Alfred, he wrote the amateur chef a bread-and-butter note: "After considerable gastric meditation, I have come to the conclusion that you set the best table I know in America." Previously, Aleck loved bantering Alfred about a leading Japanese actor, one Kikugoro. Kikugoro also prided himself on his cooking talent. During a trip to Japan in 1931, Aleck had an "entrancing supper" at Kikugoro's house. Writing to Beatrice Kaufman (Mrs. George Kaufman), he drooled over the courses and added, "The Lunts will really have to do better by me from now on." And then, for years afterward, he'd shake his head when Alfred served him some gastronomical masterpiece over which he'd labored all day.

"Sorry, clumsy," he'd say. "It's not bad, not bad at all, but it isn't really up to Kikugoro's standards."

Noel Coward would also prick Alfred's vanity on this subject. Noel claims that *haute cuisine* is a pretentious fraud. Are Alfred's fusses over sauces and *recettes* a pose? Noel affects to think so. Why, he says, anybody who can read a few simple directions in a cookbook can cook as well as Alfred.

"Even I can cook as well as you," he claimed during an argument.

"Well," Alfred challenged, "how do you roast a chicken?"

"First," Noel said, "you get the chicken cleaned, and then you get a pound of butter, and then you take this pound of butter and stuff it up the chicken's ass and then you shove it in the oven and that's all there is to it!"

In Genesee Depot there are four kitchens—one in the studio, one in the guest house, one in the poolside cabana, and an enormous one in the main house. The main kitchen, outfitted with enough electric ranges and pots and pans and casseroles and tureens to feed twenty guests at a time, is Alfred's shrine. Here he bakes bread and cakes and pastries of all kinds. He prepares cheese soufflés as gossamer as whipped cream. He concocts his own Béarnaise sauce for a steak or beats up his own hollandaise for the fresh asparagus he's picked from the garden in the morning. When he makes coffee, he often makes it Swedish style, adding a raw egg while the coffee is brewing. He sometimes enters a specialty at the annual county fair in Waukesha, and has won local fame and sometimes a ribbon with his almond cookies, currant jelly, vichyssoise, meat pastries, molded aspic jellies (I once ate a fantastic egg in aspic for lunch at Ten Chimneys), jellied madrilène, and his Swedish Meat Balls Lindstrom (fragments of chopped fresh beets and chopped fresh onions are kneaded into the meat). He grinds his own meat for sausages and for hamburgers.

Alan Hewitt remembers a glorious gastronomical weekend at Ten Chimneys. (Incidentally, the Lunt estate is named Ten Chimneys because, strangely enough, there are exactly ten chimneys on the buildings. This reminds me of the time I visited Tallulah Bankhead when she was living in Bedford Village, N.Y. Her estate, she said, was called "Windows." I asked, "And why do you call it Windows?" "Because it has lots of windows, you fool," she explained sweetly.) "They fed me up like I was a Strasbourg goose," Hewitt recalls. "The first night we had a rich soup, a sort of *potage mongole*. Alfred asked me if I liked it and I said something like wow, and he asked if I liked soup in general and I said no meal was complete without soup and he smiled in agreement. From then on I got a different soup for lunch and dinner every day. The second night, Alfred made those sensational Swedish hamburger steaks he makes. I don't know why he keeps calling them Swedish meatballs because they're not small and round. I never found out who Lindstrom is or was. He said we'd eat in the kitchen so we'd be closer to the skillet. He got it burning hot and he cooked them, a batch at a time, and we ate them right from the skillet. After dinner, Lynn wanted to finish a Scrabble game we were in the middle of and Alfred told me to go with her and he'd do the dishes alone. He said, 'I'm used to doing them. I rather enjoy cleaning dishes.' "

Like many Broadway stars, Alfred and Lynn worked at the Stage Door Canteen, a USO-operated dining and dancing club for servicemen during the war. Art Buchwald, then a publicity man for Paramount Pictures, worked in the kitchen of the Canteen, which was on 44th Street. Buchwald recalls: "Alfred Lunt is best remembered by many of us for the thorough way he cleaned the garbage pails. It was typical of him to take on the manual job of cleaning dishes and throwing out garbage, while so many other actors just came around to the canteen to take bows and get themselves photographed for publicity. The only thing that kept me going through those dark nights of garbage was the realization that Mr. Lunt was swabbing garbage pails right alongside of me."

A young Broadway player, then unknown, was also in the garbage detail at the Stage Door Canteen. Years later, at a party, Kirk Douglas approached Alfred and said, "Mr. Lunt, do you remember me?"

"You're Kirk Douglas, aren't you? I've seen several of your films."

"Well but we knew each other a long time ago," Douglas said. "We used to wash dishes together at the Stage Door Canteen."

Hewitt learned how to scramble eggs while in Louisville on tour with the Lunts in 1938. Whenever they played a date for more than one day they booked a hotel suite with a kitchen so they could cook their own meals. "Lynn and Alfred once asked me up for supper after a performance," he says. "He made bacon and scrambled eggs. He made them in a double boiler. I've been making them in a double boiler ever since. It's the best way to scramble eggs. They don't harden. They cook slowly. You turn down the heat and wait patiently and you stir them once in a while so they come out creamy—not hard, not watery—but with a perfect consistency."

I remember once visiting with the Lunts in Boston while they were trying out *The Great Sebastians*. They were staying at the Copley-Plaza; that was a surprise. The Copley-Plaza is a charming hotel, but practically all Broadway stars stay at the Ritz-Carlton in Boston. The company manager of the show had originally booked them a suite at the Ritz, but when they found out the rate was $35 a day they balked. No hotel accommodations were worth $35 a day. The Ritz refused to grant them a special "professional" rate. They at once transferred to the Copley-Plaza, whose manager was Richard Whorf's brother-in-law.

Whorf is actor, director, scene designer, and old friend of the Lunts. The Copley gave them a handsome bedroom and sitting room for $15 a day. Fine—except there was no kitchen. Alfred at once went to Filene's and bought a hot plate and some cooking utensils and crockery, although it was against the hotel rules to have a hot plate in one's room. From then on, during the two week tryout, Alfred, each morning, strolled through the Public Gardens to S.S. Pierce's and did his morning shopping. "They've got the most marvelous sweet butter at S.S. Pierce's," he told me, handing me a slice of buttered bread. "Don't you think so?" He smuggled the groceries in under cover of newspapers. The management knew perfectly well that Alfred was turning his suite into a small scale Locke-Ober's but they looked the other way. Alfred was delighted with his cleverness. He believed he was putting one over on all the Boston restaurateurs. He broiled meat and fish dishes and prepared soups, and then he slyly washed the silver, the pots, the china, and concealed them in a drawer, covering them with some of Lynn's lingerie.

Alfred enjoys shopping for cooking things. In Paris in 1953, he went about pricing pots and pans and china. He bought a lot of them. He believes French china and cooking utensils are superior to all others. He warned a friend, who was meeting his boat: "I am afraid that I shall enter New York like Red Riding Hood going to the wolf, as I shall have an enormous wicker basket on my arm. The wicker basket is full of expensive china which I just can't trust to packing in a trunk as I am afraid the pieces will break."

He will ask people about their favorite recipes. Once, during a long train ride between one-night stands, he said to company manager George Greenberg, "They tell me you're quite a chef. Do you know any good recipes?"

Greenberg said he liked cooking but he was afraid his recipes were fairly standard Jewish dishes.

"Ah," Alfred cried, "you know, I adore chopped chicken liver. I have tried to make it myself, but I can't make it so it tastes the way it tastes in Lindy's. I don't know what they put into it. Usually I can figure out the ingredients of a dish by tasting it but I can't figure out the Lindy's chopped liver."

"Well, tell me how you make it?"

"Let's see," Alfred said, "I chop up the liver and then I chop some onions and fry them in butter—"

"Aha," interrupted Greenberg, "right away you're making a big mistake."

"Why?"

"You have to fry the onions in chicken fat and not butter before combining them with the chopped liver."

"Is that it? Is that really it?" Alfred bounded up and down. "You've made me a very happy man, George."

Subsequently, he rendered his own chicken fat, fried his onions in it, chopped up the livers with the onions and finally achieved his dream of chopped liver.

When I first met Alfred, twenty years ago, he was interested in my name and inquired if I were of Russian descent. I said I was. He immediately demanded: "Tell me, please, how does your mother prepare beef Stroganoff?"

I said my mother was a career woman and had not been interested in cooking. I said the best beef Stroganoff I'd ever tasted was at the St. Regis Hotel when Serge Obolensky was its manager. Alfred said he was able to do an excellent beef Stroganoff himself but he was always trying to better himself.

Some years later, when I came to Ten Chimneys for a visit, I found that Alfred hadn't forgotten our talk. The first night he served a Russian meal. First, there was a hot borsch with *pirojki,* those tiny hot meat puffs customarily served with soup. The soup was a wonder to taste, flavored with fresh dill. Then came a beef Stroganoff worthy of Obolensky. For dessert, Alfred's *baklava.* There was even tea served in glasses with lemon slices.

Another time, Alfred met me at the Milwaukee Airport. As we were driving to Genesee Depot, he inquired whether I ate everything and I said I certainly did. He said it was a relief because sometimes house guests were peculiar about this or that food. He didn't believe in allergies, did Alfred, or digestive disorders, or cholesterol, reducing diets, or any of that nonsense. One should eat everything. And tonight we were to have *hasenschlegel,* or roast leg of hare, German style. Benny Perkins, who farms his land, had killed some fat rabbits that morning. I blushed. I admitted rabbit was one of the few foods I couldn't eat. He said I didn't have to apologize. He asked all house guests to give him a list of the foods they couldn't eat. He said the longest lists came from Lindsay and Crouse. "They hardly eat anything," he said. "Each of them sends me a two-page list of foods they can't eat or aren't allowed to eat. They don't like rabbit, either. Or turnips. I find nobody really likes turnips but Lynn and myself."

"I don't like turnips but I eat them," I said.

"You should like them. Turnips are awfully good."

Alfred likes cooking for friends. Once, for a birthday party for Crouse, he baked a dozen *Wienerbröd,* and had them packed in a Bergdorf-Goodman box, tied with a red ribbon and delivered to Crouse.

He will cook at the homes of friends and relatives. Several years ago, visiting his sister-in-law and brother-in-law, Mr. and Mrs. H. S. Wilson, in England, he prepared luncheon. He served a consommé *printanière,* then a cold boiled lobster which he had cooked and with which he served a mayonnaise sauce he whipped up for the occasion. He had brought his own pot and pan from London, Antoinette Wilson told me.

Another time, in Paris, Alfred cooked dinner at the home of Art Buchwald for a party of eight, including M. and Mme. Edmond Bory, proprietors of the finest *épicerie* in Paris. Alfred made only American specialties—clam chowder, Boston style; broiled lobster; southern fried chicken with corn fritters; apple pie and cheese. Alfred was assisted by Jules, his man Friday and all the other days of the week. "They arrived at noon," Buchwald remembers, "and Alfred was in the kitchen until eight o'clock. The food was very good. But Alfred was as nervous as if it was the opening night of a new play. He's a perfectionist about food. He chose the wines. They were French wines. He made excellent choices. I don't remember what they were."

One of Alfred's favorite television programs is a morning show over WTMJ, a Milwaukee channel. It is the Greta Greme and Mary cooking program. They discuss recipes and prepare food before the camera. "They're a marvelous team, Greta and Mary," Alfred says. "They fight and bicker over recipes and get into the most dramatic situations. Haven't seen better teamwork since McIntyre and Heath—y'know, the minstrel comics. I remember one morning they were preparing dumplings and Mary took the cover off the pot and Greta simply flew across the studio at her, screaming 'Mary what are you doing? Don't you know you must never never take off the cover when you're making dumplings?' And Mary said, 'But I only wanted to see how they were coming along.' And Greta said, 'In cooking dumplings, you must have faith. You must believe. For twenty minutes, you must believe.' "

The culmination of Alfred's culinary education took place in 1958, when he attended the *Ecole du Cordon Bleu* in Paris. He enrolled for the three month course. He went four times a week from 9:30 A.M. to 5 P.M. The students, he says, were placed in groups of twelve.

When we came in, there was a menu on the wall and raw food on the tables, and the master chef who was teaching us would tell us what to do with the raw materials. Each group had to prepare a four course meal in the morning. We ate the morning's exercises for lunch. Afternoons, there were lectures and demonstrations by different teachers. I learned a few simple things and some complicated things. One of the best things I learned was how to poach eggs so they remain soft for hours. You boil them in water to which you've added a little wine vinegar. Then you place them in cold water and as soon as they cool you put them in another pot of cold water. Now they hold all day. Damned useful if you have to prepare a large batch of poached eggs for eggs benedict.

I learned several new ways of making chicken croquettes. I learned how to make French fried potatoes as a good French chef makes them. You square off the ends of the potatoes and then you have this rectangle. Then you slice it into slices of exactly the same thickness so they all fry evenly. I remember asking the chef what he did with the ends as it seemed a waste to throw them away and he said you didn't but you put them into your *potage* for the children.

I learned how to make a flaky *vol-au-vent*, a steak *au poivre* (you get a frying pan and beat the hell out of the peppercorns on a wooden board and then you rub them into the meat), a really professional *crêpes suzette*, and the teacher showed us how to make the pancakes paper thin and how to flip them over in the pan as we weren't to use a spatula.

I learned how to make a *ragout*, but a good one. I'd been cooking stews since those boarding house days in Waukesha but this was the real thing. I learned a very good *Blanquette de Veau* and a *Bananes Flambés*. Even a *bouillabaisse*, with 17 scale and shell fish. I haven't been able to make it here because we don't have all the varieties of fish the French have.

The harvest of Alfred's theory and practice are contained in two loose-leaf notebooks, each holding 300 pages, filled with recipes and his ideas on sundry aspects of the culinary art and his experiences in his kitchen.

A restless sleeper, Alfred arises at dawn. He roams about the vegetable garden and the flower garden. He wanders into the chicken house. He goes into the kitchen, at last, and makes himself scrambled eggs and coffee and he may sit alone for hours just sipping coffee and leafing through his notebooks or other cookbooks. He likes to read other people's recipes for the sheer pleasure of reading them.

An early riser myself, I happened to be walking idly about Ten Chimneys one morning when I spied Alfred in the kitchen. I joined him for some coffee and we talked about cooking and coffee drinking and Alexander Woollcott, who drank coffee incessantly. Aleck always awakened early when he came to Ten Chimneys. When Alfred came down, Aleck was already there, awaiting his coffee.

"Aleck was never brutal to me or Lynn or Harpo Marx," Alfred said, one morning in the kitchen. "I guess we were the only three of his friends he didn't get ugly with." (Crouse, a member of the Woollcott circle, doesn't remember Aleck ever turning on the Lunts but he recalled a time when Aleck was cruel to Harpo. Aleck had gotten one of his theatrical crushes on Harpo, in 1923, when the Marx brothers came to New York in *I'll Say She Is*. He didn't care about Groucho, Chico, or Zeppo: Harpo was the only Marx brother about whom he gave a damn. You'd see Harpo around Woollcott's house all the time. In 1927, Harpo sent Aleck a Christmas present of one of the early models of a console radio—a tall monstrosity. Aleck glared at the machine. He disliked radio broadcasts anyway. He at once phoned Harpo. In menacing tones, he said, "I'll give you exactly twenty-four hours to get this goddamned thing out of my house." He didn't talk to Harpo for weeks.)

"Friendship with Woollcott was a fluctuating affair," writes Samuel Hopkins Adams in his biography of the terrible-tempered Woollcott. "He would banish a friend for any imagined insult—or a social or political or literary difference of opinion. He quarreled at one time or another with all his friends—except the Lunts."

The enduring tranquillity commenced in 1924 after *The Guardsman*. It survived all the Woollcottian vicissitudes. They called him "Ducky Dee" and "Tiddyfye." He never gave the Lunts a bad notice. Woollcott's foes said he chose for personal friends only those actors whom he could admire critically. Before Woollcott, it was considered bad form for a drama reviewer to mingle socially with actors. Was one not in danger of losing one's critical detachment? Aleck, however, was enraptured by actors. He would rather be in the company of actors than any other sort of people. Besides the Lunts, he was enamored of Minnie Maddern Fiske, Maude Adams, Laurette Taylor, John and Ethel and Lionel Barrymore, Harpo, Helen Hayes, Katharine Cornell, and Ina Claire. Even as a critic, "he was always more concerned with the player than the play, with the interpretation than the theme. In

and family life. Unable to get
life. He was a center of "fun
high price to be paid—you had
his insults. But that was only t
it was the one everybody gossipe
friends because he was kindly
in his company. They began to
Hotel des Artistes and had his
hotel's excellent kitchen via the
ful and considerate host. In 19
ments on East 52nd Street. D
End. Sunday breakfast at Aleck's
the literary and theatrical *cogn*
the gallant company which gat
and popovers and assorted hot d
of friends. Somebody once wisec
with 800 intimate friends. The
in large sentences, and making
and the world. There were passi
had eaten. Or there might be ac
was no doubt that Aleck suffered
at Aleck's often had the quality o
ous children's birthday party in v
Dean's, the ice cream from Sher
there were professional acts, ma
clever *conferencier* to keep the
cake and ice cream were all gone.

Aleck and his friends played
and Twenty Questions and Ask
They took up the new craze of
They played chess, cribbage, brid
badminton. They played to win.
played for large side bets.

Alfred never played. He hate
Lynn is good at games, and she
word games. She was good at an
the Woollcott Playground for Ad
Anagrams at one point and woul
with whom to play it. Alfred ha

his mind, the play was primarily a vehicle for the actor." * Charles Brackett once said Aleck never really liked anybody whose life story would not make a good magazine article. He constantly wrote and rewrote the lives of his friends for various publications—*The New Yorker, Cosmopolitan, Good Housekeeping* and the *Reader's Digest.*

Because of Wolcott Gibbs' notorious 3-part profile of Woollcott in *The New Yorker* and the portrait of Sheridan Whiteside in *The Man Who Came to Dinner,* a distorted picture of Aleck has come down to us. Woollcott *was* arrogant. He *was* a social tyrant. He *could* be savagely cruel in his human relationships. He was often rude. He would phone you and issue a dictum: "I can see you at my apartment next Friday between 5 and 5:30." He would tell you, "I can dine with you next Tuesday. Have Oscar Levant there. I want to ask him something." When Gertrude Stein came to the U.S. in 1932 for a lecture tour, she was introduced to Aleck. She disagreed with one of his opinions. "Miss Stein," Woollcott stated, "you have not been in New York long enough to know that I am never contradicted."

Yet the extraordinary thing is not that Aleck was querulous, vicious, nasty, arrogant, supercilious—but that so many of the most gifted and successful men and women of his time loved him and continued to love him and value his friendship. Kaufman and Hart always remained his friends. Kaufman admired Aleck so much that he collaborated on two plays with him. They did not mean their portrait of Aleck in *The Man Who Came to Dinner* to be a portrait of a monster.

Let us return to Alfred and Aleck in the kitchen—the clean, almost antiseptic kitchen, with walls of shining white tile and copper kettles. Alfred in old pants and old shirt and dilapidated shoes. Aleck un-shaven, his hair rumpled, clad in scruffy pyjamas and a silk bathrobe like a tent. He is now a grotesquely fat man—300 pounds of him on 5 feet 7 inches of height. His face is a mask of absurdity—a globular face, whose tiny features seem glued to an inflated balloon, small eyes, small ears, pursed mouth, a triangular nose on which balance his thick eyeglasses. He looks like a human owl. He smiles gently at something Alfred says. He drinks cup after cup of coffee. "He could drink coffee by the gallon," Alfred says. He talks and talks, telling amusing anec-dotes and sometimes sad ones.

"We talked until seven or seven thirty," Alfred says. "Then he'd go back to sleep until noon and I went out and worked in the garden.

* Adams, A. *Woollcott.*

He was a fascinating talker
Aleck being cruel . . . Wel
his misery drove him to be
only Lynn and I knew how
He never talked about his pr
hard it is to be charming,
pain?" Woollcott once wrote
me weep."

Afternoons, Aleck and the
guest house, also known as t
some of Alfred's family were
visiting, Aleck would comm
through a ritual of raising l
Louise had beautiful legs, a
them to the other great fem
Pennington, Gilda Gray, and

Or he would pretend to
mother, Hattie, who lived o
was charmed by Hattie. He
and tell Lynn and Alfred, "
after being with Hattie."

Independent spirits like K
Lillie, and others put up wit
he was a superb raconteur.
generous. It was also and ma
revelry. These celebrities of
were often shy, sensitive sp
other, unable to say openly
be friends?" Aleck said it to

Aleck had suffered, physica
wounded in his childhood.
until Aleck's death he learn
impotent. As far as I know,
Lynn and Alfred, who know
not explain it. What is clea
He liked women, mentally.
was incapable of physical in
sexual—though it would ha
been gay. He thought and

summer of 1933, Alfred was diverting himself by studying landscape painting and Lynn was taking lessons in French and horseback riding. Alfred wrote happily to Aleck that Lynn was making progress in equitation "and I am so grateful for that as it seems the only thing that will take her out of those goddam anagrams."

Lynn and Alfred have kept themselves emotionally youthful by always learning something new. Once, Vincent Sheean told Alfred he was celebrating his fiftieth birthday by seeing their current play. Alfred said, "On my fiftieth birthday, I took up Spanish dancing."

Lynn had trouble with the French and the riding. While riding in the fields that summer her horse fell in a hole and she was thrown on her head, almost breaking her neck. She cracked several ribs and was in bed for weeks. French—which she has been trying to master all her life—always defeated her. She was working on the conditional and she told Aleck "it has brought me *très bas* . . . I had a lovely letter in French from Thornton [Wilder] and had to look for almost every word in the dictionary. It was degrading."

Conversation was the chief diversion of Aleck and his "800 intimate friends." Aleck was, as Adams says, "the most determined talker of his time and one of the most entertaining." The conversation might become a battle of wits between Aleck and Noel or Sam Behrman or Dorothy Parker or Edna Ferber or Marc Connelly or Lynn or Alfred —and the Lunts were as good at verbal duelling as anybody in the circle. The Lunts loved going to Neshobe Island, on Lake Bomoseen, Vermont, where Aleck had a summer retreat. Describing it once to Graham Robertson, Aleck wrote, "Ours is a pine clad island a mile from shore. In summer, it looks like a green tea cosy; in winter like a birthday cake." In the afternoon there were fierce bouts of croquet. Alfred would fish or swim. In the evening, sometimes, Lynn and Alfred read a play aloud. Alfred would read poetry. Once, he read from Edgar Lee Masters' *Spoon River Anthology*.

"I want to tell you that seldom has anything I have heard stayed with me like your reading of that first poem in the *Spoon River Anthology*," wrote Aleck not long afterward. "I am now past the point of knowing whether you read it well. I only know I cannot get it out of my ears and that I want you to come back and read the whole book to me."

People often conceal their deepest feelings out of self-consciousness or fear of being thought stupid. Aleck was not afraid of showing his feelings. Call him a sentimentalist if you like, and Howard Dietz once called him "Louisa May Woollcott," but Aleck believed in pouring out his heart to those he loved.

He probably wanted more to be an actor than a writer, and to be, most of all, an actor with the style and easy grace of Alfred Lunt. Aleck acted in Behrman's *Brief Moment,* and was a great success. The role was not hard, for it was copied from life, and Aleck played himself. During most of the action he was stretched out on a couch and spoke with elegant hauteur. Convinced by the reviews that he was a potential star, Aleck began to study acting techniques, especially Lunt's.

After one performance, Louis Calhern, playing the hero, said to Behrman, "I don't know what happened to Aleck tonight. He just lies there and mutters. I can't hear a damn word he's saying. I can't hear my cues. I'm afraid to tell him to speak up."

Behrman asked Woollcott if he had laryngitis. Oh not at all, explained Aleck with an air of triumph. He was speaking quietly on purpose. He was being subtle. He now realized he had been overplaying his part, shouting his lines. He was learning how to "throw away" his lines. He had, the night before, gone to a Sunday night performance of *Reunion in Vienna.* Watching Lunt and Fontanne, he had suddenly experienced a revelation.

"I see everything now," he said, "I've been working too hard. God, you ought to see them work. Never raised their voices. It's marvelous."

Behrman diplomatically explained that the Lunts gave the illusion of underplaying, of speaking in conversational tones, but were really enunciating loudly and clearly and could be heard in the last row of the balcony, whereas Aleck had been inaudible at the previous performance. Woollcott at once ceased imitating the Lunts.

Social problems, great public questions of war, poverty, political reform—these were rarely broached at the Woollcott *soirées,* at least not until well into the 1930's, when war and fascism became threatening. Before that, the life of the circle was devoted to pleasure. The members were, if you like, selfish and self-centered and ardently pursuing sensual satisfactions—like butterflies enjoying the summer sun. Some of Aleck's friends, Heywood Broun, for instance, were politically involved, but even Broun didn't intrude politics into evenings of pleasure. The gay, the irresponsible spirit of that time, of which the Lunts were the theatrical quintessence, is summed up in this dialogue from *The Second Man:*

MONICA

But, Storey, you don't know anything about suffering.

CLARK

Most suffering is bunk, you know, Monica. Unintelligent people suffer because they want things beyond their limitations.

MONICA

How can you be so complacent?

CLARK

You're a victim of the popular prejudice in favor of agony. Why is a book about unhappy dirty people better than one about gay and comfortable ones?

MONICA

But life isn't gay or comfortable.

CLARK

Dear darling, life is sad. But I think it's gallant to pretend that it isn't!

The Lunts and their friends made of living a pattern of pleasure, in which kindness and awareness were sometimes the chief of pleasures. For many years, Aleck had made a splash wearing an opera cloak and top hat at events of a formal nature, including the more social first nights. Graham Robertson also wore them. One evening, after a performance of *The Taming of the Shrew,* the Lunts had supper with Robert Sherwood and Laurence Olivier. They told many stories about Graham Robertson.

In fact [wrote Lynn to Robertson in England] you sat in the room with us and seemed to enjoy being with us very much, thank you. You had on your beautiful evening clothes with your most beautiful cape (purple lining and all) and by the way I would like to get one something like it, only not as beautiful of course, for Aleck, as a Xmas present, lined with dark green as it is his favorite color. Would it be possible to buy one at your tailor's? It seems to me that a cape is not a thing that would require such careful measurements as a coat. If they fitted it over a large globe 6 feet in circumference, it ought to be perfect. Please, Graham darling, don't go into a dither of fury at the thought of Aleck having a cape, too, because you must admit that he will look beautiful but in quite another way, and you will always be the most beautiful.

Robertson's cape was one he had purchased in Madrid some years before. (Aleck had yearned for an authentic Spanish *capa* for years. Once he met a chap in San Francisco who had one on. Aleck offered him a lot of money but the man wouldn't sell his *capa*.) Robertson said he couldn't have a duplicate made of his cape for Woollcott. There ensued a series of letters back and forth until Lynn, as she later confessed to Robertson, "ellen-terryed you out of your capa and how willingly and how beautifully you sprang to the gift."

For Graham gave his own precious cape to Lynn to give to Aleck. A month later it arrived in New York.

November 11, 1935:
I am astounded, flabbergasted and completely slain by your magnificent gesture. For a girl who has never had any particular gift for choosing presents, this one will make up for a whole lifetime of uninspired selections. It is dear and beautiful of you, and oh, what fun! The lining shall not be touched. It shall go to him as is, and if he doesn't like red he can jolly well wear it until he's blue. I must tell you what Alfred said when I read your letter to him. I paused at the dramatic place where you offered the 'capa.' There was a trenchant silence and Alfred said in a small voice, 'It's a shame to give it to Aleck!' But to Aleck it goes and to nobody else. And nobody else will know and appreciate the beauty of it so fully . . . I am so excited about the 'capa' that I think of nothing else. Aleck is in Chicago now and as it is Sunday we are sitting in our rented furnished apartment, which includes a radio, waiting for his voice to come over the air. I have just spoken to him on the telephone. Just think, it is 1500 miles away and I called him up and he held the receiver and got through in a minute. He knows nothing of what is happening at Christmas and how different his life is going to be from then on. Isn't it fun?

December 21, 1935:
The capa is beautiful. I look at it every day to see if it is still there, the red and green lining is superb and the coloring looks very spanish. I have had it on and it really looks terribly chic. Aleck is in California and I think it better to send it to his flat to await his arrival—maddening though it is—because it might get lost on its way there and that is an anxiety I couldn't face.

The Lunts told Robertson they were attaching three conditions to the gift. Aleck must always wear it in the evening; it was to be willed to them if he should die before they did; in the event that they ever did a play laid in Spain, Alfred was to be allowed to wear the *capa.*

January 24, 1936:
Well, the witches have been flying around the *capa* and they cooked up an enraging situation in their cauldron. We left New York for Boston to play the *Shrew* for 2 weeks and *Aleck arrived in New York the next day.*

He telegraphed and is simply wild with joy, as I knew he would be, having heard from his own lips how he longed for a capa like yours. . . . If only we could have seen Aleck face to face to see every last lifting of his eyebrow . . .

March 11, 1936:
Have you seen Aleck and his capa and hat, especially made to go with it? Never has a present so perfectly achieved its purpose as that one. It has changed that darling into a sinister foreign gentleman with great hidden sources of fascination. And he is very happy.

Ignorant of how Aleck acquired his flamboyant cape, Gibbs in his profile wrote that the cloak had been given to him by a "false friend" to wear as a costume when he was playing in Behrman's *Wine of Choice*. Gibbs reported an ingénue as saying, "Every time he comes on I think, Good God it's Bela Lugosi." (The reference was to the film *Dracula*, in which Lugosi's costume was a vampiric cape.)

In its curious harshness toward the subject (who was a friend of the author and the editor as well as a *New Yorker* staff contributor for many years) this account of the cape illustrates why all of Aleck's friends were shocked by the profile when it appeared in 1939 in three long installments. Perhaps the most shocking innuendo in a biography reeking with disparaging innuendos was the intimation that Woollcott was either a eunuch or a flaming homosexual. Had the profile balanced its sarcasm with humor and a recognition of Aleck's virtues as well as his faults, it might have been digestible to his circle. But it was as slanted and as nasty a piece of magazine biography as I have ever read in my life.

The Lunts at once canceled their subscription to *The New Yorker*. They have never had it in their house since then, nor will they permit anybody to bring a copy of it into their home. Lady Duff was a houseguest of the Lunts once. In Salisbury, England, where she resided, she got *The New Yorker* by subscription and eagerly read each issue. She was upset to learn it was forbidden on the Lunt premises. Writing to a London friend, she complained: "The only thing I miss here in New York is *The New Yorker* magazine."

Several months after the Lunts broke off circulation relations with *The New Yorker*, they were visiting Aleck at Neshobe Island and there was the latest issue on a library table. "Oh, I've never stopped having it sent," Aleck said. "As a matter of fact, I'm making some suggestions now about some future articles."

Lynn and Alfred gave parties often in those days. "Some of them were pretty gay," Crouse remembers. "There was one where they hired a gypsy band. The musicians were in red uniform. What a party! I always had a good time at their parties. Everybody got high and danced and the food was good. I remember another party vividly because it was in my honor. I was leaving publicity to become a full-time playwright. They asked me to invite anyone I wanted and they had fifty of my friends over and there was a little band and champagne and caviar and Noel Coward singing *Mad Dogs and Englishmen* and Aleck Woollcott making peculiar noises accompanying him, and I danced with Irene Castle and Lynn Fontanne. Lynn was one of the best ballroom dancers of her day."

There were other parties—at Carl Van Vechten's, at Gilbert Miller's, at Condé Nast's, at Neysa McMein's, at Jules Glaenzer's. Usually you encountered the same sharp, scintillating people as at Woollcott's— except there would be more society celebrities at Glaenzer's and Miller's. But, generally, theatre people were the core of the party. "In those days," Marc Connelly says, "there was a greater sense of community in the Broadway theatre, as well as more of a desire to play. We worked hard at our jobs of acting or writing but we worked hard at having fun and my god how much fun we did have, and the fun was at people's houses because we loved to give parties and go to them and those of us who could do something did them at the parties. Sometimes before a party we went to Tony's for drinks, that was our favorite speakeasy, Tony's, also Jack and Charlie's, and after a party we usually went over to the Club Durant to watch Jimmy Durante. It was a sacred rite to watch Clayton, Jackson & Durante. We generally wound up at Reuben's for breakfast at dawn. And we went to Atlantic City for the tryouts. You didn't have them in New Haven and Philadelphia. All the gang went over to Atlantic City and then we had more parties in Atlantic City before and after the opening of the show which had been written by one of us, directed and produced by our friends, and starred other members of the gang."

Among the exhilarating moments of those parties, the Lunts remember Marc Connelly's routine. He was a living room entertainer of excellence. He was invariably called upon to do his Death of Cleopatra, which was climaxed by his calling for the asp, pantomiming the fatal bite, and then groaning, in mock surprise, "Jee-ZUS!" Robert E. Sherwood did card tricks and other bits of legerdemain. Roger Davis did parodies of French operas, playing and singing them. Bessie Love, a movie star, would do the Charleston. Noel Coward simply had to sing "A Room with a View" or "Somewhere I'll Find You" or "Mad Dogs." Sometimes people played famous jokes, like the time Clarence Nordstrom, a Follies dancer, ran into a showgirl who was being kept by a Wall Street millionaire, of whom there were seemingly tens of thousands in that year of 1928. She was flaunting a handsome silver fox stole.

"Where did you get that?" Nordstrom asked.

"You know perfectly well where I got it," the girl replied.

"Oh him, is it?" he said sneering. "Well, with all his money he might at least have given you young fox—not these old grayhaired foxes."

The girl at once went to the powder room, got a pair of tweezers, and began extracting all the silver hairs from her silver fox stole!

Once, the Lunts went to a party whose host owned a French poodle clipped in the highest Parisian style. The party was one of those ultra-fashionable gatherings where everyone is either very rich, very famous, very creative, or all three. One of the guests had brought along a provincial friend who felt out of place. He got drunk fast on side-cars, a cocktail compounded of cognac and cointreau, very popular with the smart set then. During one of those moments of mass silence which take place even at the noisiest parties, this man turned on everybody and shouted, "I hate you. I hate you. I hate you all." Then, weaving about and lowering himself until he was kneeling, he addressed the French poodle, who was observing him with an insolent air. "And you—especially I hate you in your rented costume!"

A New York publicity man and gay blade of the period, Robert Reud, was one of the few persons in Manhattan who was friendly with Greta Garbo. Once when the seclusive star was in town, she suddenly said she would like to meet the Lunts. Reud, who didn't know them personally, bragged that he could easily fix it up for her with Lynnie and Al. He assumed that when it came to a showdown Garbo would be too shy to go through with it. But she was serious. She said that she was going to see *Amphitryon 38* that night and then she would like to be taken backstage, please. Reud was desperate. He telephoned Crouse.

"Buck," he said, "I'm in trouble. You gotta help me." He described his problem. Crouse said he was sure that Alfred would understand and they would pretend they were dear friends of Reud and would be pleased to meet Garbo. "Tell Lunt about this and give him some kind of signal," Reud begged, "so he'll know it's me because if Garbo finds out I don't know the Lunts she'll hate me forever and she'll walk out of their dressing room right away."

Crouse got in touch with Alfred. Alfred said, "Instead of having this Mr. Reud bring her backstage, why doesn't he bring her up to the apartment after the show and we'll give her supper? You come too, Buck." He instructed Crouse to tell Reud not to fight the mob backstage but to proceed, after an interval, to their apartment and the Lunts wouldn't bother removing their make-up but go home right away so they'd be there first and there wouldn't be any danger of a mix-up. Crouse told him, "Alfred, now the man with her is named Bob Reud, and you're to say, 'Hello, Bob,' and shake hands with him as if he was an old college friend you've known for twenty years."

"Fine," Alfred said, "that's Bob—Bob Reud. I've got it."

"That's it—Bob, Bob Reud."

Crouse told Reud that he should stall Garbo to ensure that the Lunts got home before the group arrived. Lynn and Alfred got home first. In the party was one of Garbo's dear friends, the writer Berthold Viertel. So Garbo, Viertel, Crouse, and Reud got out of the elevator and there was Alfred waiting in the corridor and Viertel got out of the elevator cage the first. Alfred was beaming and he grasped Viertel by the hand, and crooned, "Hello there, Bob, how are you feeling, Bob?" He was pumping Viertel's hand. "You certainly are looking great, Bob."

Reud leaped in and grabbed Alfred's hand.

Alfred looked baffled. Garbo looked baffled. But she stayed for a long supper party and was animated and very talkative.

It was one of the nicest parties they ever gave, though entirely impromptu.

TEN

ESTRANGED INTERLUDE

*D*URING the season of 1927-28, Lynn and Alfred were immersed in two plays by Eugene O'Neill. They knew that he wrote with passionate intensity. They recognized the fact that his characters and situations often came alive on a stage. But they believed that his words were artificial and untrue. Lynn always said his "lines don't have the rhythm of human speech. His speeches are clumsy, stilted—it's literary dialogue not theatre dialogue." In truth, like many actors, the Lunts have no reverence for the text of a play. A text is only a rough sketch of dramatic action. It is the action underneath the words that they are reaching for. The precious words of the author—well, these are so much wet clay to be molded to their heart's desire. Acting is not the word made flesh. It is the imaginary action made flesh. O'Neill wanted his plays performed exactly as he had written them. He hated actors because they were cruel to his sacred texts. For some reason, though, he respected Alfred. According to Barbara and Arthur Gelb's biography of O'Neill, Lunt was "one of the few actors whom O'Neill did not later single out for attack." Langner, who had been attempting to get O'Neill for the Guild, managed after some years of courtship to get the rights to *Marco Millions* and *Strange Interlude*. *Marco Millions* is a formless series of episodes in the career of Marco Polo, whom O'Neill saw as a figure parallel to a modern American capitalist. He thought he was writing a satirical play, a humorous and a witty play. He said it was "going to be humorous as the devil if the way it makes me guffaw as I write it is any criticism*—and not bitter humor, either, although it's all satirical." Well, there isn't a single joke

* Did he mean "criterion" in this letter to his friend Kenneth McGowan? O'Neill was not precise in his choice of words.

in the play and nobody guffawed. Directed by the young Rouben Mamoulian, it was an oriental riot of color and scene changes, with rich costumes and scenery and a large cast. Alfred, who felt very little empathy for Marco Polo or a modern American capitalist, endowed the role with a sort of disillusioned cynicism, which, as Woollcott suggested, may have been the result of sheer physical fatigue because the Guild was working him to death.

Strange Interlude had already been rejected by Katharine Cornell, Alice Brady, and Pauline Lord when the Guild submitted it to Lynn. She hated the play. So did Alfred, who called it a "six day bisexual race." He thought it was absurdly conceived and a very elephant of verbosity. Yet he told her she would be making a mistake if she did not play Nina Leeds.

"Why?" she asked.

"It's the first Broadway play that's ever been done in nine acts."

"That's hardly a recommendation, Alfred."

"Secondly, it's an O'Neill play. He's a very well known writer. It will be the event of the season. Everyone will be writing about it and talking about it. Even if it is a flop, it will be important and you will gain something by having played in it, and besides I think you could try and make something of the part."

So she agreed to do it, though it bored her more than any play she has ever done in her life. She could not ever understand why audiences had the patience to endure the interminable and repetitive speeches of *Strange Interlude*. She thought the character she was playing quite unreal, at least as O'Neill conceived her. Why the profound psychological analysis of this woman who has many lovers and is constantly giving herself to lonely American soldiers as well? She played Nina as a nymphomaniac. "I thought she gave herself to these soldiers because she wanted to," Lynn says. "She liked a lot of sex. She didn't feel sorry for them. She just liked a lot of sex. I didn't ever feel O'Neill made her a tragic figure. I don't think he knew the first thing about women, though at the time he was very much in love with Carlotta Monterey, who was one of the most beautiful women I have ever seen. She was an actress, you know; she had beautiful ivory skin and dark hair and mysterious big eyes and then this rasping, husky voice came out of her which was such a surprise—to hear the deep voice from this divine face."

Lynn saw her the first time at a party at the Carl Van Vechtens'. Van Vechten was married to the actress Fania Marinoff, who had been in George Tyler's stock company during the short hot summer in Washington, D.C. Lynn saw an unusual looking beauty and was at once engrossed by her. Lynn was always intensely curious about the mechanism of women who were "fascinators of men," whether they were *femmes fatales* or *femmes joyeuses*. When she saw a man in the room staring at this irresistible and mysterious creature, she sat down next to him and asked, "Who is that beautiful woman?"

He looked at her, an ironic smile on his lips, and said, "Her name is Carlotta Monterey and I'm glad you think she is beautiful because she's my wife." He was, it turned out, Ralph Barton, a *New Yorker* cartoonist.

"Is she an actress?" Lynn asked.

"Yes, she plays in historical plays, you know, Renaissance period plays—that sort of thing."

"But such plays are seldom in work. She can't get very much acting if she specializes in such a narrow range. Why doesn't she play the field?"

"I don't know," Barton said.

Lynn found it impossible to play *Strange Interlude* as it was written. She asked Moeller, the director, to make cuts in it. He went to O'Neill. O'Neill refused to cut a line. She then went directly to the author, saying, "Look, we have a very long play here and I feel we would help the play if we cut it. For instance, take this speech where first I think that Ned's eyes are blue and I say it out loud and then I have to go over and say to him, 'Ned, your eyes are the bluest eyes I've ever seen.' I think the first time I could indicate it by some gesture. Please trust me to do it. I don't have to say it the first time. I can show it."

O'Neill disagreed. "That's the way I want it," he said. He would not change a syllable of the text.

So she did it herself. She went through the play and boldly made enormous cuts in her speeches. She did this without telling Moeller, Langner, Helburn, or anybody else. She "relied on the fact that the play was so long that not even O'Neill would remember what he'd written and nobody, even O'Neill, ever saw how much I had cut. Some of his scenes are ridiculous. I remember a passionate love scene I was playing with Ned and we were sporting about quite vigorously and then I was supposed to be thinking a lot of thoughts at the same time and the action was supposed to stop and we had to freeze while I was speaking my unconscious thoughts. Well, the audience would have just laughed out loud at me if I had done it. You can't stop in the middle of a nice sexual romp and have a brain-wave. I mean, it just doesn't make any sense. Later, when the Guild sent out road companies of *Strange Interlude,* the other Ninas didn't know about my cuts and they played all the lines and, well, the audiences would roll in the aisles, rocking with laughter. I didn't dare tell any of the other Nina Leedses about my cuts because I was afraid O'Neill would hear about what I'd done and make me put the cuts back."

Woollcott hated the play as much as she did. He called it a play in nine scenes and one epicene. Lynn had to play the epicene. After its success, he sneered at it as the *"Abie's Irish Rose* of the pseudo-intelligentsia." But Alfred had been right. It was a smash hit—the greatest hit in the Theatre Guild's history, until *Oklahoma!* opened in 1943. It ran for 414 performances. It was the most exhausting performance Lynn ever played. It began at 5:15. At 7:15 there was an intermission —promptly dubbed Strange Intermission by some wag—of an hour and a quarter for dinner and then the play resumed at 8:30. The curtain came down after 11. A current wisecrack was, "I'd like to see *Strange Interlude* but I don't get my vacation until August."

Alfred said, "If *Strange Interlude* had had two more acts I could have sued Lynn for desertion."

Lynn has a mystical theory of her relation to an audience. "When I am on a stage," she once said to me, "I am the focus of thousands of eyes and it gives me a strength. I feel that something, some energy, is flowing from the audience into me. I actually feel stronger because of these waves. Now when the play's done, the eyes taken away, I feel just as if a circuit's been broken. The power is switched off. I feel all gone and empty inside of me—like a balloon that's been pricked and the air's let out."

After six months, she collapsed and could no longer go on in the play. She and Alfred went to Wisconsin to recuperate, and then they went to London and Paris and bought costumes for their next play, *Caprice,* a sophisticated comedy of adultery by a Viennese, Sil-Vara. Alfred was to play Albert von Eckhardt, a middle-aged bachelor lawyer dedicated to love affairs with innumerable women. Alfred had never met any Viennese roués, young or old, but he was sure of one thing. They must certainly be heavier looking than he was. Though Alfred himself was now entering middle age he was deceptive physically. Tall, slender, debonair, with his face still unaged by experience, he looked like an innocent stripling. He must look at least fifty pounds heavier. Any other actor would have merely stuffed pillows inside his pants and shirt to put on fifty pounds. That wouldn't do for Alfred. He promptly put himself on a strict diet of rich desserts, starches, two loaves of bread daily, cream sauces, and as many deliciously fattening dishes as he could cook. He soon ballooned out nicely. Then he grew sideburns. Now he felt like an authentic Viennese roué. Lynn was playing Frau Ilse von Ilsen, a lady of impeccable immorality and voluptuous beauty, the latest in von Eckhardt's long list of conquests. The intrigue revolves about an old flame of the fat lawyer's, a certain Amalia, by whom he has had a son—illegitimate of course. The son is now sixteen. His mother brings him back to the roué in a none-too-subtle plot to get him to marry her. But the lawyer is so madly infatuated with Frau von Ilsen that he is prepared to go to any lengths—even marriage.

Was Alfred once again playing his stepfather under another disguise? Whenever he played such a figure, he was always able to exploit a rich mine of emotion in himself, as Lynn was whenever she portrayed a "fascinator of men." The play, though it was a trivial piece of theatrical pastry, became a human comedy in their hands. It was a fabulous hit in New York and later in London, where the Lunts finally made their British debut as a team at the St. James Theatre on June 4, 1929. It was with *Caprice* that the Lunts solidified their reputation as the greatest acting team of their generation. They won the world's championship that year and they never lost it. St. John Ervine, the British playwright, critic, and biographer, was reviewing plays for the New York *World*. Though accustomed to a theatre of high polish, where actors and actresses performed high comedy as beautifully as it has ever been played anywhere, St. John Ervine was fairly overwhelmed by the brilliance of the Lunts. He wrote:

It has not been my luck to see Mr. Alfred Lunt or Miss Lynn Fontanne act before. I shall esteem myself a very unfortunate fellow if I never see them again. Mr. Lunt's performance was a delightful exhibition of accomplished comedy acting: a fine and accurately observed show of manners. Miss Fontanne startled me with her brilliant artifice. I had not expected to see anything so good as this performance. Here was the essence of drawing-room, the very spirit of boudoir, the inner mood of elegant life.

Miss Fontanne can rouse ripples of laughter by the way in which she plays on sentences—even full meaningless sentences, mere lumps of words clumsily thrown at each other. Such a series of gasps as 'oh-ah-I-mean-but!' —on Miss Fontanne's lips become pieces of wit. Character flows into all she says. Her mind works in every word. No wonder people are proud of this brilliant pair. They are destined to be prominent in the history of American comedy.

Though they were the rage of London that season, there were murmurs of opposition from some reactionary critics and some of the older English actors because of certain liberties the Lunts took. They were accused of violating several so-called principles of the acting art. They were accused of deliberately going against tradition in order to be clever. They were accused of using tricks. Alfred remembers that in some sections of the press their performance was even treated as an "outrage."

It was axiomatic in that period that an actor speaking his lines faced the audience, either full face or three-quarters. He might be speaking to an actor upstage or all the way across from him, but he still had to face the audience, presumably so that his lines could be heard clearly and his facial expressions could be seen. The Lunts thought this was nonsense. They played several scenes in profile, speaking directly at each other. Alfred turned his back once and made a long speech without anybody even seeing his profile. (An English revue had a satiric song about this called "Alfred Lunt's Back.") The traditionalists were horrified at the way Lynn and Alfred "interrupted" each other's speeches in the middle of sentences or made all kinds of moves regarded as distracting to an audience and as disloyal to one's fellow actors—such as walking upstage in the middle of another actor's speech or taking out one's handkerchief and casually wiping one's brow as another actor was talking. The theory was that the audience's eyes were attracted to the white handkerchief and followed its movements like a bird hypnotized by a snake, and that therefore the speaking actor was destroyed. There was a scene between the lawyer and his bastard son in which the son had an amusing speech that always got a nice laugh. In London, perhaps to bait his disparagers, Alfred one night decided to try the "handkerchief trick" (up to then only employed by an actor who wanted to get revenge on another actor by spoiling his big moment). He flourished his white handkerchief and mopped his brow and the son, played by Douglass Montgomery, not only was heard but broke up the entire house. So the handkerchief bit was kept in.

The technique Lynn and Alfred had developed of almost simultaneously speaking their lines—*dovetailing* or *overlapping*—shocked theatrical purists. They had begun to speak like this in *The Guardsman* and perfected it in *The Second Man* and *Caprice*. They would rehearse a series of speeches so carefully that both could talk at once and yet not jam up each other's lines. Both were clearly heard and the lines meshed one into the other like the teeth of two gears. It took them many years, but they became so competent at this that they were frequently able to take a scene at high-speed and dovetail each other's lines without the audience missing a word. They did it by breaking up a line at a breathing rest; the interrupter would come in at the rest while the speaker continued talking but in a different pitch, usually lower.

They believe that this is the most difficult technical achievement in their repertoire. They were able to find only one other actor who was able to dovetail lines. This was Sidney Greenstreet with whom they played for many years, later on.

They came back to New York at the end of summer. At a meeting with the Guild, they declared they would not renew their contract unless it was stipulated that they were never again to play in separate plays. They could not stand being separated from each other even for the few hours of a play. The Guild was stunned by their decision. They were argued with and pleaded with for weeks but they said their minds were made up. They simply had to be with each other all day and all night and if the Guild did not want them as the Lunts the Guild could bloody well go out and find somebody else.

So it was. Lynn and Alfred never again played apart from each other. They were now as completely unified as two mortals can ever be. If Aristophanes was watching from heaven or hell, he must have been gratified—both by their exquisite achievements in comedy and by their realization of his theory of true love.

ELEVEN

BROADWAY SOPHISTICATES—WISCONSIN

INNOCENTS

$\mathscr{B}$ Y NOW, the Theatre Guild was producing only two kinds of plays, those with Lunt and Fontanne and those without. The ones without usually failed. From 1926 on, if one charted the annual rise and fall of the Guild on a graph, the profit line would parallel the line of plays with the Lunts. They were money in the bank. The most successful season in Guild history was its tenth, 1927-28, when it presented five new plays to the public and all were hits. Of the five hits, three featured Lunt or Fontanne separately, one featured the Lunts together, and only one was "without." Following this apogee in its fortunes, the Guild, as Langner once remarked, "began to move backward instead of forward." In its eleventh season, the Guild produced seven shows: five flops, one success, and one smash, the last being the Lunts in *Caprice*. The twelfth season was a debacle: seven productions, of which six quickly perished and only one, *Meteor*, with, of course, the Lunts, being reasonably successful. When Lynn and Alfred refused to play on separate stages, they signed the death warrant of the Guild's permanent acting company and repertory system. The Guild *was* the Lunts. Every year more and more persons were possessed of a compulsion to see any play with the Lunts. A lot of people went to the theatre only when the Lunts were in a show. This inspired Ring Lardner to write a ballad, published January 16, 1929, in the New York *Morning Telegraph*:

> There was a man who wrote a play;
> One week it ran, then died away,
> Though critics said 'twould be a hit
> And even Ervine lauded it.
> 'Twas not too pure or too obscene;

The plot was hot, the satire keen.
"It lacked two things," observed the man;
"Just Alfred Lunt and Lynn Fontanne."

A play that millions didn't see
Was one by Mr. C'on and me;
The star was Walter Huston and
He acted absolutely grand.
The piece's failure to endure
Was not his fault, yet I am sure
We could have lasted out the mont'
With Lynn Fontanne and Alfred Lunt.

The Theatre Guild takes Mother Goose,
A postcard from Anita Loos,
Professor Bore on Patent Law,
An epigram by Harry Thaw,
Or some Hungarian goulasch,
Adapted by Joe Balderdash,
And has a play you just can't pan,
With Alfred Lunt and Lynn Fontanne.

I watched a crowd one recent night
Go into spasms of delight
About a play whose claim to wit
Rests on one oft-repeated bit;
The swilling, by a profligate,
Of sodium bicarbonate.
They loved this subtly comic stunt
(With Lynn Fontanne and Alfred Lunt).

You want to pack 'em in out front?
Hire Lynn Fontanne and Alfred Lunt.
Is wounding Joe Leblang your plan?
Hire Alfred Lunt and Lynn Fontanne.
Wouldst have a smash, not just a bunt?
Sign Lynn Fontanne and Alfred Lunt.
The madam craves a Rolls sedan?
Get Alfred Lunt and Lynn Fontanne.

To hell with story and with plot,
Love interest, passion, cold or hot;
With traffic meliorations which
End one-night stands in a one-way ditch!
To hell with competition from
The rasping pictures or the dumb!

Show business needs and needs at once
More Lynn Fontannes and Alfred Lunts.

Lardner himself tried writing plays for the Lunts—but so did everybody, though until now, except for *Clarence* and *Dulcy,* the Lunts had played either in classic plays or plays written for other actors or out of an author's personal vision without an eye to specific actors (e.g., *Strange Interlude*). But almost all plays are shaped to fit specific actors. Shakespeare wrote his finest roles for Burbage. Shaw wrote *Pygmalion* for Stella Campbell. Robert E. Sherwood's first play was written for the Lunts, although the Guild wouldn't buy the play for them.

Samuel Nathaniel Behrman was the first playwright to write a play for them in which they acted. He had been admiring Alfred for a long time—since he had been a student of George Pierce Baker, who conducted the English 47 course in playwriting at Harvard and at Yale. (Among the other dramatists hatched by Professor Baker were Philip Barry, George Abbott, Robert E. Sherwood, and Eugene O'Neill.) Behrman was a slim, dark-eyed, curlyhaired, intellectual chap, with the high forehead, rimless spectacles, and brooding melancholy of a young Jewish intellectual. Despite his middle class background—he came from a shopkeeper's family in Worcester, Rhode Island—Behrman aspired to write sophisticated plays. Behrman was obsessed by the self-made sybarite, a character who has haunted his plays as well as his biographies of Duveen, Max Beerbohm, and Bernard Berenson. Alfred Lunt was the incarnation of Clark Storey, the hero of *The Second Man*, Behrman's first play. Storey is a cynic, an opportunist, a fortune hunter. He proclaims openly that "what this country needs is a dilettante class, interested in art, with no desire to make money out of it. Why shouldn't there be an amateur class in art as there is in sport?"

Alfred, playing Behrman's cynical heroes, fascinated audiences as a hooded cobra hypnotizes little birds. Percy Hammond, a hard man to trick, spoke of his "calm iridescences that seemed both calculated and spontaneous . . . the word performance is a clumsy thing to apply to any of Mr. Lunt's endeavors. Creation is perhaps better." Lynn's role was, as Woollcott said, a "mere filler," as was her role in Behrman's next play, *Meteor,* in which she again played straight to an egotist, one Raphael Lord, a financial speculator and international oil operator. Behrman wrote crisp, penetrating, witty, cerebral dialogue. He gave Lynn and Alfred the raw material for a dazzling swordplay of witticisms. But though he tried to balance the opponents, he gave the best of it to Alfred. Charles Brackett, writing in *The New Yorker*, said that three of the four characters in *The Second Man* were unimportant but that Alfred Lunt was enough to make the whole play, for he "mesmerizes one into believing the words he speaks consummately brilliant. Indeed, I think it only fair to admit that I think Mr. Lunt's Clark Storey the best high comedy performance ever given by a man."

Lynn resigned herself to playing the lesser role in any play "Berri" wrote for them. "You see," Lynn says, smiling pleasurably, "when Berri was a young man, he saw Alfred in *Banco* and he went balmy over the performance. Formed such an admiration for Alfred's technique, he couldn't see me. Kendall Frayne [in *The Second Man*] was a small part. I remember Aleck once phoning and asking me how my part was and I said oh it is not a good part at all, and he said is it really not a good part or is that just an actor's way of talking before an opening and I said my god no but it is really one of the worst parts I've ever seen anybody play let alone me and I've played my share of bad parts and Aleck saw it and agreed it was a bad part but he gave me a good notice anyway* and then in *Meteor*, well, there my part was almost non-existent."

In Behrman, the Lunts had their first experience as a team with a writer who had not only conceived his plays for them but who came to rehearsal and made changes and alterations as skillfully as a custom-tailor working at a basted try-on. Berri was a quiet, sensitive person, his soft manners giving no hint of his diamond-hard intellect and brilliant wit. After *The Second Man* became a hit, Berri wrote a Sunday essay for the New York *Times*. He told of his debt to Lynn and Alfred. He said one of Lynn's lines had been, "He never has anything interesting to say—never—never—never—never—never. . . ." He said Lynn had taken this repetition and "made it a perfectly graduating diminuendo of nevers to convey a long vista of boredom, infinite reflections in a double mirror. . . ." In Act II, Storey has a line saying that Monica is as banal as a popular song. At one rehearsal, Alfred spontaneously went over to a piano—the set had a piano—and played a few notes, and Berri kept the piano solo in the play. Toward the end of Act I, the telephone rings at a crucial moment. Behrman reported he had great difficulty with the ringing. It seemed contrived, a piece of trickery to get one character offstage so that the other two characters

---

* ". . . the art and resourcefulness with which Miss Fontanne lent color and distinction to a role that was a mere filler."

could play their necessary scene by themselves. He tried writing various lines for Alfred to bring the telephone in naturally but nothing worked until, at some run-through, Alfred picked up the phone, murmuring "Why, it's the telephone," and with just that air of disarming innocence on his satyr's face that "took the curse off the whole thing."

It was so pleasant to have the playwright at rehearsals. There was the time, during the Boston tryout of *Meteor,* when Lynn and Alfred were having supper with the author.

"I think," Alfred said, "we should have more conflict in the scenes between Lynnie and myself, don't you?"

"And, Berri dear, it would be so nice if you could give me more tenderness," Lynn said.

A rehearsal was called for 11 the following morning. Behrman had been writing all night. He wrote painstakingly. He came to the rehearsal with the new dialogue, and handed the sheets to Lynn and Alfred, saying, "Here are six pages of conflict and here are three pages of tenderness!"

Behrman was as awkward at plot construction as he was smooth at dialogue and characters. Because of Berri's concentration on character, rather than on story, he got into rows with director Philip Moeller. Originally, *Meteor* was in four acts. Moeller, a playwright *manqué,* could not help trying to rewrite the script. I suppose all really good Broadway directors—one thinks of Kazan, Josh Logan, Alan Schneider, Harold Clurman—are to some degree would-be playwrights who leap upon a new play to work out their personal conceptions. Directors on Broadway are often collaborators. Some directors make a playwright feel comfortable and others antagonize him. Moeller was an antagonizer, and he got worse as he got older, becoming more temperamental and neurotic. In Boston, a few days before the New York opening, Moeller broke down during a difficult rehearsal. He fell writhing on the stage. "I can't stand it any more!" he sobbed. "I can't stand it any more!"

Alfred at once took charge. He carried Moeller to a couch. He got the stage manager to go to a drugstore and bring some medicinal brandy. He tried to soothe Moeller. Moeller would not be soothed. Alfred commanded Langner to take the hysterical director back to the Ritz Carlton Hotel. Behrman watched the scene in disgust. He and Moeller had been squabbling every moment since the first day's reading of *Meteor.* Moeller had been trying to rewrite his play, to restructure his four-act play into a three-act play. The next day, during the morning run-through to give the actors a chance to learn the new lines, they got into another heated argument. They began shouting at each other. Behrman finally couldn't take it any more. He stalked out of the theatre. There still was no third act. There was a deathly chill in the air. Moeller was breathing hard. He watched Behrman's retreat. Then he clutched at his hair and suddenly stamped off the stage and walked out of the theatre, in his turn. No playwright, no director, no third act. "Come back, come back," Alfred called to Moeller.

Moeller trudged on.

"The play doesn't have an ending," Alfred told Miss Helburn. "We can't open tonight."

"We better," Terry said. "The house is completely sold out. We open—with or without a third act."

The script had been left hanging with a telephone call. "There I was," Alfred recalls, "with an opening night to face, nothing to say on the telephone, and not knowing how the play should end. I had a long scene talking alone on the stage into this telephone and finally I told the stage manager when I said the word 'schlemiel' in a line he should ring down the curtain and that's how we played it in Boston until Berri wrote us an ending, though the play never really had an ending even in New York."

On the whole, *Meteor*'s notices were good, the consensus being, in the words of Richard Watts, Jr., in the New York *Herald Tribune*, "it is a brilliant, provocative, and original character study set down in a frail play." But *Meteor* was not popular. Just then, brilliant financial operators were flopping all over the place, including out of windows. The stockmarket crashed three months before the play opened. Alfred and Lynn had not been hurt by the crash—they had never played the market and didn't own any common stock. All their money was tied up in cash. Lynn had hers in the Harriman National Bank, $60,000. And Alfred had his in the Guaranty Trust. She liked the Harriman because it was the only bank around that stayed open until the late afternoon, even on Saturdays.

Alfred's theory that the show must go on was put to a severe test in *Meteor*. From January on he had an excruciating pain in his neck, shoulders, and left arm. On his usual assumption that an actor's diseases will go away if he ignores them, Alfred ignored his pains. He didn't mention them to Lynn. But she saw he wasn't happy. To make things worse, he'd decided to lose forty pounds so he'd look like a jaunty young egotist. He had gone on a spartan regime of black coffee for breakfast, black coffee and toast for lunch, and lamb chops and pineapple for dinner. He didn't touch wine or spirits. He lost forty pounds and felt wretched. The agony in his shoulders got worse and finally he couldn't move his left arm. Aspirins and hot baths weren't doing anything for him so there was nothing to do but see a doctor. The doctor said he had bursitis and gave him heat treatments and massages and advised him to go where it was hot and rest for six months. Alfred refused to close the play. Then, said the doctor, he must wear his arm in a sling. Alfred played the last weeks of the run with his arm in a sling.

When the play closed in April, the Lunts went to Montego Bay, Jamaica, for two months. They did nothing but lie in the sun and sleep, and Alfred began to be converted to Lynn's view that an actor must care for his body because it is the instrument on which he plays. He must learn to take care of himself. If Alfred didn't want to treat himself properly for his own sake or for hers, then he must do it for the sake of his work. He couldn't go on playing with his arm in a sling, could he? Well, he would think about it.

At this time, John Mason Brown, now drama critic of the New York *Post*, reflected on the Lunts: ". . . without sacrificing their individualism, Miss Fontanne and Mr. Lunt manage to play together as one—sharing their control of the stage and avoiding the fatigue of those minor maneuvers for the spotlight upon which most actors dissipate their gifts . . . married though they are, the Lunts have never permitted themselves to dwindle into being a prosaic 'Mr. and Mrs.' in public . . . though they are frequently spoken of as the Lunts no one has yet thought of referring to them as Mr. and Mrs. Lunt. For the simple truth is that they have managed to remain so decisively themselves that to the world at large—and I suspect even to themselves—they are Alfred Lunt and Lynn Fontanne."

They went home to Genesee Depot in June, for more recuperation. And now they began a new pattern of working and relaxing. From now on, they would close a show in June or July and take a summer vacation on the farm, and they would travel whenever they had a chance, to refresh their spirits and their eyes. They would return to Wisconsin whenever they could—at Easter and Thanksgiving and Christmas. As Lynn once wrote to Graham Robertson, "I am mad about the country and seem only to be living when I am in it—and Alfred too is rejuvenated."

Their peaceful haven can only be described in such clichés as idyllic and pastoral and beautifully green and quiet. There isn't a depot at

Genesee Depot. The Chicago, Milwaukee & St. Paul used to stop for the whistles there but the whistles don't blow any more. You have to go to Genesee Depot by way of Waukesha. You take route 59 out of Waukesha and you turn left on Road D and proceed until route 683 and then you come to a dirt road and you follow this and then you come to a two-block main street and that's Genesee Depot. Torhorst's Meat & Groceries, the R & B General Store, the State Bank of Genesee Depot, the Outlet Store ("Pants and Work Clothes A Specialty"), Shell Gasoline, Ed Perkin's Feeds and Fertilizers ("Featuring Murphy's Feeds") and Stag's Tavern, where Alfred sometimes drops in for a seidel of draught beer and a bratwurst on a toasted roll. A few hundred feet from Main Street there's a gate of hand-hewn logs and a driveway and this is the entrance to the farm.

It is in the heart of a fertile land of pastures. It is a quiet and peaceful place, still evading the crowds and traffic of the automobile age. The farms are large and not many people live in Genesee Depot— maybe 300 in the village and another 1000 or 1200 in the outlying areas.

Behrman once said, "It's the most tranquillizing place to which I have ever been." He sometimes made long visits while rewriting plays for the Lunts. While adapting *The Pirate* he spent a month there. But the amenities of the farm made Behrman lazy. He sat around the swimming pool and sipped champagne on the terrace before dinner and glutted himself on Alfred's cuisine. They finally locked him in the studio every morning.

"We had Berri in the room all morning," Lynn later reported in some disappointment, "and we didn't hear any sounds of work so we quietly tiptoed by and peeked in the window and what do you suppose we caught him doing—reading the New York *Times!*"

The property extends along both sides of the public road. Alfred started with three acres and a smallish house for his mother and the children. Then, with each hit show, they bought more grounds and put up more buildings. I once asked how many acres they owned. My question got them into one of their amiable quarrels. Alfred said it was fifty. Lynn said it was 125. There were many references to "don't you remember when we bought so-and-so's piece of property in 1949" and "the time when so-and-so sold us the little farm he had on the other side of the creek" and she was adding up the half-acres and the quarter-acres and Alfred was finally conceding that maybe it was 105. They finally compromised at 120 acres. Most of the property is densely wooded. About twenty acres have been cleared, of which two are under cultivation. Ten Chimneys, though small, is a working farm. Lynn and Alfred work hard at caring for their chickens, fruits, and vegetables. They used to have some milk cows and pigs but now there are only the chickens. They have a greenhouse, a potting shed, a freezing room.

Once they had a mysterious lake, a vanishing lake. Lynn always fancied having a lake on the farm, so they dammed up a spring and soon there came into being a lovely lake about a mile square. She stocked it with trout and bass. They got two boats. It was fine for swimming and boating. For three years the lake was there, and then one morning when Lynn came out for a plunge there was no lake. It was like a bad dream. There was only a damp spot, a large damp spot, where the lake had been.

"Now you know," Alfred remarks, shaking his head, "we never did find out what made it vanish."

"Or where all that water went to," Lynn says. "And that was an awful lot of water to go away so fast. It never came back either."

Then they got $90,000 for playing the film version of *The Guardsman* and they put most of this into a lovely L-shaped pool and a flagstoned terrace with deck chairs and lounges and a peppermint striped tent. There was a fine cabana, looking like an oriental mosque. Informality usually is the style at Ten Chimneys. ("But often we dress up stinkin'," Alfred says.) A New Yorker making his first visit there later reported: "I was startled at how completely relaxed Lynn and Alfred are. When I got there it was a sticky afternoon and I thought of going up to my room and washing up and changing into a clean shirt and tie and coat. Alfred was peeved. He said, 'Now look here, we don't do anything like that around here.' He just went around in blue jeans and workshirt. Looked like a farmer. She didn't wear stockings or make-up. Just low heeled shoes and a nice dress. We swam every day. They said I could swim nude if I wanted. They said, 'Noel Coward swims nude, you know.' I tried it. It's all right if you like nude swimming. Breakfast is served whenever you want it. You give Jules your order the night before and then you ring when you wake up and he brings it on a tray. You can have lunch by the pool. I'm told Noel not only swims nude but lunches nude. I wasn't quite that sophisticated. It was only in Genesee Depot I was able to forget they were the greatest stars in the American theatre and see that they were not only stars, but two very nice and hospitable people named Lynn and Alfred."

You enter the main house, built of whitewashed brick, at the basement level. Alfred, designer and interior decorator, has amused himself with the main house as if it were one of his childhood toy theatres. He has added rooms and extensions, and the house, built against the slope, now has four levels. "Even the levels have levels," Lynn once cracked. On the lowest level there is a laundry room, and a large sitting room which gives out on the back terrace. Lynn loves flagstoned terraces. She would like to have dozens of little terraces all about with their chairs and tables and umbrellas. Tea is served in different places, sometimes in the basement parlor, where Lynn does much of her sewing. On level two is the enormous kitchen, a foyer giving on to another entrance, a library, a den, an 18th century dining room, and a handsome living room with chairs and couches and a concert-grand piano. I had heard that during his frequent and lengthy sojourns, Noel played the piano often and had composed several of his chansons at Ten Chimneys. He denies this however. "What would I want to play the piano for?" he inquired. "We're all too busy talking. Besides, though it's a Steinway piano, it's never in tune."

Murals embellish this living room. They were painted by Claggett Wilson. They are Biblical: David and Saul, Jacob's ladder, Rebecca at the well. The library is lined with books on three sides. On the fourth wall are two paintings: a 1915 painting of Lynn by Wilfred de Glehn and an oil portrait of Woollcott, believed to be the only painting for which he sat.

A white spiral staircase links all the levels. On the third and fourth level are five bedrooms, one of which the Lunts occupy.

A stone's throw from the main house is the enormous one-room building they call the "studio," which is where they put playwrights to work. The studio is built of 12-inch square logs. Each log is an individual tree. Until the beginning of World War II, it was a place where they went in the evenings. Lynn says, "The whole family would gather there and we'd have supper and champagne. We always drank champagne at supper. The studio is so big and high and it's like a barn you loved to go to when you were a child. We played records and had very happy moments in the studio."

After climbing a flight of stone steps outside, you come to the greenhouse, where they grow slips for flowers and vegetables from seeds. Passing borders of roses, one comes to the henhouse.

Lynn loves chipmunks and makes pets of them. "The chipmunks eat out of my hand, adorable little things.* Do we have them at home?

* Letter to Graham Robertson.

I have forgotten. They are striped yellow and black about the size of a big mouse with a fat furry tail, like squirrels. We have squirrels, too, of course. They were very shy and almost impossible to win over but at last we have them coming up on the terrace for nuts. The chipmunks don't like it and whenever they catch them, chase them right off the terrace and all the way up to the tree. Imagine that, about a third their size."

Alfred dislikes chipmunks. They are destroyers of vegetables, as far as he's concerned. He has several rifles stashed in secret places and whenever he sees a chipmunk and Lynn isn't watching, he shoots it. Like all happy marriages, this one has called for a certain amount of tolerance. Alfred has a passion for neatness, which Lynn thinks is exaggerated. He is an ashtray cleaner, a lint picker, and a pillow straightener. The barns, the henhouse, the kitchens, even the drive-ways are immaculate. Alfred at once picks up any fallen leaves or broken branches on the drive. She can't understand why he doesn't let somebody else sweep up the driveway.

And he can't see why she enjoys playing word games and card games. He doesn't ever play anagrams. But she has gotten him to play Scrabble with her, twice a day. When there aren't visitors to play Scrabble with her, she plays solitaire. "I know hundreds of varieties of patience," she told me once. "Noel taught me many. He's one of the finest patience players I've ever known."

Outside the henhouse, an elegant stone-faced building, there grows a strange thick-leafed vine. It is a hop vine. Alfred says it has the most beautifully shaped leaf in nature. "I was determined to plant hops," he says. "They're imported, you know, for beer, but I was sure there must be some growing around Wisconsin. I advertised in the rural papers and a woman wrote me from Wauwatosa that she remembered there was a farm a hundred miles from her and she'd once seen hop growing. I went up there and got some cuttings and planted them and they took."

The former henhouse, or "little house," is now a guest house. It was the first large-scale reconstruction after the Lunts planned their new design for living. The old chicken house was changed into a white frame two-story house. Lynn and Alfred painted the interior and deco-rated it. She did her own upholstery and curtains. They lived in the "little house" until 1937 when the main house was extended. The "little house" has two bedrooms, a kitchen, a bath and a sitting room with floor to ceiling murals. Some were painted by Alfred himself.

There is one panel of Adam and Eve by the apple tree. I noticed that Adam and Eve were strangely identical. "No wonder," Lynn said, laughing. "I posed for Adam as well as Eve."

Across one of the ceiling beams is painted, KUNNIA OLKOON JUMALA-LEE KORKENDESSA RAUHA HYVA TAHTO. It is "Peace on earth, good will to men," in Finnish.

Upstairs, there's a large master bedroom, decorated in stark white. White walls, white ceiling, white bed, white chairs, white dressers, white lamps, white carpet. The white vogue was popularized by Syrie Maughm, Somerset's wife, who was London's most fashionable interior decorator during the 1920's. Among her inventions were thick sheepskin rugs, dyed white. She put them on the floors of her clients' rooms. Lynn wanted such a rug for the bedroom, and inquired of Mrs. Maugham as to the price. Mrs. Maugham informed her she could furnish the perfect rug in these dimensions for $4,000. Alfred thought this was rather high. (Perhaps as an overcompensation for his stepfather's extravagance, Alfred is a frugal man with a dollar.) He went to see a woolen merchant in Milwaukee, and ordered a dozen sheepskins sewed together and dyed oyster white. The total cost: $70. It still pleases him whenever he remembers how he did Mrs. Maugham out of $3,930.00.

I once asked Lynn what she believed to be the basis of their marriage. She said it was a mutual respect for each other's privacy.

Lynn: "I think we're an utter necessity for each other. Neither Alfred nor I dislikes solitude. We like each other's company but we also cherish our own privacy. We can both be here in the house together and yet not be side by side, just aware of our presences. Alfred can be in the garden all morning while I'm going about my own affairs. The other morning, for instance, I was making shower curtains for the bathrooms with Catherine Nesbitt, one of our oldest friends, who loves to sew as much as I. Neither Alfred nor I is possessive. Nor do we take from the other. We're incurious about each other's privacy. We don't open each other's mail. We have our own bank accounts. We split all the house expenses and we each pay for our own clothes and medicines and doctors and I pay for my own maid. Consequently, we don't have any serious arguments over money."

Alfred: "I'm penny mean, if you know the expression. I am more concerned with pennies than with large sums."

Lynn: "You do object when I want to buy more clothes than you think I should buy."

Alfred: "That is only to help your bank balance."

Lynn: "And you didn't want to put up the lightning rods until the tree was struck right in front of the house and I told you I had heard that when trees are higher than buildings there is a danger of lightning fires."

Alfred: "Those lightning rods did cost us over one thousand dollars!"

Since her ingénue days with Laurette Taylor, Lynn had always desired a mink coat, but she hadn't wanted to get into a fiscal debate with Alfred about whether she could or could not afford one. Alfred was always seeing the poorhouse just around the corner. In 1939, while they were on a national tour, they were playing in San Francisco for several months, and Lynn and Ina Claire, who was living there in retirement as Mrs. William Wallace, conspired to get her a mink coat. Lynn told Lawrence Farrell, company manager, not to deposit her salary in her New York bank. He was to save it for her until she had accumulated some $10,000—which he did. And he was not to tell Alfred.

Now Alfred has a secret vice. Burlesque. He loves burlesque shows, though he doesn't think they are a proper entertainment for ladies and he never lets Lynn go to burlesque shows with him and his cronies. On tour, he never missed a burlesque show if there was one in town. There happened to be a good burlesque house in San Francisco and one Saturday he went to the midnight show. Lynn went to Ina's apartment. I. Magnin's sent over a large selection of mink coats in an armored car. Two guards and a salesman trundled the racks of coats into the apartment and Lynn tried on coats for several hours and finally chose a full-length Canadian ranch mink, costing $8,000.

When Alfred came home after the burlesque show, Lynn was awaiting him in her new coat. She modelled it for him and broke the news that it was hers, all hers, bought and paid for, cash on the barrelhead.

After he got over the shock, he agreed that she looked beautiful in it, but he said no coat was worth eight thousand dollars.

Once, lunching at Dinty Moore's, he had chopped sirloin steak. When he got the check and saw he'd been charged $4.00 he was furious. "The idea of charging four dollars for a hamburger," he said. "No hamburger is worth four dollars." And he seldom eats at Dinty Moore's.

For several years, they owned a limousine and employed a chauffeur. One afternoon, Alfred totted up what they were paying for car depreciation, chauffeur's salary, garaging, insurance, gas, and repairs, and he was horrified, since the limousine was around only to take them to and from the theatre. He decided a rented car would be cheaper. It was, but after several months of a Carey Cadillac, Alfred figured it was still ridiculously expensive. At that time, they had a butler who owned an ancient Ford sedan. Alfred made a deal with the butler to drive them to the theatre and take them home. When the butler departed, Lynn and Alfred got about in taxis. While they were in *Quadrille,* an actor overheard Alfred complaining about the hardships of finding taxis on East End Avenue and how he was always afraid of missing a curtain. (When Alexander Woollcott once asked his friends to name his East River apartment, F.P.A. suggested he call it, Little-Place-By-The-River-Where-It-Is-Hard-To-Get-A-Taxicab-From.) The actor said if the Lunts would pay him what taxis cost he'd chauffeur them to and from the theatre in the Volkswagen he was thinking of buying but couldn't afford without some subsidy. Alfred made the deal with him, since he could combine frugality with philanthropy. He didn't realize until the service started that the Volkswagen was an extremely little automobile and that he was an extremely long and large man. He was a good sport, though, and employed the amateur chauffeur during the run of *Quadrille.* Alfred uncoiling himself from the back seat of the Volkswagen and slithering out of the little car was as farcical as any scene in a play. Soon people would gather in the vicinity of Shubert Alley at 8 o'clock to watch the sight. Conscious of his large and appreciative audience, Alfred began fattening his part. Soon he had built up his exit from the little car into a wildly funny five-minute pantomime.

Growing their own food has always appealed to the Lunts because they love fresh vegetables. Lynn is not quite as enthusiastic about farming as Alfred is. For Alfred, farming is more than merely an economical way of getting food. It is one of his greatest pleasures. In 1933, he dispatched this bulletin to Aleck: "There's a great deal of country activity now. . . . I am deliriously happy. . . . Jelly making—raspberry jelly, currant, cherry, blackberry . . . and fence making and tree trimming and scrubbing and painting . . . the gardens, in late August, are fairly bursting with flowers and vegetables." The vegetables included carrots, corn, lettuce, tomatoes, string beans, onions, potatoes, asparagus, turnips, beets, cauliflower, squash, eggplant, collard and mustard greens, kale, okra, and cucumbers. Such cucumbers—enormous and succulent. "Only English seeds," Alfred once revealed, "give you really superb cucumbers. We get our seeds from Bessie Porter in London. When we play in London, Bessie is Lynn's dresser. She's a marvelous woman with a brisk sense of humor. Aleck used to say Bessie

Porter was one of the two great women in England. He never named the other. Whenever Aleck was in London, he'd have Bessie to tea at Claridge's several times a week. Just to chat with her."

Alfred is happy in Wisconsin in all the seasons—even in winter. "We've been pretty well snowed in here," he once wrote Woollcott, "and it's heaven—very cold, too—24 below zero, day before yesterday. It's a lot of work hauling in wood and shoveling paths but I don't think I've ever enjoyed this place quite so much before. The dairy chores fascinate me and at last I can make really fine butter. We have a new maid, too, a darling, who makes wonderful bread, so what with that and my butter and our milk and cream and honey and last fall's apples we're very well off indeed."

Christmas on the farm, an old-fashioned family Christmas, is a great event. In 1945, they were playing *O Mistress Mine* in Milwaukee, about 40 miles from Genesee Depot. They opened on Christmas Eve. The family—Louise, Carl Sederholm, Jr., and Karin, and their spouses and children—were all gathered at Ten Chimneys where the champagne was icing and a table was groaning beneath an opulent smorgasbord. Benny Perkins, their tenant farmer, drove their old Cadillac in to the Davidson Theatre and after the performance they began driving back to Genesee Depot. The weather got worse and worse and a heavy rain became a sleet storm which was now freezing over. The highway was covered with ice. Outside of Waukesha there was a steep grade. The car couldn't make it, and kept sliding down halfway up the hill. They all got out. The party included Susan, Mrs. Karin Bugbee's daughter, and Alma, Lynn's dresser. They trudged to the Avalon Hotel. It was after one A.M. They phoned the farm and said they wouldn't be able to get there until the morning. They were hungry and cold, and not a restaurant was open in Waukesha. The hotel's kitchen had closed hours ago. The thought of the smorgasbord was frustrating—all that smoked eel, bismarck herring, salmon, deviled eggs, Westphalian ham, hot Swedish meatballs, cheese, bread—all so near and yet so far. They asked the Avalon's night clerk if he couldn't get them anything to eat, anything at all, but he didn't have the key to the kitchen and so couldn't get into the refrigerators. He remembered having seen some apples in the basement. He got them apples. "So we ate apples," Lynn says, "and we didn't have a drop of champagne and it was so cold we went to bed in our clothes."

Their 1938 Christmas had been a merrier occasion. They had hoped

Woollcott could be with them but he was not able to come and so Lynn told him what had happened in one of the loveliest letters she ever composed:

Christmas was lovely with the family, the growing-up children are a delight—such good manners and so amusing. We sat down twenty to dinner including the two littlest nieces and one little nephew, aged eleven, twelve and thirteen respectively, Johnny the youngest. They all had milk by their places but were allowed each a glass of champagne and one of the little girls was heard to say in one of those sudden lulls—"It (milk) tastes lousy after champagne, doesn't it?" They both wore long hostess gowns and were quite blissful imagining themselves grown up. Johnny finished his dinner quickly and accompanied the dessert course on his concertina with *Jingle Bells* and *Home Sweet Home*. We played all the old favorites on the gramophone too and it was all very sentimental and lovely. Karin and Louise sang carols softly in high sweet sopranos, with their heads together, looking like the children they were when I first knew them. We left with the whole family group at the top of the stairs—three generations, from Hattie downwards, in tears, because the Christmas that they had so long looked forward to was over. . . .

TWELVE

"IDOLS OF THE AMERICAN STAGE

AT LAST IN TALKIES"

*L*YTTON STRACHEY's biography of the private life of Queen Elizabeth and the Earl of Essex was published in the United States in 1928.
Elizabeth and Essex became a best-seller, perhaps because a good many
American readers were under the impression that the title was *Elizabeth and Sex.* They were not disappointed by the text. Among its happy
readers was the playwright Maxwell Anderson, who was famous as the
co-author of *What Price Glory?*, a realistic and bawdy comedy of World
War I, and the author of *Saturday's Children*, a realistic comedy of
married life among the lower classes. His plays were noted for the
vernacular and vulgar dialogue in which his characters spoke. Now, to
everyone's surprise, his latest play was written in blank verse; it was
historical and it was called *Elizabeth the Queen.* Before it went into
rehearsal, Anderson did not conceal the source of his inspiration and
said he had chosen his theme after reading Strachey's sardonic book.
Later on he changed his story. He said he had been brooding upon the
Virgin Queen for many years and, furthermore, had long planned to
write poetic plays. During the pre-Broadway tour, Anderson delivered
himself of the following thoughts about the American theatre to an
interviewer from the Pittsburgh *Press*: "We have forgotten that beauty
is the essential element in great dramatic literature. We have gone too
far with realism and photographic detail . . . the truth we have shown
on our stage is raw and ugly. . . ." He did not see fit either to apologize for the raw ugliness of *What Price Glory?* or to justify his incon-
sistency.

The Theatre Guild had taken an option on the play as a vehicle for
the Lunts, but Lynn did not want to do the play for she thought it
had many serious historical mistakes. He had "things wrong that any

little school child would know. There is one dizzy moment in the play when Essex actually invades Elizabeth's palace and his army is waiting around outside. Actually Essex and his army never even landed in England. There was a revolt in Ireland but they were routed before getting to London." Alfred insisted that they must do the play, despite its historical errors. He thought it was a strong play with a good basic plot. Perhaps he felt guilty because *Meteor* had been so much his play. Sometimes—not always—he felt uneasy when critics rated him superior to Lynn. Her genius was a delicate thing, which manifested itself in small movements of the face and arms and torso, in a sense of timing, in the spacing of silences. But the role of Elizabeth would be a beautiful part for her. Elizabeth was everything in the play. She dominated the action even when she was offstage. Alfred convinced Lynn. Of course, she liked playing in costume, and she liked some of the play, but she thought it would have to have many revisions, especially more scenes between her and Essex, scenes of more tenderness and above all more conflict. Then they would have again their favorite story, that battle of the sexes they were to fight in one plot or another, one century or another, one duo of personages or another.

Anderson had promised the Lunts, director Philip Moeller, Langner, and Miss Helburn, that he would make all the revisions. On Broadway, it is said that plays are not written but rewritten. But Anderson was not rewriting. During the weeks before rehearsal he did not produce any new dialogue. Nor did he make any changes when the play went into rehearsal. Moeller was grating on Anderson's nerves as strongly as he had grated on Behrman's. The rehearsals were further complicated by the fact that Anderson was in the throes of a clandestine romance with a beautiful young actress, Mab Anthony, for whom he had gotten a walk-on part. Miss Anthony asked her beau to get her a better part and the playwright got her the part of one of the queen's ladies-in-waiting. Recalling the incident, Lynn once told me: "I didn't know about this, as the minor parts were already cast, and when I came to the theatre, my ladies in waiting were all there, and this little girl came on and spoke her first line, 'Your Majesty' in a harsh and dreadful voice, whereupon Moeller turned to Maxwell Anderson and said, 'I consider it an insult to Lynn and Alfred to allow somebody to open their mouth who have no experience, are complete amateurs and cannot speak decent English. How dare we allow such a person on the same stage with Lynn and Alfred?' So Anderson went out the stage door to the hotel where he was living and we did not see him for three days. It was clear as the play went along that he was in love with her and he and the young girl were having an affair. Mrs. Anderson may have known all about it. One day when she was driving in her car she had a brain hemorrhage and died. Max at once married the young girl. After he had grown used to Mab, he began having an affair with another young girl, a sixteen or seventeen year old girl, on the coast, and Mab heard of it, got into her automobile in the closed garage, and turned on the motor and let it run until the carbon monoxide of the exhaust killed her. Maxwell Anderson was not subtle or sophisticated. He could not have an affair discreetly. He was a great big cuddly honey bear. That was how he looked at himself—a hugglesome bear. He liked to be thought a great big good-natured masculine creature who didn't know anything much beyond blank-verse tragedy, but he was not worldly wise or sensitive. He was an old gentleman who liked young girls."

The Philadelphia opening of *Elizabeth the Queen* was a disaster. The reviews were shattering. Anderson had not rewritten a line. Langner and Helburn came down and talked it over and decided to close *Elizabeth the Queen* at once. The Lunts offered to buy the play from the Guild and produce it themselves. The Guild decided to risk their money on Anderson. They arranged a long tour of the play which would give him a chance to make the necessary changes. Woollcott came down and had a conference with the playwright, and made many excellent suggestions. But when would Anderson begin writing? The first stop of the tour was Baltimore where they encountered a heavy rainstorm. Anderson stayed in his room all day. Next morning he appeared with pages of precious dialogue and told the Lunts the truth about his creative problem. He could only write when it rained! At his home, in Rockland County, N.Y., he had a sprinkler device which he turned on during long dry spells. It played streams of water on his studio roof so he could write to the splashing of rain on the roof. There was rain in Pittsburgh, Cincinnati, and St. Louis. Anderson was writing at white heat and when the play opened in New York in November, 1930, it was a sensation. Lynn had transformed herself into an aging woman, with cracked voice, rheumy eyes, sagging flesh, sucked-in cheeks, and a grotesque red wig. In her costume of heavy brocaded copper colored silk with its ruff and necklaces, she was every inch a queen. Percy Hammond said it was more than acting, it was a "miraculous reincarnation" of a historical personage, and he said the audience felt not only that this queen had once actually breathed and walked and loved but that she was alive again "here and now in 52nd Street." In one scene, she waits for Essex to subdue his pride and declare his subservience to her as a queen—if he won't, he will have to die on the block. Lynn, wrote Woollcott, "was compact of all despair, as with clenched hands and twisting bloodless lips, she waits for some little word from him—crouches and waits in vain, as many a lover the world around this very day is listening for the telephone call that doesn't come."

Alfred attempted a daring piece of business in Act II. He has been waiting, waiting for letters from Queen Elizabeth, and there is a moment when he wants to show his desperation, his anxiety, his frustrated love. A messenger comes with bad news. Alfred indicates he's feeling upset. He takes a drink of water, and begins retching. He walks slowly upstage. He leans over. He goes through a realistic pantomime of throwing up.

Many persons found this altogether too realistic. When they played Chicago, Ashton Stevens, veteran Chicago *Tribune* critic, though he was the president of the midwestern branch of the Lunt and Fontanne Admiration Society, thought Alfred had gone too far and said so in an indignant column criticizing Alfred for vomiting, in effect, on a public stage. Alfred thought Stevens was wrong. He knew that in extreme and terrible moments, human beings feel violently sick and throw up.

In 1930, when the *Theatre Guild Magazine* asked all the critics to vote for the ten best American actors, Alfred and Lynn were chosen the first and second. They were now the unchallenged king and queen of the theatre in England and America.

During the run of *Elizabeth the Queen*, Metro-Goldwyn-Mayer engaged them to recreate *The Guardsman* as a "talking picture." Hiring stage actors to play in movies, even in their original Broadway roles, has rarely been done in Hollywood. But that was a period of indecisiveness in Hollywood, because the coming of sound in 1927 had revolutionized moviemaking and the studios were importing hundreds of "talking" actors from the London and New York stage, for the acting of the silent films had been not so much the projection of personality as the creation of a visual image. The Lunts were reluctant to make a movie. They had had some disconcerting experiences in films. After *Clarence,* Alfred had been signed to play a cleancut American hero, a sort of Charles Ray or Richard Barthelmess type. He made three silent films, released in 1922 and 1923: *The Ragged Edge, Backbone* and *Second Youth.* In *Second Youth,* Lynn played a society woman. Louella Parsons, back in 1923, saw Alfred as a potentially great movie comedian, and compared him to Harold Lloyd and Buster Keaton. "Comedy is his metier," she wrote. James Dean, a 1920's biographer of movie stars, stated: "Alfred Lunt is the most personable young actor since Wally Reid. All he needs now is pomade for his hair and scenes with passionate sheik stuff and he'll mount the idol's altar." Alfred found acting to a camera frightening. He couldn't get a character across in the short "takes" in which films are shot. The discontinuous method made it hard for him to surrender to a mood. He had a fear of the camera's eye. In 1923, while in Wisconsin to visit his family, he was interviewed by the Milwaukee *Journal*. "I simply can't bear to look at *Backbone*," he confessed. "Oh, it's a mess. I was too conscious of the camera all the time." He recently wrote, "The three silent films, pretty bad—though *Second Youth* had some funny things in it—Directed well." *

While he was playing *The Guardsman*, Alfred made one of the last films directed by D. W. Griffith. It was *Sally of the Sawdust,* the movie version of *Poppy,* a musical comedy hit in 1923, in which W. C. Fields became a Broadway star. Fields was hired to reproduce his Eustace MacGargle, a shady but lovable carnival shell-game operator. The movie built up the role of the ingénue, which was played by Griffith's protégée, Carol Dempster, a vivacious and kinetic young movie actress with a charming personality. Alfred played Peyton Lennox, the son of a rich man who falls in love with Sally, a poor girl who is actually, unknown to everybody but Fields, the granddaughter of a rich man who had thrown her mother out of the house when she married a circus acrobat. Through the courtesy of William K. Everson, Jr., collector of silent films and the owner of the only complete print of *Sally of the Sawdust* in good condition, I saw the movie recently. Alfred was the epitome of elegance in a double-breasted suit, a stickpin, a pearl gray fedora hat, and an air of extravagant masculine beauty. His role was, alas, rather insignificant, for W. C. Fields stole the entire picture— even from Miss Dempster, who was supposed to be the main attraction. Alfred had some scenes in the middle of the picture where he got a love relationship under way with Miss Dempster as he saw her in a street and followed her to a woods, where they embraced in an amusing kissing scene, the caption reading: "A rich young man—a homeless waif—the eternal bond of youth." Then he disappeared and was out of most of the film until he had to be brought back at the end to tie up one of the plot ends. Alfred found the whole business quite frustrating. In later years he never mentioned the picture to anybody and to

* Letter to the author, 1963. Albert Parker directed *Second Youth.*

this day many persons—even in the theatre—think Alfred made his screen debut in *The Guardsman*. Even George Freedley's scholarly monograph, *The Lunts*, fails to mention *Sally of the Sawdust* in the chronology of Alfred's screen appearances. Recalling the episode now, Alfred says: "Small leading man part in *Sally of the Sawdust*—worked by the day while we were playing *The Guardsman*—D. W. Griffith not at his best. He seemed sometimes bewildered and sometimes indifferent—I think he was ill—Said I was good in long and medium shots but didn't like my close ups!" *

In April, 1931, Irving Thalberg, the boy wonder of MGM production, and his wife, Norma Shearer, were en route to New York to take ship for Europe. They stopped over in Chicago for a meeting in Thalberg's suite at the Drake Hotel with the Lunts, who were playing Chicago. Thalberg was an unimpressive person in appearance. He was short and skinny and nervous. He spoke rapidly in disjointed sentences. He was thirty-two years old, and was to die in five years, becoming a Hollywood legend. During most of the parley, Lynn was silent, staring out of her great eyes at Miss Shearer and Thalberg. Alfred expressed their hopes that *The Guardsman* would be faithful to the original play and that it would be shot in continuous time as if the play were being photographed. He hoped there would not be any "stunt stuff."

Thalberg assured him that "we will give you a nice dignified picture, something quiet and pleasant and artistic and peaceful. You will find the picture more peaceful than the stage."

At this point, their manager, Larry Farrell, screamed, "My God, what's that?"

The Lunts looked up and saw a lion, a real lion, coming through the French doors of the sitting room. There was a leash attached to the lion and a trainer on the other end but it was all rather frightening, though they were assured by one and all that it was a polite and friendly lion who was used to posing and had never in his life eaten a single actor. They posed with Thalberg and the lion. They had gotten off to a nerve-wracking start with Hollywood and they imagined that Thalberg's definition of peace and quiet was different from theirs.

In Los Angeles, Lawrence Farrell, their business agent, had rented them a modest home in Westwood, engaged a cook, bought them a used black 1927 Ford sedan for $150, and hired a chauffeur. They got into the car, careened through Beverly Hills and into Culver City, and drew up at the gate of MGM on Washington Boulevard. The guard asked

* Letter to the author, 1963.

Lynn Fontanne as the tearful bride in *The Wooing of Eve* (1916) with Violet Kemble Cooper and Laurette Taylor

Alfred Lunt as a Greenwich Village aesthete in *Romance and Arabella* (1917)

Alfred as Clarence Smith, the saxophone-playing entomologist and war veteran, in *Clarence* (1919)

Lynn as Dulcy (1921) in a bewildered moment with John Westley and
George Alison

Alfred as Bluntschli and Lynn as Raina in Shaw's *Arms and the Man* (1925)

Alfred with Carol Dempster in a carrousel in D. W. Griffith's silent film *Sally of the Sawdust* (1925)

Lynn as Laura Pasquale beating Alfred as Joe Dermot in *At Mrs. Beam's* (1926)

Alfred as Albert von Eckhardt cajoles Lynn as Ilse von Ilsen in *Caprice* (1928)

Lynn as the idealistic girl and Alfred as the ambition-driven financier of *Meteor* (1929), with Edward Emery

The Lunts as Elizabeth and Essex in *Elizabeth the Queen* (1930)

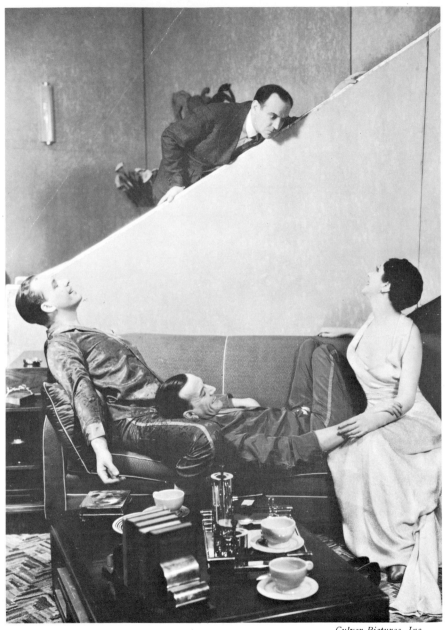

Alfred, Noel Coward, and Lynn in *Design for Living* (1933), with Campbell Gullan as the solid citizen

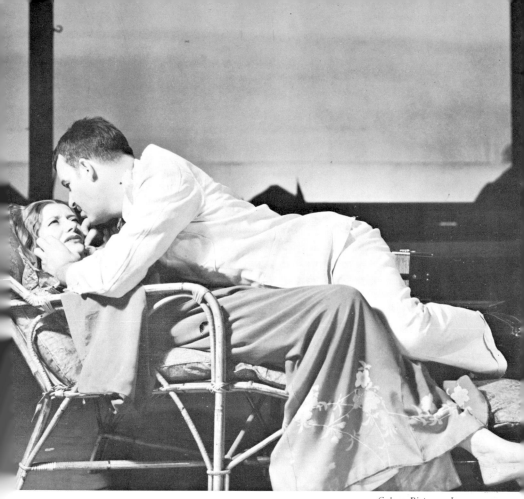

Alfred as Stefan, a passionate Russian, and Lynn as Linda Valaine in *Point Valaine* (1935)

The Lunts as Jupiter and Alkmena in *Amphitryon* 38 (1937)

AT LEFT:
Alfred as Harry Van with Les Blondes in an impromptu floor show on the set of *Idiot's Delight* (1936), with Lynn (*far left*) as the femme fatale

As Trigorin and Madame Arkadina in Chekhov's *The Sea Gull* (1938)

The beginning of the most passionate love scene ever played by the Lunts, in *O Mistress Mine* (1946)

The Lunts as a team of mind readers in *The Great Sebastians* (1955)

In *The Visit* (1958)

to see their pass. They didn't have one. He had never heard of *The Guardsman*. He told them they couldn't get in without a pass. They went away and remained in their home until Sidney Franklin, the director, got in touch with them and apologized and personally conducted them through the gate. The film was shot in a record breaking twenty-one days because the Lunts insisted on rehearsing every scene of the play thoroughly before a foot of film was shot. In his history of MGM, Bosley Crowther writes, "They still say around Culver City that there never have been on the lot two more professional people than Alfred Lunt and Lynn Fontanne."

The shooting of *The Guardsman* spawned a story which has become a classical anecdote of show business. The story goes that after the second day of shooting, there was a screening of the "rushes." Everybody went to it but Alfred, who was waiting in fear and trembling at home for Lynn's report. She burst into the room. "I was awful," she said, almost in tears. "I don't see how I can go on with the picture."

"How was I?" Alfred asked.

"You were charming," Lynn said. "You looked handsome and your voice was splendid. You'll have to change your make-up because you look as though you don't have any lips. But me—I'm hopeless. I look too fat and my voice sounds like an announcer's at a rodeo, and my eyes are too small and I'm just so gawky."

Alfred was silent, staring into space.

"I tell you I can't go on," Lynn cried. "What'll I do, Alfred?"

"No lips, eh?" Alfred said.

Frankly, I'd always believed this tale was one of those amusing fables concocted by an imaginative writer, and I once asked Alfred if there was any substance to the "no lips" story. "But it is entirely true," he said, smiling!

Lynn and Alfred loved the gay social whirl of Hollywood, and they had a high time seeing such old friends as Ina Claire (involved in a big romance with movie star John Gilbert, whom she married), Ruth Chatterton, Roland Young (who played The Critic in the film of *The Guardsman*), Laura Hope Crews, Lucile Watson, June Walker, and Ivor Novello. They went to several formal dinners. "They were very sedate affairs, held on Sunday night," Alfred told a New York *Times* reporter. "The only difference between them and a New York formal dinner is that out there you are served more avocado and less garlic."

The movie was sneak-previewed at a small theatre in San Bernardino. The next day the Lunts had a meeting with Thalberg at his office. He was studying the cards filled in by the audience. The cards were critical. The audience said the movie was boring and stupid and they hated it. Thalberg began reading the cards aloud, but Lynn finally cut in. She was quite angry.

"Don't read any more of those things if they're all as moronic as the ones you've read," she said. "I don't want to hear that particular person's opinion about *The Guardsman* because this film, in sophistication and maturity, is way outside their world, and this kind of person cannot like it. It is a subtle, brilliant comedy, and you will find an audience for it, but it won't be made up of people like the ones who wrote those nasty vulgar cards."

Variety, reviewing the film, said that the "fan public reaction is likely to be adverse . . . poking fun, not unmixed with venom, at the superficiality that makes up the lives of most actor folk, isn't going to be especially relished by a public that consumes the syrupy blurbs of a dozen or so fan magazines. . . . To the sophisticated it is all sublimated high comedy; to the commonalty of gum chewers it will be either a dark mystery or a sacrilege."

The Guardsman premiered at the Astor Theatre on September 9, 1932. For the first time, Lunt and Fontanne had their names up in lights on a theatre marquee. The studio trumpeted the event in full page advertisements which read: "IDOLS OF THE AMERICAN STAGE AT LAST IN TALKIES." From the famed Theatre Guild to the Astor screen. Tonight they make their bow from the screen. America has watched spellbound their artistry in *Goat Song, Caprice, Elizabeth the Queen* and their other stage triumphs. But now it is the privilege of Metro-Goldwyn-Mayer to bring the aristocrats of the American stage to you in the talkie of their greatest success, *The Guardsman,* named by those who have seen it as the outstanding film thus far of 1931."

But *Variety* had been right. The "commonalty of gum chewers" disliked the movie and they outnumbered the people of good taste. The movie was a great critical success and did well in the large cities, but it did not make money for MGM. Still, Thalberg, two years later, offered them a contract for $990,000 to run three years, during which they would make movie versions of *Elizabeth the Queen, Reunion in Vienna* and other stories to be chosen by the studio. It was a handsome offer, because in the depths of the Depression that kind of money was rarely offered to any actors.

They rejected the offer.

"The studio would choose the pictures," Lynn once explained to me.

"They would have the last word on everything—directors, supporting cast, costumes. We would just be their puppets. This we didn't do in the theatre and we wouldn't do in the films. Thalberg was, in his way, a clever man, and he had taste and intelligence and he seriously wanted to make good movies, we both felt. But he wanted slaves, not actors, and we couldn't be any person's slaves. We'd worked too hard for our independence."

When Carl Laemmle offered them $250,000 to play Tristan and Isolde in a Universal Film, the Lunts said no, and Lynn's remark became famous, "Mr. Laemmle, we can be bought but we can't be bored!"

REUNION IN VIENNA

AND DESIGN FOR LIVING

*I*N 1931, if you saw a line of persons standing in the street you supposed they were there to apply for a job or to get a sandwich and coffee at a soup kitchen. There was a long line every day outside the Martin Beck Theatre on West 45th Street. They were waiting to buy tickets for Robert E. Sherwood's comedy *Reunion in Vienna.* It was one of the few enterprises making any money in the city in that lamentable year. Alexander Woollcott, now a free-lance magazine writer, happened to see the play for the fourth or fifth time, and he wrote Lynn and Alfred, "When your grandchildren (on whom you have not made a really effective start) gather at your rheumatic knees and ask you what you did during the great depression, you can tell them that you played *Reunion in Vienna* to crowded houses and enjoyed the whole depression enormously."

Sherwood's play was about expatriate and seedy Austrian aristocrats who secretly meet in a private dining room of Sacher's Restaurant on the birthday of Emperor Franz Josef. Alfred played Rudolph Maximilian von Hapsburg, formerly a royal roué and now a taxi driver in Nice. Elena, played by Lynn, had been his mistress ten years ago, and is now the respectable wife of a Viennese psychoanalyst. They meet at the clandestine birthday party and for one evening resume their love affair. It was a tenderly written idyll of nostalgic love. It suited the Lunts perfectly.

And so did Sherwood. In him, they found their ideal collaborator and also a man whom they loved deeply. They had known him since 1919. He had come back from the war—in which he had been wounded and gassed—and gotten a newspaper job, but he wanted to write plays. A mutual friend arranged a lunch with Alfred at the

Harvard Club. Alfred had recently opened in *Clarence*. Sherwood came to talk about his ambitions in the theatre and his admiration of Alfred's comic talent. Instead, Alfred poured out his hopeless love for a young and unknown actress, Lynn Fontanne. He talked about Miss Fontanne all during the lunch and poor Sherwood went away without getting any advice on his dramatic problems. Some months later, Sherwood was told by Charles and Jane de Glehn, who were related to his mother, that he ought to look up an English actress, who could perhaps help him. The girl's name was Lynn Fontanne. Sherwood at once got in touch with Miss Fontanne and they had dinner, but she talked about nothing but Alfred Lunt. Eventually, Sherwood composed *The Road to Rome* as a vehicle for the Lunts, but the Theatre Guild didn't like the play and it was done by Jane Cowl and Philip Merivale for another management. He wrote other plays for them, but it was not until 1931 that they finally got together.

In *Reunion in Vienna,* the Lunts crystallized their dream of passion, playing with tenderness and animality. "It was the first time," Ina Claire once told me, "that love scenes were played so physically on the American stage. They acted like real people in real love with each other and used their bodies to express their emotions in a very intimate fashion and yet, somehow, when it was Lynn and Alfred, it was never in bad taste." John Mason Brown spoke of their "joyousness of surrender to their parts." Graham Robertson, exaggerating their homeliness, said they possessed "the power the Scots call 'glamorie'—the art of making that that is not appear to be that that is. Lynn Fontanne is a plain middle-aged woman. What she allows you to see is a beautiful woman of 29 or 30, exquisitely graceful and of ineffable charm. Lunt is an ugly, common-looking man with a podgy fat figure and a face like an uninteresting potato. He allows you to perceive this for a moment when he first enters in a very worn and dirty Tyrolean kilt and a hat that is a catastrophe, but after that minute you only see a charming fairy prince, elusive, annoying, outrageous, but wholly fascinating." *

The first moment of their reunion occurs in the middle of the second act. Lunt's back is to the audience. He is sitting in a chair before a mirror when Lynn enters, and he sees her first in the mirror. Then she becomes aware of him.

"The meeting is electric. He sees her in a mirror, turns slowly around, scorches her from head to foot with his eyes, circles silently about her,

* Letter to his friend Kerrison Preston.

comes close, lets his hand play over her bosom and buttocks, then slaps her in the face and gives her one long exhausting kiss. All that time she never speaks, never moves a muscle, but when he straightens up again, you can see that she is swooning inside. Everything about her has wilted in the heat." †

Upon first greeting Frau Sacher, Rudolf was to give her a smack on the rump and chortle, "Good evening, venerable strumpet." Then, as she coyly withdrew, he was to follow her, wondering if she still wore red flannel drawers and raising her skirt. Helen Westley was playing Frau Sacher. "The glimpse of Helen's behind incarnadined in flannel is a nightly joy to the Guild subscribers," Aleck reported. But one evening, Miss Westley forgot to put on the red drawers and when Alfred raised her skirts he—and the Guild subscribers—saw her uncostumed rear. After a brief pause for breath, Alfred got control of himself long enough to say his next line, which was, "Thank God, there's something in Vienna that hasn't changed!"

Even in May and June, though the weather was unseasonably hot, *Reunion in Vienna* was playing to standees. But the Guild Theatre was unbearable, even for a theatre in hot weather. "It hasn't an ounce of ventilation, you know," Alfred once complained to Sherwood. "The designers of that building were born in some East Side tenement without windows. How they must have loved the smell of cabbage and armpits!"

The Lunts decided to close in July, go to Wisconsin for refreshment, and then to Europe. They also decided not to renew their contract with the Theatre Guild. They decided it was high time Noel Coward wrote the play for the three of them that he had been promising to write since 1921. Noel, at the time, was voyaging about South America on a freighter. He stopped in Buenos Aires long enough to get their cablegram:

CONTRACT WITH THE GUILD UP IN JUNE. WE SHALL BE FREE. WHAT ABOUT IT?

Now Noel decided he had to stop dreaming and write a play, because he wanted to rescue his friends from what he thought were the exploiting clutches of the Guild. He brooded about plots and characters all during his travels through Chile, Peru, Colombia, and Brazil and, en route from Panama to Los Angeles on a Norwegian

† Alexander Woollcott in a letter to Paul Bonner.

freighter, the conception of *Design for Living* sprang full-blown to his mind. Lynn portrayed Gilda, a beautiful and witty woman on the lost seacoast of Bohemia. Alfred was Otto Sylvus, a poor painter who becomes rich and popular. Noel was Leo Mercure, a struggling writer who becomes a celebrated playwright. Gilda alternately slept with Otto and Leo. In one speech, Leo says, "The actual facts are so simple. I love you. You love me. I love Otto. Otto loves you. Otto loves me. There now! Start to unravel from there."

The unraveling was the play, and a most amusing play it was, though in some ways it was one of the most immoral stories ever played on a stage. I saw it and found it the most continuously amusing play I have ever witnessed. I was hardly able to stop laughing during its two hours. John Mason Brown summed up the popular feeling when he remarked that "no comedy within recent memory had the advantages of three performances equal in their brilliance [to] those given by Mr. Lunt, Miss Fontanne, and Mr. Coward. . . . [It is] a diversion which makes the moments pass so gayly one forgets about time. . . . They seem little less than miraculous."

The curtain rose on a "rather shabby studio in Paris." Nobody was on stage. Then Lynn had to enter carrying a tray with coffee and milk. Recalling the play, Noel Coward says, "All actors loathe making their first entrance—but making an entrance cold, alone on a stage, well this is an abomination. We'd been working so hard during rehearsals none of us realized the horror I'd foisted on Lynn until we were opening in Cleveland prior to Broadway. There we all stood shivering in the wings and the curtain rose and Lynn was holding the tray with the props and suddenly she realized she had to open the play cold and walk out on an empty stage and she turned to me, absolutely furious, and said, 'Noel, if your house was invaded, I believe you'd send your mother out to face the guns!' "

There is a memorable scene in the second act when Gilda has decided to leave both Leo and Otto. She writes them each a letter explaining her decision to get married to a solid gentleman and lead a respectable, normal life. Leo and Otto come back to the flat, discover the letters, read them, and proceed to get roaring drunk on cognac. Noel and Alfred played their drunk scene with a lunatic abandon. One night, Alfred forgot one of his lines in this drunk scene. So, for the hell of it, Noel spoke the line. Then, spontaneously, in midstream, both actors exchanged characters and Noel continued speaking Alfred's lines and Alfred spoke Noel's lines and each did the other's business. Lynn thought they had gone out of their minds and she looked at them, from the wings, with a horror that Noel will never forget.

Several weeks after *Design for Living* opened, Lynn got a letter from the Harriman National Bank inviting her to buy stock in the bank.

"It's very odd," she told Alfred. "It seems to me that any bank that comes to you and asks you for money is no good. It's not my idea of a bank and is very suspicious. I'm going there at once and take my money out and put it in your bank."

But when she got to the Harriman Bank, she was too embarrassed to take her money out. Instead, she wrote a check for her balance and opened an account in the Guaranty Trust Company, depositing her check. The next day the Harriman Bank closed. Lynn was relieved that she had got her money out in time but, of course, her check had not cleared and so she lost her $60,000. She got the news just before a Saturday matinee. First she felt awful and then she saw the humor of it and got rather giddy and made up a little song:

> I lost my money in the Harriman bank,
> The Harriman bank, the Harriman bank,
> I lost my money in the Harriman bank,
> And I don't give a damn. . . .

Soon she and Alfred were laughing and dancing and singing in Lynn's dressing room. Hearing the noise, Noel walked in and said, "What on earth are you singing about?"

They told him.

"I hardly think that's anything to celebrate," Noel said.

"What but else can we do, Noel?" Lynn asked. "Cry about it?"

During the bank holiday, in March, 1933, many places of business, including theatres, took promissory notes because there was not enough cash around. Noel proposed they take I.O.U's in lieu of money at the box-office.

Alfred refused.

"Lynn and I," he said, "will never play for I.O.U.'s. The theatre is a cash business. Woolworth's and the theatre are the only two cash businesses. Let the customers come with watches, eggs, turkeys, chickens, vegetables, wine, and we'll let them into the theatre. But absolutely no credit!"

Lynn's perfectionism was illustrated by an incident in this comedy.

During the scene in which she decides to begin a new and conventional life, she props her farewell letter to Leo against a cognac bottle. A few minutes later she remembers her other letter, the one to Otto, and she scampers in, hurriedly pulls it out of her pocketbook and props it on another cognac bottle. Lynn had always felt that the taking out of the second letter ought to bring a big reaction from the audience— but it never got more than a polite chuckle. On the Saturday matinee of the day they were closing *Design for Living* she happened to yank the letter out faster than usual and was rewarded with a satisfying roar of laughter.

Lynn came to Noel and said, "Now I've finally got that piece of business down right and what I want is to have one of the stagehands put a spring into my handbag so that when I open the bag the letter will jump out quickly and I will have my laugh. Oh, darling, I've finally figured out just how to do it!"

"Darling," Noel said indulgently, "I'm afraid you're a little late— we're closing the show."

She glared. *"But there's still tonight's performance."* She got her spring. And she brought the house down with the letter bit in the closing performance!

FOURTEEN

A GRAND TOUR—AND

SOME REUNIONS IN LONDON, 1934

*B*Y PREVIOUS arrangement, *Design for Living* closed after a run of 135 performances, though it was still playing to full houses. After the usual respite at Genesee Depot, the Lunts took passage on the *Bremen*. They planned a grand tour and their itinerary included a visit to the Soviet Union, which had been granted diplomatic recognition the previous year. It was the first phase of what was to become known as "peaceful co-existence" between the U.S.A. and the U.S.S.R. Lynn and Alfred were as excited by the approaching trip as little children before Christmas day. They got to New York two weeks before the sailing date and there ensued frantic days of last-minute shopping and rushings in and out of Woollcott's apartment to ask for advice and suggestions on touring in Russia. Woollcott had recently returned from a trip there. Because of his enormous bulk he looked like the epitome of the traditional American capitalist and had been hailed wherever he went as the perfect American.

Interviewed by the New York *Herald Tribune* before they departed, Lynn said, "These days you either spend your money—or lose it in a bank."

Alfred bantered: "I believe I am going to lecture the Russians on how to improve collective farming. I've got some good ideas on vegetables."

After visiting Denmark, Sweden, and Finland, they took the train to Moscow. "We've been pretty spoiled in our day but Moscow has completely ruined us," Alfred wrote Aleck. "Moscow & Duranty & Linton Wells & Rubinstein & the Tairoffs and Mme. Chekhova and the opera and the ballet and the caviar and the vodka. We went to Russia for five days—and stayed two weeks. . . . Such saluting as we receive at the frontiers. . . . The customs don't allow us to open our suitcases. I'm sorry now we didn't take out Ivan the Terrible's crown. . . . The weather is deathly cold but cold or no cold, we never miss a performance nor a supper party nor a dinner and Lynn was ecstatic every minute over the whole works."

Stanislavsky was too sick to see them, but he sent them his house seats for a performance of *The Cherry Orchard* at the Moscow Art Theatre. They were accompanied by two interpreters who sat on either side of them and whispered English translations during the performance. "It was like seeing a foreign film with subtitles," Lynn says.

They saw a magnificent production of *Dead Souls*. "Very Dickensesque and the most perfect thing ever done in a theatre," Alfred told Aleck. They saw *Prince Igor* in Leningrad and were awed by the grandeur of the production and the ballet company of several hundred perfectly trained dancers.

"Then," Alfred told Woollcott, "there was a moment in the Bolshoi Theatre . . . well, not exactly a moment either, it was 12 years. Lynnie had loosened her skirt, as she'd had too much food and vodka, in order to be nice and comfortable for the opera & at the final curtain proceeded up the aisle very grandly indeed . . . when what should we discover at the doorway but her two bare legs in a pair of underpants. . . . She'd dropped her skirt in the third row. But the most amazing thing is that all these thousands of people watching her, never smiled, never seemed to take the situation as in the least unusual. . . ."

From Moscow they went to London and cast *Reunion*. Then they went on to Paris and joined forces with Romney Brent and toured Italy and Egypt. In December they returned to London and put *Reunion in Vienna* into rehearsal. It was directed by Alfred: this was the first time he officially directed a play. He was delighted by the English actors. He told Sherwood that he was "angered to desperation that the English do not know what extraordinary actors they possess. Never have I seen small parts played so well—never have I seen actors work so hard for the play, not for personal acclaim." They were staying at Claridge's, "the most comfortable hotel I have ever been in—but the bills are too much." * So they rented a house in Chelsea in February. It was furnished in elegant style and it came with a French chef and four servants and the incredible weekly rent was a paltry 15 guineas—about $75 at that time.

Reunion in Vienna opened on January 3, 1934, at the Lyric Theatre.

* Lynn to Alexander Woollcott.

The notices were not enthusiastic. The Lunts were disparaged because they didn't "articulate" clearly and certain of their "mannerisms" were ridiculed. Lynn was miserable and Alfred, as he told Sherwood, was "suicidal." They were afraid they had played badly because it seemed that even the audiences didn't respond warmly. Graham Robertson tried to buck them up. "You don't understand our English audience. I believe Americans applaud all through an act of a comedy, which we don't—especially when the play has gripped us. But don't you see how loudly the audience applauded at the end?"

"But what's the good of that?" Alfred said. "That doesn't help us. It's too late then."

Alfred mailed Sherwood the English reviews. For years, Sherwood treasured a quote from one reviewer, who said *Reunion in Vienna* "is a trifling inconsequential bit of fluff but far and away the best play Mr. Sherwood has ever written." Alfred said, "To me, Bob, these notices seem for the most part to be pretty stupid and far from discerning or articulate. Though 'articulate' is a word I am sensitive over these days." But there had been ten curtain calls at the Saturday matinee and after the evening performance, the novelist G. B. Stern told them that not in years had she heard such an ovation for a play as they had received.

As time went on, Alfred came to have a better "feel" of the London audience and he was happier and inclined to agree with Lynn and Robertson that "the audiences still get quite swept away." Making one of his periodic visits to the theatre, Robertson noted, in February, "The play goes on as brilliantly and freshly as on the first night. The Immortal Lunts save themselves entirely for their work and come fresh to it every day." Sometimes the passion of the players broke through the normal British restraint. At one performance, when Rudolph overcomes Elena's resistance and dances her into a bedroom, a man arose and shouted what sounded like an insult at Alfred.

At his next exit, Alfred asked a stage carpenter: "What did that man call me?"

"Well, sir," the stagehand said embarrassedly, "I shouldn't like to tell you what he called you."

"Come now," Alfred said, "we may as well have it. What did he call me?"

"What the gentleman said was . . . 'lecherous mountebank.' Was it you he meant?"

"He certainly did," Alfred said, quite pleased with himself. And he went off repeating *lecherous mountebank, lecherous mountebank* under his breath.

There were reunions in London. Antoinette Fontanne, divorced from her first husband, was in difficult circumstances. Alfred took 'Toineau for a long walk during which he explained that he and Lynn wanted to get her settled. She had a company, Fontanne Ware Ltd., which did a small business in ceramics with artificial flowers backed into them. Lynn found her a large studio in Upper Cheyne Street, Chelsea. In 1936, she sold out and came to the United States—Sloane's was supposed to back her in an American factory. They wanted her, she found out too late, to mass-produce her articles. "But they're handmade," she protested, and refused their proposition. The Lunts found her an apartment near the East River and furnished it with Third Avenue antiques. For some years she was a trimmer and clipper of purebred Bedlingtons. She went back to England during the war. After the war, the Lunts wanted to build her a little house in "south forty"—which is what they call the forty acres of land south of Ten Chimneys. But by now 'Toineau was living happily in Chichester.

There was a dinner with Jane and Wilfred de Glehn. The painters had brought together many of the singers and artists whom Lynn had known thirty years before. It was a "divine evening" and suddenly it seemed as if nothing had changed and she was a shy, dreaming, tremulous gypsy of a girl, so thin and delicate, looking for work as a model and gadding about the Café Royal and Rule's and looking for her lover, who was waiting for her by the Chelsea embankment, and all the years between then and now were "like a dream."

There was a tea party with Lily and Paul Bonner, who had rented Sargent's house in Tite Street; it reminded Lynn of the time she had stood in the drawing room, this very room, but it had been Sargent's studio then, and she had brought a letter from Wilfred de Glehn recommending her as a capable and patient model, most ingenious in portraying characters. Sargent had scrutinized her and said he thought her head was exceedingly fine and he would like to do some drawings of it, but she "never found out whether he meant it or not, as he died a short time after."

They were a pride of lions that social season, Alfred and Lynn, and were invited to innumerable parties and collations and receptions, and loved them all, for the opening-night journalistic quibbles were long forgotten and the Lunts were recognized for what they were, the foremost acting team in the history of the English-speaking theatre. At various soirées they met Rebecca West, James Hilton ("he is young, dark, reserved, exceedingly polite"), Gladys Cooper (she had been the star of *My Lady's Dress* when Lynn played small supporting roles in the Knoblock play), Raymond Massey, Constance Carpenter, W. Somerset Maugham ("we are mad about him"), Sybil Colefax, Beverley Nichols, Victor Cazelet. Cazelet, twenty-seven years old, was a wealthy patron of the arts and a sportsman. The Lunts went to many of his parties. H. G. Wells was at one of them with his latest *amie* whom Lynn remembers only as Maura, an Anglo-Russian translater who translated Russian plays into English and was, at the moment, translating *Reunion in Vienna* into Russian. The conversation got on to Czarist Russia and then the murder of Rasputin by Prince Youssopoff.

"I don't see why Youssopoff was so nervous after he'd done it," Maura said.

"Then," remembers Lynn, recreating for you the people at the table and instinctively putting on a face for H. G. Wells and mimicking his high-pitched voice and the sly look, "then Mr. Wells at once remarked, 'Oh, I don't know, Maura. If we all took Victor Cazelet into the garden and shot him, we'd feel pretty nervous afterwards.'"

Noel Coward was in London playing *Conversation Piece* with Yvonne Printemps, whom Lynn found one of the most interesting of "fascinators" because of the curious discrepancy between her strong animal sexuality and her "tall, thin, child's body." After *Conversation Piece* opened, Noel got a letter from a duchess saying she wanted him to arrange for Yvonne Printemps to sing at a party. Could he give her an idea of how reasonable her fees were? Noel said she had two performances the day of the party and would be too tired to sing later but he was sure he could arrange for her services on some other occasion. As for the fee, oh she charged reasonable prices: 500 pounds for the first song, and 250 pounds for each additional song.

They encountered J. M. Barrie at the dress rehearsal of *Conversation Piece*. The rehearsal went on until two in the morning and they gave Barrie a lift home in their limousine.

"When we got there," Lynn recalls, "he insisted that we come up and see his flat. We couldn't resist, though we knew he liked going to bed early. It was indescribably beautiful—lots of books, a great inglenook, a marvelous chimney corner, queer shaped rooms, mostly green, and great bow windows looking out onto the Thames. He was shy and sweet and sly and quite adorable. A week later he had us to a simple supper of cold corned beef, salad, fruit, and rice pudding. He told us a story about a little boy who went to see *Peter Pan*. The minute he got to his seat, he stood up and looked around the audience of children and then announced in a very loud voice, 'I'm not going to clap when Tinker Bell is dying.' When Peter came on he yelled out, 'I'm not going to clap, Peter, I'm not going to clap.' And then when the great moment arrived and Peter said, 'You do believe in fairies, don't you?' the audience clapped uproariously. And when the applause had died down, a triumphant voice was heard to say, 'I didn't clap.' "

But their happiest social conquest was of W. Graham Robertson, then sixty-eight years old, a pre-Raphaelite painter, poet, playwright, charmer, *flaneur*, conversationalist. He withdrew from the contemporary world around 1914 as he considered it was becoming vulgar and brutalized. He hadn't seen a play since 1912 when Ellen Terry retired. He was a dedicated recluse. He made a career of reclusion. He had very few friends and these cherished him as if he were a rare specimen of Chinese porcelain.

In 1931, Woollcott, returning from London, told the Lunts, "Well I've met the most enchanting man that ever lived. Graham Robertson. English writer." Aleck sneered in his mock-hostile tone. "Of course, *you'll* never meet him, I'm delighted to say. You don't stand a chance. He never sees anybody. Graham Robertson's the hardest Englishman to meet. No—Kipling is. Of course, you'll never meet Kipling either. Nobody has ever met him. Even I have never met Kipling."

"I am sorry to destroy you, Aleck, dear," Lynn said. "But I have met Kipling."

"I was referring to Rudyard Kipling, the author," Aleck said sharply.

"We met him when we were doing *Caprice* in London."

"How did two strolling players, two wandering minstrels come to meet Kipling?"

She explained that Lady Bland-Sutton, who had known her during her ingénue days, had given a party for them in the "Persian Garden" of her Belgravia house. (The "Persian Garden" was a drawing room whose floor was in a mosaic of tile with an oriental motif.) Kipling was among the guests.

Hamish Hamilton brought about the meeting between the Lunts and the "most enchanting man in England." The first work published by Hamilton in 1931 was Robertson's book of reminiscences, *Time Was*. Hamilton was a friend of the Lunts. He knew Robertson would like

Reunion in Vienna and persuaded him to break his rule and go to the theatre. Robertson fell victim to the "glamourie" of Lynn and Alfred. He told a friend that he "had never been reduced to such a state of helpless idiocy since the days of Ada Rehan, who could raise one to heaven in heavy, witless, and vulgar German-American farces, to avoid seeing which one would normally have paid large sums. I also realized that even Ada never concealed all the machinery so triumphantly as the Lunts. . . ."

Hamilton took him backstage. He wore his *capa*, and was in a state of bliss which he did not conceal. He came to see the play many times and Lynn and Alfred loved him. He came to worship the Lunts, calling them The Ineffables, The Adorables, The Immortals. Alan Dent, drama critic and friend of Robertson, said that he "had a divine gift of making people expose themselves."

Lynn and Alfred often went to Sandhills, Robertson's country place. He lived in a rambling old farmhouse with many servants but no electricity, running water, telephone or radio. He hated all such "modern" improvements. As Dent once phrased it, he "was a drifting spar of the 19th century." In the evening, illumination was provided by candles. If you wanted hot water, you rang for a servant, who brought you a basin. If you wanted a bath, servants filled an iron tub with warm water and you took a hip bath. Robertson was a dedicated rose grower and liked raising other flowers, fruits, and vegetables. He was an apiarist and produced his own honey. He had cattle for milk and chickens for eggs and pigs for meat. He even made his own wine, a bitter doleful *pinot noir* which he dubbed Chateau Sandhills. His friends humored him by drinking it and pretending to like it.

Among the animals he bred was a species of longhaired sheepdog. Every year, Robertson sheared his dogs—and then had their hair woven into a tweedlike cloth, out of which he had his jackets made!

Once, he gave Lynn a lovely necklace of beryl stones, and told her, "Wear them always—but if you hear the sound of weeping, take them off instantly and put them away and you will break the spell of some evil that is about to befall you and the people you love."

But Lynn was afraid to do this and she never wore the necklace, not once.

Robertson was drawn to the Lunts because they shared his love of nature, animals, children, growing things, quiet, and solitude, and "yet they are full of humor and fun." He loved to quote Lynn's remark when he was showing her around his vegetable patch one afternoon.

"It is curious," she remarked as she regarded a row of cabbages, "that people do not realize what *fun* it is to be a vegetable!"

Unexpected things upset Robertson. "He was a very strange man," Alfred says. "I remember once describing some trees that grow in Grenna, Sweden. They are lilac trees and they are trained to grow in the shape of umbrellas, and they line the streets and have lamps set in them and are most beautiful at night. Well, for some reason, this annoyed the hell out of Graham."

"He was always jealous of something he hadn't got in his own garden, you see," Lynn adds.

"And he insisted there were some lilac trees in Hyde Park trained like umbrellas and even bigger than the ones in Grenna, which he'd never seen. He was very cross. 'I want you both to come with me and see them now,' he said, and so we three wandered all around Hyde Park, miles and miles, while Graham was trying to remember just where those umbrella lilacs were planted and finally he found a few scrubby little lilac bushes and said, 'You see, there they are,' and I said, 'They are very pretty indeed,' but they weren't even comparable to the Swedish lilacs. I didn't dare say so. I don't know what he'd have done—probably imported hundreds of lilac trees from Sweden."

When it was time to return home, in June, Alfred wrote to Graham Robertson: "I am six foot two and have been on the stage for 20 years but in the last act tonight when Lynn said, 'You'll be traveling in the morning,' * I burst into noisy sobs. It will give you a rough idea of how I feel about leaving England."

* An actual line in *Reunion in Vienna*.

FIFTEEN

A CRISIS WITH COWARD—A SUCCESS
WITH SHAKESPEARE

*T*wo PROBLEMS troubled Alfred that summer, one, artistic, the other, agricultural. He was unable to grow good stringbeans. He could grow strawberries and raspberries by the bushel; on good days he picked thirty quarts. His tomatoes and cucumbers flourished, as did his radishes, parsley, corn, turnips and potatoes, but he couldn't get anywhere with the stringbeans. "I can't grow good beans and it breaks my heart," he wrote to Woollcott.

His artistic problem was to learn the accordion. Their next play was Noel Coward's *Point Valaine*. Lynn was to play Linda Valaine, a lusty mature woman. Alfred was Stefan, bartender and waiter in her Caribbean hotel. Stefan was also her lover. He was a Russian. He played the accordion. As we have seen, Alfred was not one of your actors who will fake some instrument while, offstage, a member of the musicians union is really playing. "The saxophone," he informed Aleck, "was a cinch compared to this goddam thing. I have to learn the accordion for *Point Valaine* and it's breaking my heart. My practising, however, is a great joy to my niece and nephew—they beg to hear me and roll around on the floor when I strike a sour note—they wait for the sound and simply scream with delight when it pops out—this goes on for hours—and is breaking me down—awful."

They were so close to *Point Valaine* that they couldn't be detached about it. Noel had told them the plot and even recited some of the speeches as he was making it up back in London, and "by the time he had finished," Lynn wrote, "we knew as much about it as if we had written it and were as little able to judge its chances of success—but we think it is good. Alfred's sister, Karin, read it, and proceeded to have a miscarriage right away—which may or may not be a good omen." *

Coward directed the play which was well cast and mounted, Osgood Perkins playing a writer and Louis Hayward making his American debut as a young man with whom Lynn has an intense sexual interlude. Perkins, now remembered (if he is remembered at all) as the father of Tony Perkins, was, in his time, one of the finest players of saturnine sophisticates. According to Noel, things did not go well from the first, and he and Lynn and Alfred "were irritable with each other, which we had never been before." Much of the action took place during a tropical rainstorm. The rain machine went berserk at the dress rehearsal and it rained and rained and rained and the machine couldn't be shut off until the entire stage was flooded. It had to be abandoned.

They opened on Christmas Eve in Boston. The audience had come to see a light-hearted comedy by Noel Coward in which the Lunts would happily disport themselves. They witnessed a tragedy of sex. Their Lynn was sleeping with a dirty savage Russian who doesn't say clever things because he mostly grunts. And their Alfred was this dirty Russian and he also spit full in Lynn's face twice during the play. Audiences were hostile. You could feel the resentment radiating from them like a physical, a tactile phenomenon. It was a horrible experience for the Lunts to feel they were actually hated by the audience. The audience would not allow them to be serious actors, driven to explore the many facets of human existence. As a play, *Point Valaine*, in its savage examination of the sexual drive, was twenty-five years ahead of its time, and one had to wait for Tennessee Williams to create an audience for such stories. It was a good play, one of Noel's finest. And Lynn's performance was simply stupendous. Not Jeanne Eagles, not Lenore Ulric ever played a siren more powerfully than Lynn in this play.

She once explained to me, "When you are playing a woman with heavy sex appeal and you don't produce that sex on the stage, then you have failed as an actress. When I played Linda Valaine, I imagined I had slept with ten different men in the previous year and I found I could produce this quality."

Point Valaine was doomed on Broadway. The Lunts began frantically seeking another play. They were desperate. Alfred wrote Graham, "I wish Bob [Sherwood] would write one for us—something with a lot of music & costumes & dash & go—something even with villains

* In a letter to Woollcott.

and a death scene—Lynn gets so upset when I die on the stage and it's enormous fun for me."

Guthrie McClintic was contemplating an all-star production of *Candida.* His wife, Katharine Cornell, would play Candida, Burgess Meredith would play Marchbanks, Alfred would play Reverend Morell and Lynn would play Miss Prism, a minor though significant character in the charade. Lynn, being a star of a magnitude equal to that of Mrs. McClintic, asked Guthrie, "But why should Kit play Candida and I Miss Prism? Why shouldn't I play Candida and she Miss Prism?"

With diplomatic brilliance, McClintic replied, "Lynn, you would make a superb Candida—but, you see, Kit couldn't play Miss Prism!"

They didn't accept the play.

Finding a good play in which the leading roles were equally balanced was becoming more and more difficult. When, some years later, Howard Lindsay and Russel Crouse made their adaptation of *Life With Father,* producer Oscar Serlin offered the Lunts the play. Serlin once said, "A producer always starts trying to get Alfred Lunt and Lynn Fontanne for his play and he is eventually happy to finish up with anybody on the stage." They read the play.

"I've been seducing you in the theatre for fifteen years," Alfred said. "Here's a chance to marry, settle down, and have children. I think it's about time."

"After all these years," Lynn replied, "I don't think I'd want to spend every evening wondering whether or not you're going to get baptized. No, thank you very much."

Lawrence Langner was not exactly broken-hearted over the failure of *Point Valaine.* He had "never given up hope that one day they (the Lunts) would return to the Guild." The Guild was sorely beset that season. Out of six shows (five plays and a musical revue) they had staged to meet their obligations to the subscribers, not a single one had succeeded. Now was the time to come a-courting Lynn and Alfred, and Langner came with Helen Westley and sang sweet songs of giving them artistic freedom and a choice of plays. They could even do Shakespeare, he promised, for he knew that doing *Twelfth Night, Troilus and Cressida,* or *The Taming of the Shrew* was close to their hearts.

They returned to the arms of the Guild.

The Taming of the Shrew was to be their first venture. They dreamed of a completely new acting version. When they got home after talking with Langner backstage they at once sat down and each wrote his ideas. They threw out every traditional conception. All revivals of the play went back to David Garrick's production, using his cuts and scene arrangements and his prompt script. The Augustin Daly-Ada Rehan version and the Ada Rehan-Otis Skinner version were both variants of Garrick's script, in which an arrogant woman is subdued by the physical superiority of a man and is rendered a helpless Victorian maiden. The Lunts would have none of this. They showed their outline to Alexander Woollcott and to Margaret Anglin, who had been a memorable Katharine in a 1914 production of the *Shrew*. They were both encouraging. "All we did," Alfred wrote Graham Robertson, "was to take a play and put it on as you would a brand-new script. There is no business indicated except 'strikes him' and 'enter' and 'exit.' So we just did what we thought was appropriate, amusing, or picturesque. Neither of us had seen the play since we were children, so we had no tradition to fall back on and then why should one? We did not jazz it up either. In fact, I think we play it as it was written —a troupe of actors playing for a drunken tinker."

The program read, "Directed by Harry Wagstaff Gribble, from a scheme of production devised by Mr. Lunt and Miss Fontanne."

They played the Induction scene—in which the drunken Christopher Sly is discovered by the lord and his huntsmen—which was usually left out of modern revivals. Sly was retained as a motif throughout the play, which was done with a simple setting but a carnival riot of costumes. It opened with a sort of circus parade led by dwarfs and then acrobats and tumblers and Sidney Greenstreet beating a bass drum and a girl riding in a cart and playing a harp. Alfred came on riding a "horse" (two men in a horse costume). Alfred's hat was tricked out not with a feather but with a whole rooster.

Stark Young, writing in *The New Republic*, praised their daring and imagination. They had shown not "irreverence" toward the Bard of Avon, but the truest reverence, because "they believe in the delight inherent in the piece they undertake for us, in the deep power of joyous humor; and they know that nothing is less Shakespeare than a good deal of the Shakespeare tradition. . . . They were quite right to invest that play within the play with a contrasting palatial elegance and rich riot. Such was the renaissance and nobody could know that better than Shakespeare. Such was England, bawdy, magnificent, dirt and brocades."

Their stage direction* for the wedding scene describes the snow and

* The prompt script is in the Theatre Collection of the New York Public Library.

wind noises and adds, "The churchbells shiver. So does the church music. So should everything throughout the scene until after the ceremony."

Their stage direction for the end of Act I is "Music-Bells-Bagpipes-Acrobats-Ring-Around-the-Rosy and What have you?"

The Lunts made of *Taming of the Shrew* a carnival of a performance. When Shaw first saw the Lunts in *Caprice*, Langner asked him, "Would you like to meet Alfred and Lynn backstage and congratulate them on their acting?"

To which Shaw replied, "It is more than acting. It is performing."

They indulged in the most outrageous and rollicking acts of amorous sadism they had practiced since *At Mrs. Beam's*. She broke a lute over his head, threw plates at him, bit him, ground her heel into his foot. She did everything but knee him in the groin, and would have done that if they hadn't felt there had to be a limit to everything. As for Petruchio, he threw her on the floor, dragged her around, pulled her, slapped her, kicked her in the rump, sat on her stomach, and at one point literally kicked the breath out of her body. And it never looked like play acting when the Lunts were beating each other up. It was a reasonably frightening facsimile of the real thing. It was a case of all hell breaking loose in Padua, observed Joseph Wood Krutch in *The Nation*.

Lynn has always regarded Kate as one of the most difficult roles of her career, because "she's supposed to be fiery but her actual lines are not really at all hot." Beyond this there was the simple fact that our conception of woman has changed so much that the David Garrick version would have been ridiculous. In the "transformation" scene Lynn gave it a tongue-in-cheek treatment, implying, ever so slyly, that her spirit had not been broken, that though she finally was in love with Petruchio at the close she considered herself his equal and would never be a slave to his whip.

The play ran for 129 performances. Lunt thought the 127th performance was ragged and called a complete rehearsal—everything, music cues, light cues, all the stagehands—though there remained only two performances.

Crouse, then publicity man for the Guild, remarks, "This is real love of theatre—to want to do the best possible performance you can even though you know you're closing tonight." Was it "love"? Or was there an element in Alfred's nature, a demon of the absolute, which seized him and changed him into another person before your eyes? When this "second man" took over, Alfred would become like one possessed, flying into terrible rages, brooking no opposition or criticism, hearing nothing, caring for nothing, thinking only of some "ideal" performance, driving his company of actors as relentlessly as he drove himself, screaming at stagehands, at scenic designers, at the whole world which could not understand his own vision of perfection. To the actors in *The Taming of the Shrew* who were not possessed of Alfred's divine urges, his calling a complete rehearsal the last day of a run was a useless torture.

In September, 1935, he was made a member of the Board of Directors of the Theatre Guild. Alfred now hoped he would learn the financial secrets of theatrical production. But meetings of the board began at half-past four, and Alfred had to leave at six or six-thirty because he was playing. So the other directors saw to it that fiscal problems were not raised until it was time for Alfred to depart. "I never did get to hear one bloody word of the financial side of the theatre," he says, "though I got to see some statements of costs on the productions." But he learned no financial secrets. The inner workings of the Theatre Guild still remained a mystery. He ceased attending meetings, and, in 1940, he tendered his formal resignation, asking that it be kept "entirely confidential" as "I would like to slip away as quietly as possible."

Looking back over their association with the Theatre Guild, the Lunts believe that the Guild was, on balance, a powerful force for good in the American theatre, though it had great defects, defects not of theory but in the personalities of those who ran the organization. They were arrogantly critical of playwrights and they were unnecessarily cruel in their treatment of actors, "many of whom came away with inferiority complexes for the rest of their lives." But the Lunts continued to play for the Guild because "it changed the shape and sound of the whole English-speaking theatre. It raised the tone of the theatre. It produced plays that were literature, plays that were written by good writers, plays that had a mind back of them. The directors, they were all people with a vision. Yes, they were bitches and bastards and all this, that, and the other, but they had a vision in 1919 and they made it come true. And in a business way, they were honest. If they made a promise, they kept it. You got paid on time. They lived up to the letter of their contracts. They never asked us to take a salary cut. There was only one promise they broke. We did not wish to be starred in their plays—but only on condition that nobody else was starred. Well, we were out on the road with *The Guardsman* and *Arms and the Man* and we came into Cleveland and we were signing into the hotel when we looked around and there in the lobby was a poster advertising George Gaul and Florence Eldridge starring in *The Guardsman,* which the Guild had sent on tour. We put down the pens and didn't sign the hotel registration. We telephoned them and Terry and Lawrence came out right away and they assured us it was a mistake and they burned all the posters, so, you see, they were honorable people."

SIXTEEN

MILTON BERLE GIVES
ACTING LESSONS

*M*ILTON BERLE, master-of-ceremonies at the Paradise cabaret on Broadway during the winter of 1936, had become conscious of a tall, handsome gentleman who came, accompanied by a beautiful and elegant lady, night after night, occupied the same ringside table, and laughed at all his jokes with gusto. One evening, the headwaiter told Berle that an Alfred Lunt would like him to sit at his table after the floorshow. Berle was naturally gratified by this unexpected admirer. After he was introduced to Alfred and Lynn, Alfred said, "Mr. Berle, you could do me a favor."

"*Me* do *you* a favor?" Berle replied. It was as unbelievable as T. S. Eliot asking Nick Kenny for help in versification.

"I am going into rehearsal in a new play by Robert Sherwood. I am playing a night-club performer, a song-and-dance man, and he does introductions rather like the sort you do, Mr. Berle. I think your timing is brilliant. I have been studying you. But I can't get your moves right. Do you suppose we could meet a few times and perhaps you'd show me how to do that swagger you do and how you snap your fingers? Just the moves and how you work yourself up into the proper frame of mind before you enter."

Alfred paid four or five visits to Berle and was tutored in the tricks of the trade. Later, Sophie Tucker coached him in the art of night-club singing. Alfred once remarked, "I envisage Harry Van as a guy with a pastyfaced expression—the look you see on men around Times Square who don't get out enough into the air. A man with black shiny hair, slicked back, with a few white streaks. I spend an hour before each performance covering my hair and face with grease to get just the effect I want. Perhaps it's foolish. I could get away with hardly any make-up, but it wouldn't *feel* the same."

For years, Alfred had been badgering Sherwood, Noel Coward, and Behrman to write a play in which the Lunts would play a husband-and-wife vaudeville mindreading act. They couldn't do it, though Sherwood attempted to sketch out a story. Then Alfred said he would also like to play a song-and-dance man, like Harry Richman. Sherwood discarded the notion but it lay in his unconscious and apparently germinated slowly. Sherwood, like most of the hedonists of the 1920's, was shaken by the Depression, the violence of fascism, and the danger of another world war. The idea of writing another light-hearted sex comedy like *Reunion in Vienna* repelled him. Behrman has described Sherwood's evolution into a "fiercely militant liberal . . . an impassioned New Dealer . . . a fanatical devotee of Franklin D. Roosevelt." He wanted to write a play against war, against fascism, against the international trade in munitions, against the "merchants of death." Alfred's yearning to play a Harry Richman character fused with Sherwood's hatred of war.

The creative personality works in mysterious ways. While going to Europe, once, Sherwood made a shipboard acquaintance, who told him of the mixture of nationalities living in the leading hotel of Harbin, Manchuria, and how these refugees, people without even passports, were always looking up at the sky waiting for the bombers that would start the next war. The following year, Sherwood went to a Budapest cabaret, the Club Arizona, and saw an American act—a troupe of six dancers and a hoofer. They were stranded in *mitteleuropa*, trying to work their way back to the States. The images combined and recombined, shifted and changed patterns in his creative kaleidoscope, and out of it emerged *Idiot's Delight*. The year 1935 was Sherwood's *annus mirabilis*. He had fallen in love with Madeline Hurlock (formerly married to Marc Connelly). He divorced Mary Sherwood in Latvia and married Madeline in Budapest. In one year he finished *The Petrified Forest*, adapted Jacques Deval's *Tovarich*, wrote the screenplay for *The Ghost Goes West*, dramatized *Pride and Prejudice*, and, in two weeks of impassioned writing, composed all three acts of *Idiot's Delight*.

The Lunts began rehearsing *Idiot's Delight* while they were playing Katharine and Petruchio. They were afraid that if Hitler or Mussolini were to die the play would lose its immediate impact, "although the story is quite separate from that and does not depend at all on politics." * Bretaigne Windust, the Lucio of the *Shrew* company, was made director, because they liked his ideas, though he worked closely under

* Letter from Lynn to Graham Robertson.

the "supervision" of Lynn and Alfred. Most of the actors were cast right from the players in *The Taming of the Shrew.*

But there were no chorus girls playing Shakespeare, and they needed six of them, known as "Les Blondes." Since Russel Crouse had written musical comedy librettos, Alfred asked him where he could get six chorus girls in a hurry. Crouse knew Jacqueline Paige, who had danced in *Anything Goes;* she was amused by the idea of "Les Blondes" and said she would be able to lay her hands on five other dancing girls. Miss Paige was a brunette. Alfred said the role called for a blonde.

"For you, Mr. Lunt," she promised, "I'll dip my head in the barrel every night."

It was Miss Paige who taught him to tap-dance. By the time the rehearsals were done, Alfred was able to do quite an impressive time-step and had learned all the brash mannerisms and the kinetic vocalizing of, respectively, Milton Berle and Sophie Tucker. It was acting within acting. He had first to act a convincing song-and-dance man, and then he had to act the character of this hoofer involved in a social and personal situation. An insight into Alfred's genius as a director and his own secret of creating truth in acting is revealed by a suggestion he made to Richard Whorf. Whorf played Quillery, a French communist working for a "united front" against war and fascism. The action took place in a ski resort in the Italian Alps, where a group of persons are stranded. Whorf had a scene in which he had to spew out his disgust at fascism while fighting with several fascist army officers. He was having trouble with it and told Alfred he couldn't get enough emotion into the speech.

Alfred said: "Under the words you're speaking, try *thinking,* 'you son-of-a-bitch, you son-of-a-bitch, you son-of-a-bitch,' and I think you'll get the emotion you want."

During the rehearsals Lynn became depressed about her role of Irene, the mistress of the munitions maker. She was playing her like Valentina, the vivacious Russian-born costume designer who was a good friend of the Lunts. But Lynn didn't feel a rapport with Irene, at first. Irene seemed entirely too theatrical and manufactured. Outwardly, Irene was "interesting," but she had no inward reality for Lynn, and Lynn couldn't relax in a role that was so artificial. Katharine had been the same sort of part. Oh, how she longed for a role that was true and good, and that she could enjoy playing. But she didn't say anything to Alfred. She had to work out the problems of Irene by herself. And this, after all, was inevitable when one played "in double harness"; one season she would have the better role, as in *Elizabeth the Queen,* and another season it would be Alfred's, as in *Idiot's Delight.* And yet how thin and unresolved Irene's part of the action seemed. Langner, watching a run-through, suggested that the love story of Irene and Harry Van was not related to the "serious implications of the coming war." Lynn, Langner reported, solved the problem by suggesting that Sherwood write a new scene between her and the munitions maker. Her denunciations of her rich old lover became an artistic balance to her revelation of her love for the cabaret emcee.

Harry Van is sure he and Irene have met many years before, when she was in a Russian vaudeville act and he was doing a mindreading act, and he suspects Irene isn't really a blonde. (Lynn wore a blonde wig in a page-boy bob.) Van's line went, "No matter how much you may lie, you can't deny the fact that you slept with me in the Governor Bryan Hotel in Omaha in the fall of 1925!"

The dress rehearsal in Washington, D.C., was a shambles. Actors fluffed lines; cues were missed; the sound effects—air-raid sirens, roar of planes, crash of bombs—were bungled. Alfred was keeping himself under control, but in the last scene, in which he plays the piano while he and Lynn are sipping champagne, he suddenly blew up. The demon took over. He got up, his face turning red, and smashed his glass of champagne against the piano. Slivers of crystal flew all over. Everybody watched him, in dead silence. He was frightening to see. His eyes were cold and hard. "We will now *start* to rehearse," he said, grimly. "From the beginning. Places, please." It was now three in the morning, and everybody was dead tired, but he was flailing at them with his invisible whip and so they all—the cast of thirty-five plus fourteen stagehands plus stage manager and assistant stage manager plus three sound effects technicians—began rehearsing. He worked them until eight in the morning, and they were to open that night at the National Theatre.

And open they did, giving a stupendous performance which brought them sixteen curtain calls. But Alfred was still seething. Later that week, Crouse, on a publicity assignment from the Theatre Guild, came down to take pictures for the New York papers. Lynn wanted to pose on Thursday and Alfred said Friday. The pressure was too much for them and they began shouting at each other. Crouse thought he had better go away until they calmed down. He returned an hour later and suggested they go out to supper at Harvey's Sea Food Restaurant, which they did. In the middle of supper, Lynn narrowed her eyes and said, "Alfred, I should not be sitting here. I'm mad at you. I shouldn't even be speaking to you."

And with that she rose, marched over to an empty table, and ordered a waiter to bring the remains of her supper. She finished her meal in solitary hauteur.

The next stop before Broadway was a week's engagement at the Nixon Theatre in Pittsburgh, beginning Monday, March 16. Spring came early that year and the waters of the Allegheny and Monongahela had been rising for three weeks. Pittsburgh is at the confluence of these two rivers, where they join to become the Ohio River, which flows into the Mississippi. The Nixon Theatre was in the "Golden Triangle," the heart of the shopping and amusement district. It was under several inches of water when they came. By Monday, the Nixon's basement was flooded, but they played to a good house, though many waded through several inches of water to get there.

By Tuesday all trains in and out of Pittsburgh were canceled. The telephones were dead. Telegraph service was stopped and there was no mail delivery. The water was unsafe to drink. There was no hot water in the hotels. Three of "Les Blondes" came down with intestinal malaise from drinking the water. Then all the electricity failed. But they gave a show anyway on Tuesday and on Wednesday, though automobiles and street cars were in water up to the roofs. The stage-hands improvised an auxiliary power service to light the show. In one scene with "Les Blondes," even the auxiliary power failed, and Alfred lit his cigarette lighter so they could finish the number. The various actors were scattered in different hotels—the William Penn, the Fort Pitt, and the Pittsburgher. The Lunts had a suite with kitchenette at the Schenley.

Some of the actors were panicking. They wanted to get out of town by car or train or boat. After the Wednesday performance, which they played to 100 people, most of whom had come in rowboats, the cast had an emergency meeting with the Lunts. Several spokesmen demanded that they cancel all performances at once.

"As long as there is a single customer in the house, we shall play," Lynn said firmly.

Alfred, like a general under fire, rose to the occasion. He calmed the hysterical and fed the hungry. "Those who can't get back to their hotels tonight will either be put up at our place or can sleep here in the theatre," he said.

"We have a responsibility to those who have paid for their tickets and waited to see us. And now let's not have any more talk of quitting. Let's all of us come and have supper," Lynn added. Everybody got into hip boots and trooped over to the Schenley.

"The Lunts had prepared for the refugees a large dinner of beef stew which was the only thing they [Lynn and Alfred] could cook on one gas burner, but everyone was raving about the far-famed Lunt cuisine," noted the actor Alan Hewitt in his diary.

Only when martial law was declared and the police would not let ticket-holders through the lines, did the Lunts close the show. It took them twenty-two hours to get to Pennsylvania Station. They opened in New York to an enthusiastic audience and beautiful reviews. But Sherwood was not elated by the tone of the critics. They praised *Idiot's Delight* as entertainment, but they had not been able to see it as a call to action against the warmongers and the fascists. Lynn tried to console Sherwood, saying one ought never to read reviews because "no matter how they praise you, they'll always find something to say which is offensive and it is just this bad thing which remains in your mind and you forget the good things in the reviews."

Sherwood was somewhat placated when *Idiot's Delight* won the Pulitzer Prize for 1936.

They were doing capacity business, but Alfred felt comfortable only when there were standees. "Al," Crouse says, "is nervous about even a single empty seat. He goes nuts. He pictures the play closing next week. The poorhouse is waiting for the Lunts. I used to tell him there were plenty of hits that ran a year without selling out but it didn't comfort him. One day I saw a few empties. I was afraid Al would be upset. I remembered in *Mourning Becomes Electra* there was a dummy used as General Mannon in a wheelchair. General Mannon was still down in the basement."

Crouse got the General some modern clothes and stood him up in the back of the house. Then he went backstage and told Alfred that they had standees. Alfred was pleased. After the performance, he told Crouse, "There was one standee who was so interested in the play, why, he hardly moved during the whole performance. Most gratifying."

It was only when they went on tour—and they toured *Idiot's Delight* many times during the next years—that they encountered censorship troubles. In San Antonio, the Legion of Decency wanted the play cut in sixteen places and the title changed, since they said it implied that God was an idiot. There was worse trouble in Omaha, scene of the brief encounter between Harry Van and Irene in the Governor

Bryan Hotel in 1925. The first intimation of trouble came when they were playing Des Moines. Lawrence Farrell was informed by the Drama League of Omaha, sponsor of the local engagement, that the mayor had said that unless *Idiot's Delight* was a lot less sexually delightful the show would not go on. (Farrell, a stocky urbane gentleman, has been the business arm of the Lunts since 1930. He had originally been hired as Alfred's dresser. The first morning he made them toast and coffee for breakfast. They declared it was the finest coffee they had ever tasted and he has worked for them happily ever since.)

The mayor was convinced it was an obscene play. He did not think it was nice for a man, even in a play, to sleep with a woman he wasn't married to. And if such acts had to take place, it was certainly an insult to the sovereign state of Nebraska that they should take place in Omaha. The mayor insisted on a number of cuts and above all the deletion of this line, "No matter how much you may lie, you can't deny the fact that you slept with me in the Governor Bryan Hotel in the fall of 1925. (*Irene laughs heartily again.*)" Dorothy Parker called it "Idiot's Delete."

Alfred despatched a frantic telegram to Woollcott:

WE BROKE THE RECORD HERE IN DES MOINES WITH A FEW DOLLARS LESS THAN EIGHT THOUSAND IN ONE PERFORMANCE. TOMORROW WE GO TO OMAHA AND ALTHOUGH THE HOUSE IS SOLD OUT WE MAY NOT BE ABLE TO PLAY BECAUSE THE MAYOR THINKS IDIOT'S DELIGHT IS INDECENT. WE WISH YOU WERE NEAR AT HAND TO ADVISE US. WE ARE SEEING HIS HONOR TOMORROW BUT WE NEED YOUR WORDS. I HAVE GOTTEN OVER MY FLU AND I SUPPOSE THAT IS SOMETHING.

When they got to their Omaha hotel they at once began phoning Woollcott. They had originally intended to accept the censorship and make a curtain speech explaining the cuts. Woollcott was outraged. "I denounced them both as poltroons not fit to be trusted with a play by Sherwood or anybody else if they didn't have the gumption not to play at all," he told a friend. He gave them advice on what to tell the mayor.

Which Alfred did.

"Mr. Mayor," he said, "if you want any lines cut, you will have to speak to Mr. Sherwood. He has created these characters. Now we have played it all through the country. A play is a person's property, just as your house is your property. If anyone damaged your property, you could sue them. So it is illegal for me to tamper with Mr. Sherwood's property."

"Where is Mr. Sherwood?" asked the mayor.

"In Europe."

"How do I get in touch with him?"

"I don't know."

"We can't have any dirty shows in this town, sir."

"In that case," Alfred said curtly, "we will cancel the performance. Thank you. Good-by."

He stalked out. At the theatre, the electricians were setting up the overhead pipes of light bulbs. The scenery was already in place.

"Take the pipes down," Alfred said.

"What?" inquired George Greenberg, stage manager.

"Strike the set. There'll be no show."

"Why?"

"The mayor won't let us play unless we make cuts. We have refused to make the cuts."

The stagehands had begun dismantling the set and loading it into a truck when a committee of breathless ladies from the Drama League arrived and said they had been arguing with the mayor and he had finally agreed to let the show go on without deletions!

Alfred wired Woollcott:

THE PERFORMANCE LAST NIGHT A RIOT. NEVER SAW OR HEARD ANYTHING LIKE IT IN THE THEATRE. WHOLE THING SEEMED ONE GREAT FAMILY JOKE AND A PERSONAL PROTEST AGAINST CENSORSHIP. READ MAYOR'S SPEECH AFTER PLAY TO HOOTS, JEERS AND CATCALLS.

SEVENTEEN

CONVERSATIONS WITH ECKSTEIN

*B*EING CONVINCED, perhaps by General Mannon's dummy, that *Idiot's Delight* was a palpable hit, the Lunts decided it was high time they settled down in a permanent Manhattan domicile. For many years, they had been staying at hotels or apartment hotels. In April 1936, they leased a luxurious abode at 130 East 75th Street, where they lived and loved and entertained for a decade. As usual, they threw themselves into the delights of interior decorating with great gusto. For the master bedroom, Lynn, after some deliberation, concluded that since fate had made of two such morally impeccable persons as herself and Alfred the theatrical symbols of upper-class adultery, it was fitting they have a bed worthy of their reputation. She ordered a bed six feet long and six feet wide, adorned with a magnificent headboard.

"It is the best bed in America—and why not?" she inquired of Vivien Leigh.

The apartment—which boasted seven rooms—was painted in various colors. There were murals by Richard Whorf. The dining room walls were decorated with Swedish motifs and the drawing room was something to behold—unfinished pine woodwork and walls of "rich greeney blue," beige wall-to-wall carpets, white velour draperies.

"And crystal light fixtures on the walls, all over the walls and oh how I love them," Lynn wrote to Graham Robertson.

In these two rooms, during the next fifteen years, they gave many dinner and supper parties. Conversation was the chief pastime, for the Lunts believe with the Chinese writer Shih-Nai-An that "of all joys nothing brings more joy than friendship, and the most joyful part of friendship is quiet talk together among friends." The friend whose conversation delighted them most perhaps was Dr. Gustav Eckstein who was then and is now a professor of physiology at the medical college of the University of Cincinnati. He is a small man with a large head and thick glasses, shrewd eyes and a sly shy smile. Author of a famous biography of the biologist Noguchi, he has also written many amusing books about birds and animals. "Gus," Lynn explains, "is the greatest conversationalist I have ever known, the greatest inasmuch as he has the widest information on more subjects than anyone I ever knew. He knows something interesting about everything that ever comes up. I never stumped him once. He is of course terribly brilliant and yet he has a deep human sympathy. He looks about the size of a boy of fourteen. A strangely small body with such a large and handsome face. But it is his mind that draws you. He has the strangest way of seeing things and making them visible to you in a way you never saw them before. He studies human foibles. He talks so well, so brilliantly, that you find you have been listening to him three hours but weren't conscious of the time passing but only felt a mental excitement."

There was an instantaneous affinity between the Lunts and Eckstein. They first met at a dinner Woollcott gave in honor of the zoologist in 1936. Eckstein had just published *Canary*. Aleck cherished Eckstein's books as masterpieces, and Aleck would crusade for a favorite author as other men crusade for a social reform. The whole world had to love the books he loved. He sent the Lunts a copy of *Canary* and warned them that if they did not love the book they could consider their friendship with Woollcott finished.

They loved *Canary*. When they met Eckstein at Aleck's house he seemed rather quiet and withdrawn. He left early, but an hour later, there was a phone call for Lynn at Aleck's. It was Eckstein. Rather timidly, he said he had liked her and Alfred and hoped they could meet again.

When Harper & Brothers accepted the manuscript of *Noguchi*, they had asked the author for the usual autobiographical sketch and he wrote the following: "Born, practised dentistry, studied medicine, taught physiology, learned not much, read two or three men, learned a little, came to know two or three women, learned a good deal, made friends with two rats, learned prodigiously, wrote about the rats, continued to write."

Whether it was his experiences with rats or with women, Eckstein remained a bachelor.

After the meeting at Woollcott's, the friendship ripened rapidly, though Eckstein lived and worked in Ohio and came to New York infrequently. "We never asked anybody else to the house when Gus was visiting us," Lynn says. "Since we had so little time with him and that time so precious, we could not afford to waste any time when he came to New York and we never asked anyone else to come over when he was with us for if we had invited other people we would have been talking to them and not to him."

A sense of empathy with animals was one of the bonds between Lynn and Eckstein. Lynn's rapport with animals was manifested when she was a baby. Wandering away from home when she was merely three, she didn't come back at night and a search got under way. She was finally discovered fast asleep sharing the kennel of a ferocious German shepherd dog, the terror of the neighborhood. She and the dog were curled up against each other. No one, not even the dog's master, was able to go in and get her, as the dog menaced all those who came near. So she slept with the beast all night.

During their 1933 tour of Russia they had also visited Finland, and one day, near Hansko, had taken a lengthy promenade in a forest, where they were set upon by several wolves, who showed their teeth and indicated they were sizing up the Lunts as a dinner possibility. Lynn murmured soothing words to the four or five wolves and they kept their distance and stared and finally Lynn and Alfred slowly walked away. "I assumed," Lynn explains, "that since they hadn't attacked us at once, we weren't exactly to their taste. They had smelled us out and we were not a prey they liked. So if we didn't startle them or make them think we were going to attack them, they wouldn't mind our going about our business—and they didn't."

Eckstein's empathy with animals extended beyond the usual dogs and cats to include mice, rats, turtles, parrots, pigeons, and even cockroaches. He was a scientist and a clinical experimenter but he was also a man of feeling. Woollcott compared him to St. Francis. He said Eckstein's most important piece of laboratory equipment was his "listening heart. If you must also have a name for the medium, the temperature, the conditioned atmosphere in which the observations are made, only one occurs to me. The word is 'love.' "

Lynn says: "All his friends took their broken animals to Gus and he healed them. Somebody's cat once had a raw place on a paw and it got infected and would not heal and the cat was to die in a few days but Gus put something on it that healed it and I don't believe it was only the medicine he put on it—but it was the love he gave the cat. I think one of the most wonderful things anybody ever did for a friend was what Gus did for me when I had a little dachshund, Elsa. She was very fond of Gus. She was close to me and walked wherever I walked, followed me in and out of rooms, and stayed by my feet when I sat down. She was always backstage, waiting in the dressing room, and she would know when it was time for me to exit and come pattering out and wait for me in the wings. Gus was the only other person she would accept. Then she became very ill, for she was quite old. We had to go on the road and she was too sick to go with us. I telephoned Gus and told him the situation and he said, 'Don't worry. We'll let Elsa stay with Marguerite [a servant at Genesee Depot] until she is uncomfortable, and when she's uncomfortable, I'll take a plane and go and put her out humanely, the way we would all like to go—without pain, without tasting death.' And it happened. He called the house each day to get a report on Elsa and when she got bad and was in great pain, he flew to Milwaukee and went on to the farm and he put her on his lap and he gave her a shot which made her sleep and then something stronger and then she did not wake up again."

He often came to Wisconsin for visits, sometimes in summer or spring, sometimes in winter, when the snow was knee-high and the weather was 20 below zero for weeks at a time. He loved taking long walks with the dog and with Lynn and Alfred and he "discoursed beautifully" about all things, both great and small. The present dog, Lisa, also a dachshund, met Eckstein when she was new to the household and suspicious of everyone. Eckstein came in the front door. Lisa stood on top of the stairs, studying him. He peered up at her. Then he held out his hand. She slowly descended and smelled his hand and she was his friend at once. The following morning she made as great a fuss over him as she made over Lynn. Then he was away for a year.

"And," Lynn says, "when he came back she remembered him. She still loved him and loves him to this day."

EIGHTEEN

ROBERT SHERWOOD'S REVELATION

*I*N FEBRUARY, 1940, the Lunts, who had just completed two years on the road, returned to Broadway in a one-week revival of *The Taming of the Shrew* at the Alvin Theatre, for the benefit of the Finnish Relief Fund. On the closing night, Robert E. Sherwood came backstage. He said, "Here is a new play I have just finished. It is called *Revelation.*" Lynn and Alfred presumed it was still another revision of *Acropolis,* an old play about the Peleponnesian Wars. Sherwood had written it in 1933 and had been revising it constantly. It had never been produced in America. It had failed in London. The Lunts had never liked *Acropolis,* for it lacked characters and dramatic color; it was an intellectual dialogue between "Athenian democracy" and "Spartan totalitarianism." Nevertheless they packed *Revelation* in one of their suitcases. They promised to read it at once, but now they had to rush to Pennsylvania Station. They were taking the midnight sleeper to Chicago.

For the first time in many years, the Lunts were not looking for a new play. They didn't even want to read a new play. They were exhausted as they had never been before.

In the last five years, they had worked harder than any American actors before them. They had created four new plays, all difficult, all intricate—plays of Sherwood, Giraudoux, Chekhov, Shakespeare. They had traveled the length and breadth of the country, making a thousand-and-one night stands, bringing the living theatre to cities that hadn't seen a Broadway play since the road died in 1930, playing in towns where there were no longer legitimate theatres, often playing in places where there were only four walls and a ceiling.

"The SPCA wouldn't allow animal acts to appear in some of the theatres where you've booked us," Alfred once complained to the Theatre Guild.

They had played in high-school gymnasiums and college auditoriums, in churches and synagogues, in dilapidated movie houses, in Shrine auditoriums, in tobacco barns and stock pavilions, in vast civic stadia so enormous that the first row was fifteen feet away from the stage. Sometimes they played in houses without a stage. Once they played in the War Memorial Auditorium in Louisville, Kentucky, capacity 6,000. The band pit was so broad that the first row was a dozen yards from the stage and Lynn said, "I don't think they'll hear us or see us in the balcony." But they were seen and they were heard and without microphones, for they knew with uncanny intuition how to pitch their voices to the dimensions of any theatre.

They had been seen and heard in Jackson, Mississippi (where they played in a high school and used empty classrooms for changing costumes), in Little Rock, Arkansas (where the stage entrance was too narrow for the scenery, and it had to be carried through the front entrance), in Amarillo, Tyler, Ft. Worth, Kansas City, Wichita, Oklahoma City, Waco, Dallas, Austin, San Antonio, Memphis, Chattanooga, Atlanta, Montgomery, Birmingham and New Orleans (where they were served, at Antoine's, a huge Baked Alaska, with their names spelled out inside a heart and arrow in pink icing). Back and forth they had wandered, sometimes by automobile, sometimes by railroad with three baggage cars for the scenery and props and luggage and two sleeping cars for the actors ("It is such fun to feel the train wheels rumbling under one," Lynn wrote Alexander Woollcott), and 150 costumes, four for everybody in the cast. They were playing a repertory of four plays, north and south, east and west, Cedar Rapids, Davenport, St. Paul, Milwaukee, Cincinnati, Indianapolis, Columbus, Pittsburgh, Des Moines, Salt Lake City (where they arrived five hours late because of a blizzard and Alfred said, "Let the doors be opened and the people come in and watch the scenery being set up," and the matinee didn't start until half past four and there was only time for a sandwich between shows), and sometimes they lived in second-rate hotels and ate in cheap restaurants, playing Boston, Toronto, Chicago ("I hope to be like Mrs. Fiske in one way and spend my old age doing one night stands," Lynn wrote Aleck Woollcott), Youngstown, Seattle ("Wherever they go," scene designer Robert Edmond Jones said, "they bring with them all the excitement of the theatre. It radiates from them. It glitters like a Christmas tree. The whole town is at their feet."), and

Los Angeles and Sacramento and San Francisco, many times in San Francisco, in 1936 and again in 1937, 1938, 1939. San Francisco: "After the play last night, Lynn and I went up to the roof of the Curran Theatre and we sat upon the roof until we were put out," Alfred wrote Aleck. "We sat there in the darkness and looked across the bay. We decided this was what we want: San Francisco. Lynn says every person should pick out the town or city in the United States he loves most and stay there for ever. For us it is San Francisco at this moment, we felt. Silence fell upon us. We were at peace with the world."

But the world was not at peace with them or with any person who lived for beauty and private happiness. They were haunted by the fear of death closing over their world of beauty. They were oppressed for the people they loved. Lynn had written to Graham Robertson, in October, 1938, "Oh dear, now we are in for another war, and God knows what effect that will have on our being able to elude mines and torpedoes and get to London for a season soon. Don't let England go to war, Graham, please! Write one of your beautiful letters to the Houses of Parliament and stop it all."

But Nazi Germany was on the march and the Soviet Union, which became its partner in a strange alliance, was on the march, and the democracies were recoiling or paralyzed. France had fallen. Finland was invaded by the Red Army, which one had believed to be the vanguard of antifascism. England alone, sustained by our ships and arms, stood against tyranny. On the morning after the Nazi bombing of Warsaw, Noel Coward put through a call to Genesee Depot. The connection was bad. Noel's voice drifted away intermittently but they heard him say, "War has been declared. So nice to have known you." And they went into that small house they called the "studio," which was where they had gone to hear music and sip champagne so many times with Noel, and they drank a toast to Noel and to England and they could not hold back their tears. They held each other's hands and they wept. Then they went out of the "studio" and locked the door and they did not open it again until 1958. Sherwood's premonitions of disaster in *Idiot's Delight* had come true, more horribly than had seemed possible. There seemed nothing to sustain one's hope except one small island of free men. There was nothing Lynn and Alfred could do now but be entertainers, so they threw themselves into their work as if they were young again. Lynn wrought two characterizations, one after the other, that were among the finest ever achieved by an actress: her Madame Arkadina in *The Sea Gull* and her Alkmena in *Amphitryon*

38. Alkmena is a loyal Grecian wife who refuses to betray her husband even with Jupiter himself. Her acting was a thing of delicate humor and tender nuances, in which she spoke with a classical perfection the aristocratic speeches written by the greatest modern French playwright, Jean Giraudoux. "Though she was human, she was divine," Behrman once remarked to me. Her acting was a thing that actually shimmered on the stage. She had worked at the inside and outside of her character. She let her fingernails grow long and painted them white for she had learned that Grecian women did this. Theresa Helburn, going to England, asked if she could do anything for her, and Lynn said, yes, that Floris, the Jermyn Street parfumeur, put up a certain attar of roses which she hadn't been able to buy in New York and would Miss Helburn please bring her several bottles of this attar. She wanted to rub it into her skin, since it gave her the feeling of Alkmena.

Valentina designed Lynn's costumes for *Amphitryon 38*. They were made of silk jersey. Now they had been rehearsing the Giraudoux comedy while they were touring with *Idiot's Delight* and the costumes had hung on hangers many weeks. Consequently, the jersey material had stretched. On opening night, in San Francisco, Alfred, during Act II, became aware that Lynn's left breast, because of the sagging silk jersey, was bared to the audience. It was hanging out in full view. Alfred was playing a long scene with Lynn at a table. His eyes opened wide. He attempted to get her attention. He coughed. He raised his eyebrows. He nodded his head in the direction of the bare bosom. But she ignored his signals. When the act finally ended—to Alfred's great relief—he told her, "Did you know your left breast was bare to the audience?"

Lynn frowned and replied: "Don't bother me with little things like that until I really know my lines!"

We get an insight into how Lynn took the measure of a character in something she wrote Graham Robertson. She is describing that scene between herself and Jupiter in which she tries to discover whether or not it is he with whom she slept last night and whether he had assumed her husband's shape. "I take that bit in the last act—from the moment I say 'Are you sure that you've never taken the shape of Amphitryon?' and carry on from there with a note of suspicious interrogation through 'Jupiter, take me in your arms' and 'You see, it seems quite natural for me to be calling you *darling*' and 'What is this pleasurable sensation that flows through my body when I am near you—whence does it come?' and finally topped by 'Confess, Jupiter, wasn't it you, yourself, that came to me after the great fire in Thebes?' All this is taken with one line of thought behind it and a definite plan of tricking him into confessing. I have brought that whole suspicious motif behind that scene up very high and it is much—much more dramatically effective."

Alfred, as Jupiter, wore a beard of golden ringlets. "It makes me look," he observed, "as if I'd swallowed Shirley Temple."

In the prologue, Jupiter and Mercury are seen on Mt. Olympus looking down on Alkmena, and Jupiter is describing his yearning for this lady. Originally, the scene was played on the stage level, the gods pretending they were in heaven and making believe they were looking down on earth, locating it below the stage, as it were. Alfred decided they must play it up high, ten feet, fifteen feet above the stage. He wanted a cloud built so he and Richard Whorf, who was playing Mercury, would be discovered lying naked on the cloud. Impossible, Lee Simonson said. So Alfred drew a design, and it was executed to his specifications: a large papier maché cloud, with two "cutouts" in papier maché showing bare buttocks. When the actors placed their heads in openings in the "cloud" it gave the illusion of their heads being attached to the nude rumps. (At a party, later, a woman told Lynn she had figured out how Alfred and Whorf had done the prologue. "I believe," she said, "they do it like magicians—with mirrors." "Yes," Lynn agreed, "they do it like magicians—but not with mirrors. They do it with false bottoms!")

While in Boston, columnist Leonard Lyons asked Charles Washburn, the show's press agent, to summarize the plot of *Amphitryon 38*. Washburn replied, "It's the old story of a guy making a pass at a dame— but we do it differently."

Lyons wanted to know, "What's so different about a guy making a pass at a dame?"

Washburn explained, "The difference is—we have a harp in the orchestra."

Washburn's joke, alas, became truth for the critics, who judged it a "bedroom farce" instead of a noble comedy of the ironic contrast between divine and earthly love. Burns Mantle, summing up the critical consensus, said, "The reviews may be generally spoken of as having sounded a note of restrained rapture. *Amphitryon 38*, plus the attraction of the leading players, did offer an unusual and delightful evening in the theatre. However, a bedroom farce is a bedroom farce, however classic, they said, and the stretching of a single anecdote to cover three acts of time was obviously a stretch."

The Lunts were wounded by the critics. Alfred expressed their anguish to Woollcott:

The press yesterday was a terrific blow. The acting came out magnificently but the play was dismissed as bedroom farce and not a very funny one at that. We are so puzzled by the reviews, as we had no inkling of what they'd say from the reaction of the audience, the response had been perfect as far as we were concerned. They laughed in the right places, they were intensely quiet in the right places, and at the close they sat and called the curtain up and down 25 times which is a record for anything we've ever been in and then the next day the press reports of something we never dreamed of or had experienced. The scenery and costumes they adored (the music too and the acting) but all this we had done ONLY to complement the lines, and those they found, for the most part, dull. I am worried because of the influence of the daily printed word. I love this play. I think it distinguished writing, gentle, witty, and at times profound, and I would like people to see it and hear it unprejudiced by such fanfare as "bedroom farce." If there had been any indication of boredom, either on opening night or during the 50 performances that preceded it, I wouldn't be as bewildered as I am.

But in England, both the play and its production were accepted as an artistic masterpiece. The Lunts took *Amphitryon 38* to London chiefly because it was Graham Robertson's favorite play and they wanted to please him. They placed a comfortable chair in the wings on opening night. Graham was the only outsider ever permitted to watch them from the wings, as Gladstone had been given the privilege of watching Ellen Terry and Sir Henry Irving from the wings of the Lyceum Theatre.

It is thanks to Robertson that we have a vivid picture of Alfred's stage fright, which is a real and a chronic thing for him. Robertson reported that as Alfred and Whorf were in their places in the cloud this is what they said before the curtain rose:

(Jupiter *and* Mercury, *in their birthday suits and visibly quaking, recline high in air upon a thunder cloud, over the edge of which they peer.*)
JUPITER (*in a hollow whisper*): How do you feel?
MERCURY (*ditto*): Feel? I feel I've lost my voice. Supposing I can't speak?
JUPITER: You must speak. Gawd—I'm afraid I'm going to be sick.
MERCURY: You can't be sick! There goes the curtain.
(*Curtain rises*)
JUPITER (*apparently apostrophising himself*): Oh God, we're off.

"And then," Graham added, writing to his friend Kerrison Preston, "when all was over and Alfred-Jupiter had stridden up the sky to his waiting cloud and Lynn-Alkmena had returned to domesticity and Amphitryon, it was lovely to find the dear things quite unchanged— simple, kindly and affectionate as ever, as if four years' parting had never been."

The opening night was one of those spectacles that only a British audience puts on for special performers whom they have taken to their hearts. Seats were torn up, hats flung in the air, and there were cheers and shoutings and applause and cries of "Bravo" and "Welcome Home" and "Why have you stayed away so long?" and Alfred, coming out to make a little speech, found himself weeping with happiness. He suddenly decided that London audiences were the finest audiences to play to. One day, the call boy brought a letter backstage, addressed to the Lunts, from a complete stranger, who wrote, "I thought perhaps you might like to hear a bit of conversation which I overheard between two old ladies who were sitting behind me at the matinee of *Amphitryon 38.* When the curtain fell, one said, 'Well, it was lovely, wasn't it?' 'Oh, lovely,' replied the other. 'But, oh my dear, when we get home what shall we tell them the play was about?' "

One Sunday they went out to Robertson's farm, Sandhills, to spend a charming nineteenth century day without electricity, running water, radio, or telephone. It was a stormy rainswept day but they put on boots and warm clothes and then walked in the woods and visited a nearby farm, Redlands, which Robertson rented to three aged women. The beldames owned a cat which was, at the moment, extremely pregnant. "Alfred," Robertson said, "was in character as Jupiter for he stroked the Redlands tabby and she had four kittens almost immediately after." The kittens were named Hercules, Castor, Pollux, and Helen, in deference to their Grecian *accoucheur.* Then Alfred-Jupiter returned to Sandhills and visited the pigpen, where he was introduced to Sarah, a sow. Jupiter smiled upon Sarah. Sarah was delivered of "nine little pigs on the same evening. All Sandhills, as it were, is bursting into blossom."

There were visits with Noel. Noel gave a supper party for them at which the Duke and Duchess of Kent were present. The Duchess was a very beautiful woman, perhaps the most beautiful princess then alive. The Duke of Kent was killed in 1942. At supper, Anthony Eden sat on Lynn's left and "you can get a rough idea of his charm when I tell you that he was asking me exactly what he should do on his return to the House [of Commons] and what his line of attack should be, and you can get a rougher idea of my gullibility when, nothing daunted, I gave him my advice, which he received with the utmost respect." *

They followed *Amphitryon 38* with the delicate ironies of Chekhov's *The Sea Gull.* Alfred's Trigorin brought that world-weary sensualist to life and Lynn's Arkadina was one of her most sublime performances. Maria Ouspenskaya, who was then one of the leading teachers of acting as well as a fine actress, said that Lynn's Irina Arkadina was "better than the original creation of the part under Stanislavsky."

Robert Milton, a Russian-born disciple of Stanislavsky, was the director of record, but Alfred was doing most of the directing. At the dress rehearsal, designer Robert Edmund Jones lighted the play. (It is customary for the scene designer to work out the light plot and supervise the actual lighting.) Jones believed a soft, chiaroscuro lighting enhanced the mood. It was so dim you could hardly see the actors. Alfred played the first act, but then began criticizing the lighting so harshly that Jones broke down in a fit of weeping. It took hours to calm him. Alfred and Lynn believe in light, as much light as possible—though they will accept dimming at moments to stress the mood of a scene; but essentially they believe the faces and bodies of the actors must be clearly seen from every part of the theatre. Alfred believes full lighting at its highest power is especially important in playing comedy. If he had his way, he would bring the footlights back in every theatre. He believes if you have a well-lighted stage you can play comedy under any circumstances, even in an enormous setting. Lee Simonson had not wanted to design a wide sweeping set for *Idiot's Delight,* for which Alfred wanted a lot of furniture and a long sweeping staircase. Simonson said, "You can't play comedy in a twenty-four–foot set."

After the premiere, Simonson said, "I'm still right. You can't play comedy in a twenty-four–foot set—except when the Lunts are playing comedy."

And now it was 1940, and they had journeyed 39,000 miles in five years and 300,000 persons in 80 cities had seen them in *Idiot's Delight, The Sea Gull, The Taming of the Shrew* or *Amphitryon 38.* And they were going home to Wisconsin and they were going to take a rest for a year, at least. In their compartment, Lynn and Alfred had a nightcap of scotch-and-water. Lynn undressed and prepared to go to sleep. She has the gift of being able to fall asleep at once, no matter where she is, and now she felt she had five years of sleep to catch up with. As she was taking out her nightgown, her eyes fell on the blue-bound script.

* In a letter to Woollcott, June 23, 1938.

Revelation. A play in three acts by Robert E. Sherwood. Idly, she opened it. She riffled the pages. *The action takes place in Finland at* . . . Ah, it was not that play about Athens in the age of Pericles, after all . . . She turned another page. *Scene 1. Living room of the Valkonens' house in Helsinki, early in October, 1938* and now it was too late, for she was captured. She was not to sleep a moment that night and for a long time afterward her sleep would be fitful and uneasy, sometimes broken by the sound of air-raid sirens and war and death.

For the final title of the play she was reading was *There Shall Be No Night.* She finished the play as the train pulled into Harrisburg. There was a thirty minute stop. She handed the script to Alfred and said, "I want you to read it." Then she rang for the porter and sent a telegram to Sherwood: THIS HALF IS COMING BACK TO REHEARSE.

Then Alfred read the play. From Chicago he wired the author: AND THE OTHER HALF IS COMING TOO.

But Sherwood came to them. He flew to Wisconsin on Monday. Richard Whorf, hurriedly appointed as designer, came on Tuesday. And at once they got down to business.

There Shall Be No Night was inspired by a 1939 Christmas broadcast over CBS from Helsinki, Finland, by foreign correspondent W. L. White. Sherwood wrote the play in January and February. Russia's invasion of Finland had shocked Sherwood. In his postscript to the published version of *Idiot's Delight,* he had written of his hope of a united front of England, France, the Soviet Union and the United States to "defeat Fascism in Germany, Italy, and Japan." Now, he wrote that what he thought was "the mightiest opponent of Fascism" seemed to be its ally. "But with the assault on Finland the last scales of illusion fell," he said. Why did the American isolationists not come to help "brave little Finland"? He wrote the play as a deliberate work of propaganda, to arouse Americans to realize that the invasion of any free country was a threat to all other democracies. He wrote in great haste, and the play was still in a rough form when he came to Wisconsin. The Lunts shared his sense of urgency. They thought it a "beautiful and moving play" and a call to arms. There was a battle of ideas as well as a battle of armies and this play was a weapon in the ideological conflict. While working with Sherwood on the rewrites and planning the settings with Whorf, they were casting the play, mainly from the actors who had been touring with them. Lynn and Alfred were rejuvenated by the challenge. Alfred had believed in the theatre as a place to express high ideals; he had won Lynn to his view, and this was a play that said something that had to be said. Alfred directed it himself. He knew Finland and the Finns. He and Mrs. Sederholm gave the playwright many of the small details that fleshed out the characters. In a week the play was cast—by telephone. Many of the regulars were back—Sidney Greenstreet, Thomas Gomez, William Le Massena, Phylis Thaxter, Charva Chester, Ralph Nelson, Robert Downing. In the crucial part of the son, Erik, they cast an unknown young actor, who had been playing juveniles for several seasons in comedies and musicals, without making his mark. He was tall and quite lean. His eyes were pale blue and tortured and he had about him what Yeats called a "terrible beauty." Later, women of all ages were to feel tenderness as they watched him in the movies. He was Montgomery Clift. It was under the inspiration and guidance of the Lunts that he developed from a clever handsome juvenile into a sensitive observer of life and an actor of depth. One of Clift's proudest possessions is a photograph of the Lunts, inscribed, "From your *real* father and mother." And they were, in a personal as well as a professional way, his parents. He is their most successful disciple. When he was studying the role of Prewitt in *From Here to Eternity,* he learned boxing, bayonet charging, and bugle playing, because Prewitt could do these things. Alfred, who had learned the saxophone, the accordion, the piano, and tapdancing and cabaret singing to strengthen the verisimilitude of his various roles and to identify with his characters, had indeed found his real son.

Two weeks after reading the play, they were in rehearsal. Four weeks later they opened in Providence. Even while they were rehearsing, Finland was beaten. Soon Denmark and Norway were conquered, and then Holland, Belgium, and France were conquered. But even in the saddest time of the war, those who saw *There Shall Be No Night* came away with a sense of hope about the final outcome of the struggle. Because the play was so immediate, Alfred strove for simplicity in directing it. Never before, Woollcott told him privately, had he and Lynn played with such "serene simplicity."

For a long time, Aleck had been ailing. He didn't see the play until late in the run, "tottering to New York, a still shaky convalescent, who was defenseless as the play unfolded. I had thought myself quite safe emotionally as it went along, and was the more unprepared, on my way backstage for the sudden and violent need of privacy. I bolted for the nearest cover, which turned out to be Lynn's dressing room." Her dressing room was crowded with well-wishers but she saw how wrought up Aleck was and she politely dismissed them all and now they were alone. He wept openly, his body shaken with sobs. "But if she counted on being allowed to stay and enjoy the scene she was in error. I threw her out and wept noisily amid her costumes." *

Though the Lunts were now in the late afternoon of life, they preserved their youth, especially on the stage. Lynn's agelessness was incredible. Robertson remarked, "If things go on like this, Alfred will soon be too old to act with Lynn." In 1942, Lynn visited Woollcott at the Peter Bent Brigham Hospital in Boston, where he was recovering from major surgery. Aleck wrote Katharine Cornell that "Lynn came over to spend the following afternoon with me, looking very lovely, and, at a rough guess, about 27." And Alfred, given a few weeks of vegetable growing on the farm or a week on a transatlantic liner, could look like a man of 30.

On May 26, 1941, they celebrated their nineteenth wedding anniversary, quietly and alone. He awakened her in the morning with a long kiss and announced, "This is our wedding day. I have a surprise dinner for you tonight." She went down into "my" cellar. Up she came with a bottle of Chateau d'Yquem. "We had a grand dinner and drank the whole bottle. The next day we turned on the radio and a voice boomed forth, 'And it is also the wedding anniversary of Alfred Lunt and Lynn Fontanne.' We were very surprised, but felt their head for figures was probably better than ours, and so we celebrated again— brought out another bottle of wine and had a wonderful time. The next day we had a letter from that old Louise, our first cook. She congratulated us on our anniversary. We felt that this was more authentic and so we celebrated again—did ourselves up brown. The following day was the sinking of the Bismarck which seemed to me an even better excuse than any, and so now we are rather tired, chastened, on the wagon, and very good." †

How much do the varieties of love, licit and illicit, which the Lunts have played all their lives, mirror their own mutual adoration? Is their dream of passion an artifice of the imagination? Or does it reflect their own experiences?

Now, a long and happy marriage is not usually supposed to be typical of good actors. In fact, many actors honestly believe that many romances and many marriages are necessary to stimulate an actor or actress. Words like "fidelity" and "married love" and "monogamy" are not commonly found in the lexicon of teachers of acting. Yet no less a man than Con-

* Letter to Graham Robertson, Nov. 20, 1940.
† Lynn, writing to Sherwood.

stantin Stanislavsky believed that conjugal romance was a vital part of an actor's equipment. Lawrence Langner once had a discussion with Stanislavsky in which the Russian master described the exercises he gave to young actors.

"But," added Stanislavsky, "do not imagine one can become an actor by exercises. Above all, there is the basic personality, and more is learned from actually living a rich and deep life, so as to gain understanding, than in any classroom. In loving, suffering, discussion, interest in the arts and in the poetry of marriage, the soul of the artist is developed."

Langner pricked up his ears. Poetry of marriage? He could not believe he had heard Stanislavsky correctly. He asked the Master to explain this unconventional theory and Stanislavsky explained: "Marriage —a true marriage—has a poetry of its own which gives a background of harmony to the artist for his creative work."

The conjugal felicities of the Lunts certainly enriched their acting. But did not their acting, their artistic expression, make their private lives more fascinating, more complex? Did it not help them avoid that ennui of the everyday which kills so many marriages with monotony?

In the love and marriage of Vivien Leigh and Laurence Olivier, the Lunts had seen themselves as they were twenty years before. Vivien and "Larry" met while both were married to other spouses. They had fallen madly in love. He was twenty-eight, she was twenty-one. She was slender and refined, with deep gray almond-shaped eyes. He was a muscular youth, stunningly handsome, with one of those voices that vibrate like a violoncello played by a master. They had acted together and tried not to accept their love, but in the end they had to divorce their spouses, and they married each other. They were in New York to play in *Romeo and Juliet*. The play had been a miserable failure and the reviews, Miss Leigh remembers, were "simply appalling, devastating, oh we were crushed, as it was our first play together since marriage." Lynn and Alfred remained up with them all night, endeavoring to console them. After that, the Lunts and the Oliviers became an inseparable quartet whenever they found themselves in the same city. In wartime England and afterward, there were innumerable visits to the Oliviers' country place, Notley Abbey in Buckinghamshire. There were long and exciting conversations about acting and discussions of the leading actors of the Edwardian age. Larry was as deadly a mimic as Alfred. He could, for instance, do a sardonic impersonation of Henry Irving in *The Bells*. They talked about marriage. The Lunts believed that the Oliviers were their spiritual heirs. Vivien, who was passionate about sports, even got Alfred to play bowls. And she shared Lynn's passion for anagrams, Scrabble, and patience. Noel Coward taught them some of his advanced variations. "Oh, some of them take weeks to finish, just one game," Miss Leigh says. "I think Noel makes them up purposely to frustrate Lynn and myself. But I am afraid I do not have Lynn's calmness. She doesn't get ruffled, ever. Larry and I hoped we would be like Lynn and Alfred. We thought our marriage would last as long, but our natures were not as angelic as theirs. Lynn and Alfred have angelic natures. When my marriage was breaking up, I'd ask myself, *But the Lunts worked it out, why can't we?* I was never able to find the answer."

On the Lunts' silver wedding anniversary, the Oliviers sent them a Georgian tea service. In that same year, 1947, Larry was knighted. Alfred wrote them: "I doubt if a day goes by that we don't speak of you. For one thing we use the beautiful tea-set every afternoon and its grandeur must necessarily recall you both very much indeed—tea service or no tea service. . . . Thank God, the knighthood came when it did, as I really think we should have burst if it had been held off any longer. . . . We send our love and devotion and everlasting admiration. Your kindnesses to us during those two years can never be repaid—certainly they have never for a moment been forgotten—and the only regret I have is that we cannot impose on you a little oftener."

Lynn's reaction to the knighthood was that "he and she are so beautiful that knighthood, instead of being an absurd and rather dubious honor, seems to come in flower again with them, which makes me think of *The Forest Lovers* by Maurice Hewlett. I wonder if that could be dramatized or made a picture of? How perfect they would be for it. I must write them and suggest it, but as I have not read it since I was a little girl, I expect it is not sensational enough or exciting enough for present day consumption." *

I spoke about the Oliviers with Lynn in 1959. She knew then of the stresses and ever-longer separations of Larry and Vivien, but she didn't believe the marriage had gone bad. She sensed in the Oliviers that "poetry of marriage" whose verses their own lives recited daily—sometimes in heroic couplets, sometimes in triolets and rondelles, sometimes in anarchic *vers libre,* and most often in the ordered harmonies and ironies of Meredith's sonnet-sequence, aptly called *Modern Love.* Even as late as 1959, Lynn thought the love of Larry and Vivien was roman-

* Letter to Alexander Woollcott.

tic, as in Hewlett's novel. Lynn is in some ways more of an intellectual than Alfred, at least in a literary sense. She reads widely and knows the best writing of all countries. Though she is vague about time and place, being the sort, as S. N. Behrman told me, "who doesn't know what year it is," she has a sharp sense of literary art, and a "good ear for style" in Behrman's opinion. "Her taste for good writing is impeccable and she knows a great many books you wouldn't expect her to know and she's one of the few persons I've ever met who can really be 'sent' by a book or a poem the way some people are said to be 'sent'— you know, 'excited'—by jazz music."

From *The Forest Lovers* she went on to speak of other roles for the Oliviers. In her mind, everything becomes transmuted into acting. "Another novel I always thought was perfect for them was Somerset Maugham's *Liza of Lambeth*. It was Willie's first book. They would have been so right for a dramatization of it. Also *Ondine*. Giraudoux had given us the play after he wrote it, but we felt we were too old for it and we urged Larry and Vivien to do it but they didn't. She can play a gamin when she wants to—oh, she can look sixteen on a stage and he was ideal for the knight."

But it was not to be *Ondine* or any other play. Larry fell in love with Joan Plowright while they were playing in *The Entertainer*. In August, 1960, after months of rumors, Vivien Leigh gave out this statement: "Lady Olivier wishes to say that Sir Laurence has asked for a divorce in order to marry Miss Joan Plowright. She will naturally do whatever he wishes."

It was like losing a friend, for though the Lunts continued to see Larry and Vivien separately, it was not the way it had been when they were a quartet.

But in the 1940's the Lunts did not foresee this outcome. They held on to their image of the Oliviers as the quintessence of romantic love all during the war years. In December, 1941, *There Shall Be No Night* was forced to end its run. Russia had been invaded by the Nazis and was now fighting with England. We had been plunged into the war by Pearl Harbor. Lynn and Alfred worked in the kitchen of the Stage Door Canteen. They were wondering whether to go out on a tour of the army camps and naval bases with a play. They had to do something. They couldn't sit still. Over in England, their dearest friends were undergoing the terror of the nightly bombings. Lynn wrote to Woollcott that she had heard from Jane de Glehn who "tells me that the house in London is now a heap of dust. The studio that I posed for Wilfred in all my growing years. That lovely old house with its apple green door. . . . It was opposite Battersea Bridge and my best beau used to stand on the bridge looking over at the boats going underneath, waiting for me to finish my day's work. He was killed in the last war and the house he used to watch for me is now gone, but as Jane says, 'Nobody can take our memories from us.' " An incendiary bomb had fallen outside Antoinette's house, almost killing her. All their friends had suffered in one way or another. They had to do something. Sherwood suggested they help to sell war bonds. They went on a campaign. Alfred introduced Lynn, who read a speech written for her by Brooks Atkinson. When Alice Duer Miller wrote *The White Cliffs of Dover* Lynn went about and recited it to the accompaniment of a symphony orchestra. Alice Duer Miller, the witty and lovely woman who was such a vital part of the Woollcott circle, died in September, 1942. Lynn wrote Aleck:

I went to Alice's funeral. I'm glad you weren't here. I think you would have found it very upsetting, that familiar room and all our old friends standing around—George and Beatrice [Kaufman], Irving and Ellin [Berlin], Frank and Esther [Sullivan] . . . but no Alice. It was so difficult to believe. As Frank said, we had had so many good times in that house and now it is gone forever.

Gone forever . . . Woollcott was very ill. In San Francisco, in 1940, he had a coronary thrombosis, and was on the point of death. Then he rallied and lectured all over this country and in England and fought hard against the isolationist viewpoint in the middle west. He suffered a brain hemorrhage, and had gallstones, but he kept his spirit waving like a banner. He came to Genesee Depot at Christmas in 1941. Lynn told Graham Robertson that "we had the most wonderful twenty-four hours. That angelic mood has been going on ever since his illness. I think it is that he was just about to leave us all for a long time and suddenly realized how much he loved us. . . . There are occasional flashes of the old devil, but it's mostly a rather chastened little boy, infinitely tender and loveable. . . ."

In January, 1943, their great friend and warmest admirer died of a heart attack. His admiration for them as human beings and as actors had been intense and unreserved. In 1939 he had said, quite simply, "I know that if I were to spend the next five years in a town with only one theatre in it, but would be allowed to name the personnel of that theatre's stock company, the first players I would choose for its roster would be Alfred Lunt and Lynn Fontanne."

NINETEEN

THEY WON'T LIKE IT

*F*OR MANY years, Alfred had been asking S. N. Behrman to write them a frivolous play in which he could do magic tricks and walk a tightrope. *The Sea Robber,* by the German playwright Ludwig Fulda, had the germ of an idea, and he wanted Behrman to use it to make a long play. The idea is that a notorious pirate becomes a fat and banal bourgeois in middle age, and retires to a small town where he marries Manuela, a romantic beauty. She dreams of an exciting love affair with a man like the famous pirate Estramaduro. Bored by her dull husband, Manuela falls in love with Serafin, "a strolling player," who comes with his troupe to give a show. Serafin passes himself off as the famous pirate. It could be a fine vehicle for the Lunts, and they thought of having gorgeous costumes by Miles White, splashy settings by Lemuel Ayers, choreography by Felicia Sorel, and a score by Kurt Weill. Alfred would do Spanish dances and magic tricks and even walk a tightrope. Everything worked out as planned, except that Weill did not write the score. Alfred directed the play. The dialogue was "cued in with music, but it's harder than a musical comedy, where you can rehearse the dancing in one place and the lines somewhere else and then combine them; but we have to do this all together, and it's been the toughest chew we've ever bitten off." *

And the writing was not easy. John C. Wilson, who was producing *The Pirate,* came to Genesee Depot and they all had meetings about the play. "Berri" was writing it under their noses, so to speak. He wrote all during June and July. Alfred became high-spirited and tense, like a thoroughbred race horse, getting ready for an important race. Only his cooking seemed to relax him.

* Lynn writing to Robert Sherwood.

"I believe," Behrman says, "that cooking is for Alfred what golf was for Eisenhower. Alfred is at peace with the world only when he's in the kitchen preparing a meal. And the only time when he verges on conceit is when he's cooking. It's the opposite feeling to the one he has about his acting. He doesn't feel any certainty about his acting or about a new play. But food—ah, he *knows* his food is going to be good and 'they're' going to like it. He hands you a plate of food with such a look of self-satisfaction. He watches you closely while you're eating it. Eating one of Alfred's dishes in front of him is like writing a piece with a magazine editor looking over your shoulder. But the only thing that quiets his nerves is cooking."

Whenever Alfred wanted Berri to change something in the play, he'd point to a line and say, "They won't like it."

That's all.

Behrman says, "I kept hearing this expression for so long I finally asked him, 'Would you mind identifying for me this mysterious "they" to whom you are always referring? How can you be so prophetic and say "they" won't like it?' And Alfred would answer, 'Because I *know* they won't like it.'"

Behrman has concluded that "they" is "an unseen cavalcade of enemies, who, it's fixed in his mind, is a cabal, a platoon of unseen and undefined enemies, whom Alfred seems to know intimately, both individually and as a group and he knows that 'they' are not going to like it. It could be a line 'they' won't like or a scene or a costume, most often it's the whole production which he knows 'they' are not going to like, and he's constantly being ambushed by this corporate hostility and Lynn cannot do anything about 'they,' neither can I, neither can anybody else."

If there is one thing the Lunts hate about "them" it is when one of "them" begins coughing. A cougher exasperates them the most because he may cough on an important line and then the whole scene, even the whole act, may lose meaning. Lynn can usually stop a cougher by placing him in the theatre and then glaring him into silence when he begins coughing. Once, while they were doing *The Pirate*, a cougher began barking away during the last act. He had one of those uncontrollable coughs that go on and on and get louder and louder. Lynn couldn't paralyze him with her glare and finally Alfred stepped out of character. He walked downstage, looking straight at the cougher, and declaimed, "It was a cough that carried him off. It was a coffin they carried him off in."

235

The cougher got the idea and departed.

"Once and once only," Lynn says, "did I have a cougher in the hollow of my hand. I had injured my knee in *The Taming of the Shrew* and had diathermy treatments from a doctor. He was a great fat man and his wife was a fat stupid cow of a woman. Well, we were playing *O Mistress Mine*. At one matinee, the play was ruined for ourselves and for the audience by a woman who hacked, hacked, hacked all through the performance. Now this doctor and his wife had come to the matinee and they came back to see us and as they were going upstairs some of the actors were going up and somebody said, 'If I had that bitch that coughed all afternoon I'd wring her neck.' The doctor's wife thought this was funny and when she came into the room she quoted the actor."

Then the woman said, "I must confess I'm the woman who coughed all afternoon."

"Why?" Lynn asked.

"Well, I had this sort of tickling in my throat."

Lynn was outraged. "Then why didn't you go out?"

"Oh, I thought it would get well any minute."

"It didn't get well for the entire performance. Do you realize that the audience sat there hearing only one word in every ten of this particular performance? Every one of them wasted their money, and some of them came a very long way to see this play and you ruined the performance for them. Do you know that? I am just saying this, my dear lady, in the hope that the next time you have a cough you will leave the theatre right away—at once—*immediately!*'

TWENTY

ACTORS DO NOT THINK OF DEATH

*I*N JANUARY, 1944, a silver-haired gentleman whose moustache gave him a vague resemblance to Thomas Mann, and who had about him that air of frayed gentility which characterizes that breed of Englishman known as the "Chelsea pensioner," answered a help wanted advertisement in the London *Times*. The advertisement had been placed by St. George's Hospital, near Hyde Park. Because of the manpower shortage, the hospital was seeking orderlies. It pleaded for ablebodied men, or even those whose bodies were not especially able, to come out of retirement. The tall, large-bulked gentleman applied for a position, giving the name Karilo Vlachos. He was at once taken on at a salary of five pounds weekly. He stipulated one condition, that he not work on Saturdays and Wednesdays, though he would work Sundays. The labor shortage being what it was then, the superintendent didn't cavil. Vlachos was at once put to work sweeping corridors, emptying bedpans, and making beds. One afternoon, when he returned home quite done in, his wife inquired what he'd had to do at the hospital that day and he replied:

"I washed down Louise."

It turned out that the orderlies nicknamed each ward and Vlachos had been washing the windows in "Louise." At the end of his first week, the superintendent complimented him.

"By the way," he said, "I see we don't have your address. Where do you reside?"

"The Savoy Hotel," replied the old gentleman.

Some time later, the superintendent took his wife to the Aldwych Theatre on the Strand to see Lunt and Fontanne playing in *There Shall Be No Night*. (It had undergone a geopolitical change; the scene of action moved from Finland to Greece, and the aggressors were now Fascists.) In the hero, a Greek neurologist who has won the Nobel prize for medicine, the superintendent recognized his new orderly. It was, of course, Alfred Lunt. This curious Mr. Lunt had taken the name of his character in the job. Nor was the resemblance to Mann accidental. Alfred had seen a full-color photograph of Mann. This was how he had seen Dr. Valkonen-Vlachos and he made himself up to look like the German novelist, even to growing a brush moustache.

Alfred's work in the hospital was one of the strange incidents of the strangest adventure in the career of the Lunts. When *The Pirate* closed, they felt they had to go to England and be "in it, for we could not be at peace when they were fighting for their lives." They at first thought of playing a comedy. In the words of a character in *O Mistress Mine* who learns that two actors expected for dinner are rehearsing a new comedy: "I do think that in times like these it's far better to make people laugh than to make them cry." But then they changed their minds. It was better to give people some sense of the war's meaning. Most of their friends thought they were crazy to go over, but Woollcott said they were right. "The Lunts have played in England once every five years," Aleck told the circle, "and why the hell should they let the goddam Nazis stop them?" Robert Sherwood, now head of the Office of War Information, also stood with them, and revised *There Shall Be No Night* to suit the new situation.

It is paradoxical that Alfred, who stands so much in fear of "them" that he still gets a nervous stomach almost every night before he makes his entrance, is in real life a man of moral courage. All his life he has gone on living and laughing, though his body has been racked by serious diseases that would have made most people take to their beds. He has a spiritual strength that goes beyond courage, because, being a nervous, sensitive man, he has had to fight against fear in himself, and so his triumph is the more extraordinary.

It was hard for the Lunts to get passports. They had to go to Washington to see many important people, and use the influence of Sherwood and Harry Hopkins, and be vouched for by everybody of any power. After numerous meetings, they went to the State Department, and filled out many forms, and were granted passports. They went to Union Station to take a train and then somebody from the State Department came rushing on the platform and wanted to know why she had signed "Lynn Fontanne" instead of "Lynn Lunt" on her papers, and was she or was she not married to Mr. Lunt, for the government could not condone moral turpitude. Mrs. Lunt gave the anxious bureaucrat a piece of her mind and then filled him in on the story of her marriage. He bade them wait. He telephoned somebody at State. The Lunts missed a train. Eventually, the problem came to a woman in the Passport Division. She, being a career woman herself, sympathized with Miss Fontanne's situation. She said that a married woman could travel with her husband under her maiden name.

They finally got to Philadelphia, where they boarded a small Portugese freighter taking some British children home from Canada. Near Bermuda, the ship ran into a hurricane in the Atlantic Ocean. The captain, faced with the choice of either going into the eye of the hurricane and riding it out or attempting to go around it and risk being wrecked by the waves striking the ship's sides, had chosen to go into the storm. The ship creaked and quivered. It was an old ship and the Lunts were sure they were going to be wrecked. It didn't seem possible the ship could stand such a beating. There was one moment when the ship rose very high, on the crest of an enormous wave, quivering frighteningly. At last it got steadier, and they were fine.

It was a slow trip. It took them twenty-two days to get to Lisbon. From here they had to take a plane. They both hate flying, but they flew. They arrived in London on Sunday and went to the Savoy. On Monday, they heard for the first time the screaming of sirens and the thunder of bombs, the rumbling and crashing and then the crackling noises of buildings coming apart. And they saw the blackout. Several bombs fell within a few blocks of the Savoy, but the hotel was not hit.

They opened on December 15.

Alan Dent, drama critic of the London *News-Chronicle,* was called up for service with the Royal Navy, though he was over forty. Dent mentioned this to Vivien Leigh, and she cried, "But they can't possibly call you, Jock—why, you'll miss the Lunts' first night!"

In private, the Lunts lived as if there was no war on. They dined mostly in their hotel, as if they were touring the states. They had only a suite at the Savoy, but they installed a spirit lamp in the bathroom, and Alfred prepared austerity meals with as much panache as if he were in Genesee Depot. Once, Yvonne and Hamish Hamilton came to dinner, and Alfred said, with his usual culinary confidence, "Oh, I've got a rare treat for you tonight. Managed to buy two pounds of calves' liver. I've made you a liver stew with a fine brown sauce. You've never tasted a better brown sauce than I've made." It happens that Mrs. Hamilton detests the "inner organs" of animals, but she closed her eyes and forced herself to eat the whole portion of liver stew. Her husband, however, pronounced it a masterpiece.

Though Goering no longer could send over fleets of 300 bombers every night, for now the RAF controlled the skies over London, there were some hit-and-run air raids every night. One night, after they came from the theatre, there was a long bombardment with bombs falling very close. The desk called to say they must go down to the air-raid shelter in the cellar. Alfred got out of his pyjamas and put on some trousers and an overcoat. Lynn went to the dressing table to put on her make-up. Outside, there were the hideous sounds of crashings and crumblings, and Alfred was sure the Savoy was likely to be blasted to rubble at any moment. He kept waiting at the door for Lynn, but she was still putting on make-up.

"Good God, Lynnie," he cried finally. "What on earth are you taking so long about?"

"I'm not going to face my public without looking my best," she said serenely.

There were rows of cots in the basement and the Lunts went there several times, but they couldn't sleep because of the sounds of snoring, and since you were allowed to sleep upstairs if you wanted to risk it, they slept upstairs. Once, there was a direct hit on their floor and two guests were killed; they were in the theatre at the time. On another occasion, they'd gone up to Windsor Castle, at the invitation of the Dean. They had given a performance without scenery or properties or lighting for the royal family and some of their friends, an audience of fifty, crowded into a long drawing room. In order to cross the "stage" the Lunts had to step over the feet of the spectators. They gave the play after lunch and then took an early train back to London for a 7 P.M. curtain at the Aldwych. As they got into Waterloo Station, the alert sounded. They waited in the air-raid shelter until the all-clear, and then took a taxi to the Savoy. Had they been in their room during this raid they would have been killed: a bomb had fallen on the hotel and every window in the room was smashed by the explosion. The floor was littered with broken glass.

Even during the worst days of the blitz, the London theatre had carried on. At the Aldwych, there were two electric signs, one on each side of the stage. As soon as the sirens wailed, the signs flashed: AIR RAID WARNING—ALERT. Anybody who wanted to leave could go to the basement. The actors also had the option of making an exit and staying away until the all-clear sounded. Not once did Lynn and Alfred give way to fear. Not once did they panic. "Nothing ever floored them," Binky Beaumont, their English producer, recalls. "They gave their performances every night and matinees as if they had been acting during air-raids all their lives."

Lynn and Alfred had to admit that from one viewpoint there was some dramatic value in the raids. They raised the tension to a breaking point that enhanced the emotions of the play.

"Why," Alfred would say sardonically, "we've got the highest-paid stagehand in the world. We've hired Adolf Hitler to make our offstage sound-effects."

One night, during the schoolroom scene, in which Dr. Vlachos has a long oration about the meaning of civilization and the goal of the war, he was well into the speech when, almost on cue, the sirens began screeching and bombs fell. The speech began with the doctor replying to an American soldier who asks whether the nobility of the war isn't an illusion, and he speaks of the nature of evil, in rather a lofty tone, and then—this was Sherwood's dialogue and stage direction—he goes on, "Forgive me gentlemen. I forget myself. I think I am lecturing at the Medical Institute. But (*He pauses to listen to the guns*) the Germans are only a short distance away. This may be my last lecture. So— please permit me to finish. . . . Listen!" And continues his discourse.

The audience, admiring Alfred for what they thought was quick thinking, was sure he had improvised the line, "This may be my last lecture," because real bombs were exploding outside.

Were they afraid when they were playing in London? Alfred once told me, "No. An actor wants to hold his audience more than he wants anything in the world and by God that night when I said, 'This may be my last lecture,' I held that audience and I gave a wonderful performance."

"An actor," Lynn said, "doesn't think of death when a performance is going well. He thinks of the performance and of the audience."

"I don't think I was heroic," Alfred said. "An actor trains himself to give a performance any time—when he's feeling tired, sick, unhappy, whatever troubles he's having in his personal life. The fact that a bomb might have hit the theatre didn't change it. There was another scene where I'm drinking coffee, which Lynn pours. One night there was a bad raid. The bombs were falling quite close. One of the things I'm proudest of as an actor is that my hand didn't tremble. The cup didn't shake at all. I held it steady."

At another time, Alfred was offstage, preparing to enter during a scene in which Erik, their son, is saying goodbye to Lynn just before going to join his regiment. At this juncture, the sirens began whining. The warning signs flashed ALERT on stage right and stage left. The bombs began to crash down. It happened that the young actor playing the son got the wind up and scuttled offstage when a nearby explosion was heard. Lynn started talking to her "son" and suddenly he was gone. Alfred still had to wait for about two "sides" of dialogue before his cue, but since there was no "son," Alfred, after a pause, came on stage, and his first lines were, "It was awful, not being able to telephone. But are you all right, darling?"

Later Lynn said, "Alfred, in all the months we've been doing this play, that's the first time you ever read that line properly!"

One evening, General George S. Patton and General Maxwell Patch came to see the play. Afterwards, they all went out for supper. A discussion of the play ensued and the question arose as to the meaning of war and why men fought bravely in combat. General Patch had recently given a morale lecture to American soldiers in a Devonshire base. "They didn't understand the purpose of the war," General Patch said. "I told them they were fighting for democracy and for the free way of life."

When Lynn tells the story she becomes General Patch, delivering a noble oration, full of fine phrases worn threadbare. Then General Patch stops quoting from his speech and turns to Patton, saying, "George, isn't that true? Isn't that what we're fighting for?"

And General Patton—here Lynn assumes the bulldog face of Patton and imitates his high piping voice—shrills back, "Hell, no. I'm fighting because I like it!"

After this, Patton became "their" general. They followed his program and the program of his armored division from then until D Day, when they saw him again in London.

The Aldwych Theatre had been hit directly several times but not severely enough to close it. On Friday, June 30, 1944, an enormous bomb fell on the Strand, just in front of the Aldwych. The doors were blasted. All the glass was blown out. A pile of rubble blocked up the front entrance doors. The next morning Beaumont inspected the disaster.

"I think," he once told me, "that the hardest thing I have ever had to do was to go to the Savoy and tell the Lunts that they could not play the matinee or the evening show on Saturday because the Aldwych was ruined and I couldn't find them another house in London. We'd have to close. They looked bewildered—as if I'd said to them, 'You can't breathe.' Finally they glanced at each other and Alfred said, 'When and where do we reopen?' I said that if they'd give me a little time I would arrange a tour of the provinces and then they were happy again."

Alfred once remarked, "Do you realize that we played Sherwood nine years of our lives? We played *Reunion in Vienna* here and in England. And *Idiot's Delight* here. And we played *There Shall Be No Night* a total of one thousand six hundred times!"

TWENTY-ONE

THE MINISTER'S MISTRESS

ORIGINALLY, Terence Rattigan had written *Love in Idleness* as a vehicle for Gertrude Lawrence. He met her while she was playing the USO circuit in England and told her his idea; she loved it. Rattigan is a tall, handsome, athletic-looking man, with the manners and sophistication of an aristocrat, by birth, breeding, and education. He is the best writer of drawing-room comedy since Noel Coward. At twenty-three, he wrote his first comedy, *French Without Tears,* and three years later, *While the Sun Shines.* Both were long-running successes. He served with the Royal Air Force during the war. In spare hours, Rattigan wrote his comedy about a beautiful widow having an affair with a war minister when her seventeen-year-old son returns from Canada suddenly. The boy is one of those high-strung sensitive Marxian chaps and he dislikes his mother's lover on moral and political grounds, since the lover is both a Tory and a rich businessman.

Having finished the play, Rattigan told Binky Beaumont the good news that Miss Lawrence's next play was all ready to go. Beaumont, in high spirits, got in touch with Miss Lawrence. To his surprise, Miss Lawrence said that though Rattigan was a very charming man, she didn't remember the conversation, she had never encouraged him to write a play for her, and she was returning to America where she had other irons in other fires. Beaumont communicated the dismal news to Rattigan.

Rattigan could not believe it. He was desolate. To think she had completely forgotten the play! As originally written, it revolved around the woman. It was a comedy of a woman suffering from a conflict between her need for her lover and her love for her son, and it needed a superb actress of a certain flash and flair. He couldn't see anybody but Lawrence in the role. Every line had been written with Lawrence in his mind. The bottom had been kicked out of Rattigan's world.

He confided his sorrows to his fellow drawing-room comedy playwright, Ivor Novello. Novello had a country place, Redroofs, in Maidenhead. The Lunts often came there on Sundays to get a respite from the "doodlebugs." (The Nazis had begun the V-1 and V-2 terror campaign as the war entered its final phase.) Novello told Rattigan to buck up. If his character was a good role for Gertie Lawrence it should be an even better role for Lynn Fontanne. Rattigan had not dared to think of Lynn because there wasn't a worthy part for Alfred. But Novello invited Rattigan for a week-end, and the Lunts for a Sunday. Rattigan spoke about the play. Then he and Alfred went for a long walk in Novello's garden.

"Frankly, Mr. Lunt," Rattigan said, "I have strong qualms about showing you and your wife the script. I'm afraid you'll think I'm insulting you. Your part is insignificant—and that's the truth of it."

In this version, the son's role was equal to the lover's. And the minister was portrayed as an unwholesome sort, of dubious financial reputation, who had engaged in dishonest manipulations while making his money. In fact, Sir John Fletcher was a thoroughly unsympathetic character.

"Well," Alfred said, "Lynn and I, we don't worry about whose role is bigger. Sometimes Lynn has the play and sometimes it's my play. Mr. Rattigan, if your play is good, I'll be satisfied to hold a tray and let it be Lynn's play. The play is what matters."

Touched by this unusual actor's self-abnegation, Rattigan gave him a copy of the play. Two days later, the Lunts rang him up, and they had lunch. For two hours, they told the euphoric playwright what a lovely comedy he had written. It was charming and witty and the character of the woman, Olivia Brown, was tender and true. Alfred would direct it himself. And he and Lynn would play in it. Oh, there were a few little things that needed to be fixed. A line or two in Act I, a few speeches that should be cut in Act II, some tightening in the last act. What they would like to do was put it into rehearsal at once, while they were touring with *There Shall Be No Night*, and then open it in London in the fall, perhaps. Was this agreeable? Rattigan cooed his assent.

Sam Behrman arrived to gather material for a *New Yorker* piece about London under fire. He remained in London several months. His only relief from the horrible V-2 buzz-bombs was visiting the Lunts.

"Whenever things got too much," he says, "I'd go over to the Savoy and see Lynn and Alfred. And they would tell me about the play and do some of the speeches and act out scenes. I was afraid to leave their room. While I was with them I forgot I was in London. I forgot there was a war. The buzz-bombs didn't matter. I didn't hear the noises. Nothing mattered except these two miraculous actors. How I hated to have to go back to Claridge's, back into the real world."

Rattigan was polishing his play. The "polishing" turned out to be a total reconstruction. Rattigan, looking back, thinks he was getting what he calls the "treatment" from Alfred. It was the old story of "they" and their "dislikes."

Rattigan recalls: "I had the sort of post with the RAF where I was permitted to take time off. Well, I'd go up to Glasgow or Leeds and watch Alfred directing the play and he'd naturally ask me to make a few changes here and there. He was so subtle about it that I didn't realize he was making me write a new play. In the end he was right. I wrote a far better play because of his suggestions. But at the time it was rather a trying experience. He'd begin by saying, for example, Act II and Act III are perfect but there were a few, oh very minor, little things in Act I that bothered him. Sir John Fletcher, the minister, that was Alfred's role, well wasn't he a little too brutal here? And my but he was a dreadful reactionary, and in this passage here he was such a disagreeable Tory and 'they won't like it, you know.' And he'd lose the audience in this scene here. As I'd written it, Olivia's son was constantly scoring off Sir John. Gradually—so gradually I didn't know it myself—the minister began scoring off Michael, the son. In fact, Michael became rather a snotty character, while Sir John changed into a fine fellow, good hearted, a worldly chap doing his best for God, for England, and for Lynn Fontanne, and having to put up with this beastly little bugger of a left-wing socialist."

When Rattigan had finished rewriting Act I, then Alfred would sigh and observe that Act I and Act III were now in good shape but there were a few minor points about Act II that required a little fixing. After Act II was altered, it suddenly developed that Act III had a few weaknesses.

The Lunts were now playing in Edinburgh and Rattigan visited Alfred's dressing room there. Rattigan was uneasy about the play and Alfred was upset about his anxiety. Had he been right after all? Was he betraying the play? Had he lost his sure instinct for the audience? He suddenly didn't know. He only knew that Rattigan had written a perfect gem of a play and he and Lynn believed in the play. He asked Rattigan to forgive him and then he began to choke up with emotion and Rattigan began crying, and then both men, weeping profusely, went arm in arm out into Prince's Street. Seeing a haberdasher, Alfred went inside and, wiping away his tears, he purchased a striped tie and gave it to Rattigan.

Speaking of Rattigan, Alfred once remarked to me, "Not since Sardou has there been a writer with such a gift for plot construction as Rattigan. You know, the plot of *O Mistress Mine* [this became the title of the play] is so tenuous, it's almost invisible. You can hardly see it, but it's there all the time, like a very fine silk line, binding the whole play together. Rather like fishing for tarpon. You use a very fine line and yet the line is so strong you can catch a six hundred pound fish with it."

They opened to bad reviews in Liverpool. The next week they played Leeds and the reviews were terrible. The Yorkshire *Post*, Rattigan says, "gave us a drubbing on the grounds that the play was against youth and was full of pro-Tory propaganda." Noel Coward, who had invested money in the play, was coming up to take a look at his investment. Everyone dreaded his arrival. What would they do if Noel didn't like it? Rattigan finally telephoned Noel and said, "Please, do not be too harsh or severe when you see the play, because I'm still working on the last act."

"Don't worry," Noel said. "I'll love it. I love everything you write and I love everything Lynn and Alfred do, so I have to love this play."

Noel saw the play. After the performance, Rattigan was in Alfred's dressing room when Coward went to see Lynn. Only a thin partition separated both chambers, and Alfred and Rattigan couldn't help overhearing Noel's voice uttering phrases like "a total mess," "second act doesn't work," "not very funny," "hopeless." Alfred and Terry sat like men sentenced to die. Alfred, Rattigan says, "looked as if Noel had plunged a dagger into his heart." Alfred finally got out a bottle of whisky, which the two men polished off. Then they joined Coward and Lynn and they all went to the Lunts' suite at the Queen's Hotel. Supper was ordered, but nobody had an appetite. Alfred ceased drinking. Rattigan went to work on a new bottle, but he couldn't seem to get drunk no matter how much he tried.

Noel said that what he had to do was very hard for him to do, but "There's no use my saying this play is anything but bad. It's hopeless.

The first act's amusing, but you've got no second and third act. Don't open in London. It will be a disaster. I think you should close it this week."

As Noel made a scene-by-scene analysis, Alfred sank lower into his armchair. Suddenly, Rattigan was aware that Lynn was signaling him. He followed her into the bedroom. "Look," she whispered, "nothing that Noel has said or will say can affect me. This is an enchanting play and we're going to do it in London. I know Alfred will want to close it. But don't worry. I shall talk Alfred around. I have faith in the play."

Rattigan went back to the sitting room. An hour later, Alfred said he had to go to the bathroom. He got up, and when he was out of range of Lynn and Noel, motioned to Rattigan, who followed him into the bathroom. Alfred closed and bolted the door.

"My boy," Alfred murmured, "as you can see, Lynn is disheartened by Noel's reaction. She's going to want to close the play. But no matter what Lynn says, we shall do it. It's a good play. Now don't say anything. Leave it to me to talk Lynn around to my way of thinking. I have such confidence in your play that I'm going to buy Noel's share in it."

Noel felt terrible about his bluntness, but he wanted his old friends to appreciate his honesty. "I want to be cossetted, comforted, and pampered because of this awful thing I had to do," he said.

Lynn glared at Noel. "*You* want to be cossetted, do you? Here you've come and killed us and you want to be cossetted?"

And now Lynn and Alfred rolled up their sleeves and went to work. The Lunts never lost faith in the play, but Coward's criticisms had opened their eyes to some of the weaker places in the production. Alfred rehearsed the company all morning and afternoon, and Rattigan rewrote furiously. Lines were cut; the tempo was speeded; Lynn developed new bits of pantomime; Alfred worked out some new delicious pieces of action. In Glasgow, they played a special matinee for members of the armed forces, including naval officer Alan Dent. "Every man jack of us," he once told me, "had been to the Glasgow pubs and we'd drunk ourselves high when we got there. The play opens with Lynn making a telephone call. She has a long scene, all by herself. She was in a negligee. Looked a regular smasher. Looked like the most beautiful woman you ever saw—about twenty years old, she looked. Every man in the theatre started whistling and calling to her. It was the most unruly, drunken audience an actress ever had to play to.

Couldn't hear a word she was speaking. She got absolute silence. She raised one finger, as if she were chiding a little child, and that entire theatre of soldiers stopped whistling. Never saw anything like it in my life—how she dominated the audience with one gesture."

The London audience, when the play finally came to the Lyric Theatre, was equally dominated, and nobody was happier than Noel, who told them they had performed a miracle. The Lyric became known as "the theatre you couldn't get into." During the six months' run, there was never an empty seat. And they played under the nerve-wracking tension of the stepped-up rocket bombardment. The doodle-bugs could be heard whining and then a silence, and then the explosion, and you never knew where it was going to hit. During that silence before the hit the whole audience would instinctively crouch down and when the rocket exploded and they were still alive they would exhale with relief and laughter. They would always laugh at the next line of the play even if it wasn't funny.

The Lunts didn't miss a performance. They weren't afraid of death. They were only afraid of a scene being spoiled by a rocket exploding at the wrong time. They asked Rattigan to invent several "protection lines" which they would speak to cover an explosion during an important scene. Lynn fell in love with several of her "protection" speeches and Rattigan has always thought she rather hoped a doodlebug would drop in Shaftesbury Avenue so she could try out one of the speeches on the audience.

The war ended, finally, in May, and Lynn wrote of their emotions on VE Day to Robertson, who was in the country:

The great day has come and it seems that a load has been lifted off everyone's back. Most of the people are tired, of course, but already one has a sense of freedom. We wake up in the morning with a what shall we do today feeling, instead of what is going to be done to us today. The lovely Sunday that we spent with you in the sunshine and that rude galaxy of flowers seemed to be a promise of what began to happen on Monday. That night all the lovely buildings were flood-lighted. Big Ben, Westminster, the National Gallery, all the government buildings, Buckingham Palace, the revolving ball on the top of the Coliseum and some of the lovely old churches. The darkness hid the scars, and London was bathed in such beauty that one stood weeping to see it. Big Ben was especially beautiful; the floodlights made him disappear in vapour around the base so that he looked like a sturdy honest ghost. The people walked the streets in an orderly fashion, some singing and dancing, nothing rowdy. Young couples who had been walking the streets all day lay asleep in doorways looking very childish and innocent. We saw one or two young girls lift their swains onto their shoulders and walk along quite easily with them. . . .

Graham had been quite sick and he did not see *O Mistress Mine* until it was about to close. Instead of his chair in the wings, they gave him a box to himself. After the performance, a table was laid in the box and they had tea and sandwiches. It was the last play he ever saw. Not long afterwards, he had a stroke which left him paralyzed. "When Graham was dying, in 1948," Lynn remembers, "Alfred and I and Jamie [Hamish Hamilton] went down to see him in the country. Poor Graham could no longer speak and we don't know if he could hear us or knew who we were or even if we were there, but I think he did, because his eyes were alive, and we just sat by his bed and we talked to one another and Graham sat propped up and I prayed he'd understand us and know how much we loved him."

After taking the play on a tour of army camps in France and Germany, they opened in New York at the Empire Theatre on January 23, 1946. It was Broadway's first glamorous opening after the war. The charm of the play and the iridescence of the players captivated the audience. *O Mistress Mine* was the biggest hit of their careers, and their longest Broadway run—four hundred fifty-one performances. All in all, they played it, in New York and Europe and on the road, for almost four years.

Now their English friends were coming for visits—Edith Evans, Hamish Hamilton, Noel Coward. Lynn was indignant when Hamish wrote that he was making a business trip and could not take Yvonne, because taxes were so high and her expenses weren't deductible. She wrote that pleasure was more important than budgets: "Pleasures are so few we should snatch them when they come and when he is 80 and looks back on it, he will be glad he did not save that little, because he will know by then that he never missed it," she wrote Robertson. "Of course, if he thought like that about everything he would probably be a pauper but I don't think Jamie would, so he will be quite safe."

They gave a dinner party for the Hamiltons. Edna Ferber came, and Thornton Wilder, and John and Natasha Wilson. "We had steaks, sauce Béarnaise and all the things we hadn't seen in England for a long long time, and champagne," Lynn reported to Robertson. "It was a gay evening. We drank a toast to you and you responded with one of the wittiest speeches I have ever heard and we all fell under the table with delight."

In September, when Noel was to arrive, Lynn was waiting for him in his apartment when he opened the door, to present him with two enormous ripened avocadoes, one of his favorite delicacies and something he hadn't tasted since 1939. And Alfred had baked a handsome three-layer chocolate cake, rich and creamy. Noel was usually in an exuberant state, even when his affairs were going poorly—but now he was positively euphoric. He had never expected to see Lynn and Alfred again.

Before coming to New York, he had visited the Riviera. One night, in a Cannes casino, he had been playing roulette with stacks of what he thought were 100 franc chips. They were, however, 500 franc chips, and he found he won a million francs in 15 minutes.

"I collected my money," he once told me, "rushed madly out of the casino, trampling several women to death who were standing in my way, and ran with the money." On the ship he won 500 pounds more on the horse races. And when he departed from New York in December, his friends had loaded him down with so many "dubious commodities" that he told the Lunts since the British were limited to spending 50 pounds outside England "the simplest thing for me to do is order a car to meet me at Southampton and take me directly to prison."

They were nearing the three thousandth performance of *O Mistress Mine,* in Seattle, when Alfred got a bad case of Virus X. He kept on playing, though at one time his fever got as high as 105°F. Alfred is not the first man who has triumphed over physical pain by force of will. But, to me, what makes him so rare an example of human courage is that he has had to do the work of his life in public. While experiencing intense pain, he has had to be smiling and charming to audiences. From the time at age twelve when he was operated on for appendicitis and lost a kidney, he has lived with pain every day of his life. Sometimes the pain is bearable and sometimes it is unbearable. But he has never allowed suffering to stand in the way of his becoming his ideal of an actor. He had dedicated himself to his ideal in youth and he held unswervingly to his course, in good times and bad, in sickness and in bad health, in depression and prosperity, in hits and in flops. In San Francisco, he was given a massive injection of penicillin, which not only cleared up the influenza but also gave him a sensation of well-being. The tour ended, they returned to the farm. Later, in the summer, he had several operations, and Dr. Edward Bigg, their personal physician, prescribed a strict diet and no alcoholic beverages for six months. And he wasn't to act, either. For a time, Alfred enjoyed the compulsory leisure, rereading all the novels of

Dickens and working in the garden. There was a heat wave in August. "The gardens are burning up," he wrote Olivier. "And the grass is like fine shavings. The trees alone are left green, and even so, some of the leaves are beginning to turn brown and falling like burnt paper. Nothing to do but sit and hope for rain."

By February he was feeling like a new man, cooking dinners for guests and drinking Pouilly Fuissé, and looking for a new play. Could Sherwood write them a new play? But the thread of Sherwood's artistic continuity had snapped during the war. His work in politics and in war propaganda had drained him dry. He could not recover his dramatic powers. He showed them the script of a historical comedy about the Mormons. Lynn was to play a dressmaker in a Mormon community; Alfred a U.S. army captain in love with her. They were too old for the parts, they said. They told Bob they were long past the "age of romance. We can't act parts that young."

"Nonsense," Sherwood replied, "you can act any age you want to be and the audience will believe it."

Then he wrote another play for them, *Small War on Murray Hill*. It was New York in the time of the American revolution. Lynn was a married woman having an affair with General Howe, obviously a variation on the theme of *The Road to Rome*. Alfred said, "Bob, I can't play an English officer. I'll do a Chinese general, a Russian, a Finn, a Greek, a French, a German general—but I can't do an English general."

But the play was not good, really, and finally they thought it was the better part of true friendship to reveal what was wrong with it. Lynn put down their criterion for evaluating a play in the following letter, which was very hard for her to write:

You were so wonderful—and made it so easy for Alfred and me—as I expected—like the great man you are. It never entered my head that you would be hurt by our criticism, but Alfred and I both know the blood, sweat and tears that go into a play—and remembering you had said you would have thrown *There Shall Be No Night* into a wastebasket if we hadn't liked it—we felt and still feel doubly responsible. I have been thinking ever since and cannot find anything wrong—except the most important and the thing that makes or breaks—and that is *no story, no situations* [underlined in original]—no drama, no tears—and not enough laughter to cover. For my particular taste, I must have some of all. One cannot say *Present Laughter* was not funny or witty—but it was all one color and I did not like it at all. . . .

TWENTY-TWO

THE RAIN AND THE SHINE

OF THEIR LIVES

*D*ESCRIBING THEIR new play, *I Know My Love,* to Graham Robertson, Lynn said, "It is laid in Boston and the first act begins with two old people over 80, celebrating their 50th wedding day. Then after that, it goes back through the years and you see the rain and shine of their lives. It is very moving and very interesting."

In *Milestones,* so very long ago, Lynn, then a young actress, had to impersonate a girl, a middle-aged woman, and an old lady. Now she was again playing the three ages of woman, except here she was herself an old lady. Yet she was able to project the illusion of youth in her sixty-third year as skillfully as she had imitated old age when she was twenty-four. For she had not only retained the physical vitality and sparkle of a young woman, she knew every trick of the acting trade. She could make you believe she was anything she wanted you to believe. And Alfred, who as a young actor in Boston had been forever playing old men, was now an old man himself and yet, playing young Thomas Chanler to Lynn's Emily Chanler, by God, Alfred *was* a young man and you didn't have to make any allowances. Sherwood knew what he was talking about. They could, at sixty, have played any age, even Romeo Montague and Juliet Capulet. Making every allowance for their artistry at make-up and their psychological trickery, Lynn and Alfred *were* young in spirit, and the life force rushed through them as vigorously as it had in the fullness of their youth—though perhaps they were not as quick on their feet as they had been when they played in *The Guardsman* in 1924. Like prizefighters and ballplayers, actors begin feeling their age in their legs first of all. During the run of *I Know My Love,* Lynn told the stage manager to tell Alfred, during a performance, that "he is to come downstairs a little more quickly in the next scene than he did in the last, because he is holding up my lines and my timing is badly off."

And Alfred replied: "Tell Miss Fontanne that if she wants someone to come downstairs faster in that second act scene, she should have married a younger man."

Emily and Thomas Chanler were a happily married couple, as were Lynn and Alfred Lunt. The Chanler marriage was clouded by the husband's flirtations and love affairs. This was the "rain" in their lives. But such rain never damped the love life of the Lunts. In plays, the Lunts are the archetypes of sexual dalliance. In life, they are paragons of marital fidelity.

Once, on tour, they had supper with Tallulah Bankhead, who was touring in Chicago with *Private Lives.* They were sitting in the Pump Room of the Ambassador East, and present, besides the Lunts, were Donald Cook, Ivor Novello and Robert Andrews. Tallulah looked about her and cried hoarsely: "I've slept with every man at this table—except you, Alfred—and *you're next!"*

Alfred's look of horror was something to see. If it was Tallulah's desire to dally with Alfred—which I doubt—it was an unsatisfied desire.

Strangely, though they are so conventional in their personal lives, they have rarely played a husband and wife. When they did, as in *The Guardsman* or *The Doctor's Dilemma,* it was a bohemian and adulterous couple, more or less. *I Know My Love* was one of the rare exceptions in their gallery of matrimonial portraits. I suppose it must have been that the role of the profligate stirred Alfred's imagination as the *femme fatale* stirred Lynn's. Yet they were truly noble when they spoke the tender lines of *I Know My Love.* They spoke with the feeling that came from their own hearts, their own marriage, when they played a little scene alone in the closing moments of the play. Then they seemed to go beyond acting, to reach a plane of emotional truth, and many in the audience wept with bittersweet pleasure as they listened to the dialogue, Lynn speaking low and Alfred raising his voice, for "Emily Chanler" was hard of hearing.

THOMAS. Today, I think you might call me darling.
EMILY. I don't wish to be sentimental, darling.
THOMAS. Well—it's been all right with us, hasn't it?
EMILY. So far.
THOMAS. As good as you expected it to be?
EMILY. Fully as good.

THOMAS. And today you still love me?

EMILY. Of course I love you. And I shall go on loving you. Maybe not for very long, but at least forever.

THOMAS. Are you happy that you lived for this?

EMILY. Very happy.

THOMAS. In spite of everything?

EMILY. Why do you say that? It's always been wonderful with you.

For a long time, they had wanted a town house and finally they found it, in 1950. "It is tiny," she wrote to Vivien Leigh, "and situated off Gracie Square, facing the East River, with a little park between. We have done some remodelling and it is almost ready for us to go into. All our furniture has gone to be re-upholstered and our carpets to be cleaned. We have been haunting auction sales and if you enjoy all that kind of thing you must know we have been having a delirious existence. . . . The house was built around 1882, horrid but old and quite quaint for New York. It is one of a row of little houses with brownstone stoops. We have knocked ours off, and made a lot of use of the ground floor. . . ."

The house is so narrow—not even 15 feet wide—that scene designer Stewart Chaney, who helped them decorate, suggested they mirror the walls solidly to give an illusion of space. Alfred enjoys watching visitors looking at themselves in the mirrors.

"You know," he says, "I've always noticed that men stare in mirrors more than women, regardless of what is generally believed. Yes, I think men are more vain of their appearance than women. Men seem almost to pirouette with their reflections. I've known only one man who didn't look in mirrors. Somerset Maugham. He never looks in a mirror. Never. Why? I never asked him."

The national tour of *I Know My Love* (season of 1950-1951) was, in Alfred's words, "a long and terrible nightmare." And Lynn wrote a friend, "I think the witches are around us." In Hartford, Conn., where they played a split week, a sneak thief cleaned everybody out of their cash backstage. In Springfield, Mass., somebody attacked the chief prop man's wife in a street when she resisted his overtures; she was severely beaten and given two black eyes and a broken nose. On closing night in Springfield, Esther Mitchell, an actress, was putting her make-up case in the large prop box when the lid fell on her head and gave her a brain concussion. The next stop was Portland, Maine. Going down the steps of the hotel on the way to the theatre, Lynn caught her heel in the hem of a long skirt. She put out her arm to break the fall and broke her left arm. "I had never seen a broken arm before," she wrote Antoinette, "and it is without doubt the horridest sight. I didn't believe it was mine. My hand looked more like a foot and Alfred gave a high strangled 'Oh' and ran away for a doctor." He took her to the hospital. There, a young doctor gave her a stiff dose of novocaine and temporarily set her arm. She played that Friday night and both performances on Saturday! The Portland *Evening Express* hailed her as "gallant Lynn Fontanne" on the editorial page:

> Far beyond the call of duty, Miss Lynn Fontanne's performance in *I Know My Love* last evening at the State Theatre here—with her arm in a cast for a wrist fracture suffered in a fall barely an hour before curtain time.
>
> Miss Fontanne need not have gone through with the scheduled performance, following her painful accident. But she did go through with it without a murmur of self-pity, great actress, great trouper that she is. She asked, through another, merely that the audience "please ignore" her arm. She hoped they would enjoy the play.
>
> We salute this brave lady who thinks first of others' happiness and, with that in mind, makes light of her own misfortune.
>
> Would that more of us were capable of similar self-effacement, gallant Lynn Fontanne.

After the Saturday night performance, she returned to the hospital. The cast was removed. Her arm was then set again, with an injection of pentathol. "It took three doctors to get it straight and they did a miraculous job," Alfred wrote Lynn's sister. "She is in a plaster cast from her fingers almost to her shoulder and the weight of it seems terrific and must be very exhausting. She doesn't complain at all, but now and then she goes awfully white. . . ."

But on they went, to Boston and Montreal, she playing Emily Chanler with her arm in a cast; then in Pittsburgh there was a blizzard, thirty inches of snow immobilizing the whole metropolis. They were supposed to leave on a 12:40 A.M. train. It didn't leave until 7 A.M., and it took twenty-two hours for a trip which usually takes seven— and there were no diners on the train. In Detroit, the next stop, their costumes and sets had not yet arrived from snowbound Pittsburgh. (Alfred asked the audience if they wanted to see a naked performance— they could pretend it was a rehearsal. The audience was delighted.) And in Chicago, the company manager slipped on the ice and fell, bruising his head badly.

"I think God is trying to break us up in little pieces as a punishment for discovering the atom bomb," Lynn wrote to Hamish Hamilton.

But they completed the tour—Cleveland, Cincinnati, Dayton, Columbus, Toledo, Indianapolis, Louisville, New Orleans, Atlanta, Richmond, Baltimore, Washington, and Philadelphia.

Because they were actors of training and discipline, because they were troupers, the Lunts were often baffled by the new breed of actor and actress, who seemed to be amateur psychoanalysts, wasting time at rehearsals, arguing with the director, raising philosophical questions about "motivations," contemplating their navels, obsessed with personal neuroses, imagining that a rehearsal was a session of group psychoanalysis.

"When I was a young actress," Lynn once remarked, "one of the hallmarks of the greenhorn actor was that he stopped a rehearsal to explain why he did it this way instead of that way or he took too much rehearsal time talking about himself and his problems. Holding up a rehearsal—good lord, only amateurs did that sort of thing."

Sometimes they wondered if the new Broadway theatre were not completely out of joint. There were new playwrights after the war, principally Tennessee Williams, Arthur Miller, and William Inge, and a new school of actors and actresses who operated on the springs of nervous flutterings and intuitive spontaneities, perhaps suiting the themes of sexual disorder and social confusion of the new playwrights. Sometimes audiences complained that the new breed was inaudible, but their defenders claimed they were playing realistically and therefore conversationally. The name of Stanislavsky began to acquire talismanic powers. Some of the new breed, like Marlon Brando, seemed to have the divine spark, and there were others of great talent. There were splendid directors, like Elia Kazan, Robert Lewis, and others of the mystical elect, especially the high-priest of the "method," Lee Strasberg, now dominating the Broadway scene. But this did not seem to be the theatre of disciplined professionals in which the Lunts had been trained.

Could they really function in this new world of chaos?

They remembered Marlon Brando. He was one of innumerable unknown actors whom they read for the role of the boy in *O Mistress Mine*. He had come on the stage sloppy, unshaven, scowling. He held the script as if it were a dead insect. He didn't seem to have the dignity and the pride in himself that they had hitherto believed was part of the actor's equipment. He glared at them sitting in the theatre.

"You may begin now," Alfred said.

Brando looked at the script. "I haven't studied it," he said.

"Well, just give us an idea of your voice," Alfred suggested. "Say anything."

"Hickory, dickory, dock," snarled Brando and marched out of the theatre.*

When producer John C. Wilson sent young Brando the script of *Present Laughter,* one of Noel's new comedies, Brando returned the script with this note: "I have read it. Do you know that millions of people are starving in Europe and Asia?"

Was there no longer any knowledge of the nature of comedy? That it was written by serious men, whose hearts were so broken by life's tragedy that they laughed in order that they might not go mad? Did they not see that beneath the laughter of Shaw and Giraudoux, of Chekhov, Molnar, Behrman, Barry, Sherwood, and, yes, Noel Coward and Terence Rattigan, there lurked a deep sadness about the human condition?

And after all what did the theatre expect of them now? They would read, with a certain pain, that at the Actors' Studio, the temple of the new breed, Strasberg had said, in a lecture:

"A man like Alfred Lunt has more equipment as actor and director than Laurence Olivier. But what do the Lunts do? Fool around with tired Noel Coward. What is their total impact? They make nice nostalgic pictures in the Sunday supplement. But what does Olivier do? He's got the Old Vic to work with, and he is in a position to *create*." †

Repertory—repertory, that was the war cry. But why did everyone forget that the Lunts had played five seasons of repertory with the Guild in the 1920's and then organized their own company, that they

* Though Brando has told this story on himself often, and with great relish, Lynn and Alfred do not remember Brando saying "hickory, dickory, dock." As Alfred recalls it, "He walked across the stage for us. He looked too old for the part. He looked at least 20 or 22 and Lynn thanked him for coming and explained it was important that the boy be around 16 years old or at least look 16 and that he appeared to be too old and that the young man's age was vital to the story. Marlon Brando was polite and thanked us for hearing him. I have heard this hickory-dickory-dock story many times and I imagine that when he became famous, Brando decided to make a character for himself, and rudeness was part of this character—what is nowadays called one's 'image.' But I must tell you in all honesty that he was not in the least rude to us."

† Quoted by Frederic Morton, *Esquire*, December 1954.

played four seasons of repertory in the 1930's and without patrons or foundations to back them? Did Strasberg and Kazan believe they had discovered a panacea for our theatre when they cried, "We must have repertory to save us from the commercial theatre"? Curiously enough, when the Actors Studio played its first season on Broadway, in 1963, they revived *Strange Interlude,* with Geraldine Page playing Nina Leeds, the role Lynn had created thirty-four years before. When Kazan and Whitehead started their first season of the Lincoln Center Repertory Company, their second play was *Marco Millions,* which Alfred had done thirty-six years before. And the third play was *But For Whom Charlie,* by S. N. Behrman, who had conceived the play with Lynn and Alfred in mind.*

They had done so much and worked so hard in their time, and now it seemed they had written in water. Yet they could look back on lives rich in achievements. They had met every challenge nature, art, and society flung at them, and they had won. Out of the raw material of shyness and a sense of inferiority, Lynn had made herself into one of the most glamorous women of her time. Beginning with small technical knowledge, she had ripened into the most powerful actress in the world. Alfred, taking the clay and straw of his middle-class middle-western American background, a most uncongenial stuff for the artist, had formed himself into the leading dramatic personality of the age. He had not attempted to reform the world or the commercial theatre. He had acted everywhere and in whatever material came to his hand. In Wisconsin, before farm audiences on a lecture circuit. In Boston, in a stock company playing crime melodramas. In vaudeville. In Broadway plays. He had never bemoaned the problem of being a serious actor in America or cast aspersions on Broadway producers. He had simply gone about the business of acting, trying his best to live up to his ideal of the theatre as a church in which actors presented the great issues of life to an audience of communicants. And when their accidental collaboration with the Theatre Guild gave them, finally, a platform, the Lunts brought to life a gallery of men and women in a variety of great plays. They had never betrayed the theatre, while the new breed, who made the high-sounding noises about starving millions and how the theatre should be a vehicle for social improvement, somehow forgot their own nobility and became movie stars when they were tempted by money and power and publicity.

Lunt and Fontanne remained faithful to the theatre in good times

* In a conversation with the author, January 1964.

and bad times and in all kinds of seasons and in all states of health. By 1957, they had already outpaced, as an acting team, the previous record-making partnerships of Ellen Terry and Henry Irving, and of Julia Marlowe and E. H. Sothern.

In the 1956-1957 season, they played *The Great Sebastians,* by Howard Lindsay and Russel Crouse, on the road and on an NBC television program. They earned $400,000—more than they had ever earned in any season before. Now, in the spring of 1957, exhausted after the long tour, they believed the time had come to hang up their armor, put away their weapons and go no more to the wars. When Theresa Helburn sent them a new play, *The Old Lady's Visit,* adapted by Maurice Valency from the German of Friedrich Duerrenmatt, they returned it. They were two very tired old troupers and now they were going to spend the rest of their lives traveling to Europe, to Mexico, to Asia, to Africa, seeing their friends and relatives, tasting the peace of the pastoral life in Genesee Depot, Wisconsin.

In the summer they went to Paris. For the thousandth time, Lynn was studying French and trying to communicate with French people. And Alfred was going to the Cordon Bleu school—after he had taken the examination he was awarded a *"Diplome de Cuisine Bourgeoise et de Patisserie Courante."* (He wrote me: "The best one can get in six weeks.")

They stayed at the San Regis, on Rue Jean Goujon, a small elegant hotel near Place François Premier. Alfred went to cooking class from 9 to 5 and Lynn to French from 10 to 12, "but I have much homework to occupy me in the afternoons." Strolling along the *quais* of the Seine on Sundays or through the park of the Champs-Elysées between the Rond-Point and the Place de la Concorde, they reminisced about their experiences in the theatre. They were sure it was all behind them, lovely memories, some ugly, but all so interesting. It was past, it was finished. They were in love with the soft lights and changing moods of Paris in the morning and the early evening, her twisted streets, her old buildings and gabled roofs, and with the French admiration for beauty—in clothes, in flowers, in sensual things, in artistic things. Sometimes they talked about the new theatre—Beckett, Ionesco, Pinter —and they wondered. Could they? Once more, perhaps. Once more. To show a new generation that acting, as they acted, was more than make-believe, it was life on a finer plane. Ah, if only the work of an actor endured like the work of an artist, a writer. But so little remained of an actor's work—his memories, and who else's?

"When the painter or the writer wakes, his work, good or bad is still there," Sothern once said. "He can erase in one place and touch up in another. The actor wakes to nothing. Each night he must do it over again. And as the years pile up and he is doing it over and over, there comes a time when for all his labor and love the work is faded and dim. He has no longer the power to make it vivid even for the brief hour of the play. He is done for and has nothing left—no remembrance of a life's work except a few notices in a scrapbook, which none but himself, not even the men that wrote them, remembers or would care to read."

TWENTY-THREE

A HEAVEN IN HELL

ONE AFTERNOON, Moss Hart encountered Peter Brook outside The Ivy, a theatrical restaurant in St. Martin's Lane. Hart was in London to stage *My Fair Lady*. Brook was directing Lunt and Fontanne in *The Visit*, the seventh play written by Friedrich Duerrenmatt. Hart's limousine was outside and he gave Brook a ride. When he asked Brook to tell him the plot of *The Visit*, Brook replied: "There is this old woman who is very rich and she comes to Güllen, a little town in Europe, and she has a black panther, an empty coffin, two American gangsters, two blind musicians, and she's prepared to pay a billion marks to get a man killed because thirty years before he had given her an illegitimate baby and then he—"

But Hart cut off this ridiculous précis. He assured Brook he didn't really want to pry into any secrets and if Brook didn't want to tell him the plot he didn't have to invent fantastic tales. Hart knew perfectly well this was not and could not be the story of the play the Lunts were preparing!

That *The Visit* was ever done in English at all seems, in retrospect, to be the result of a series of lucky accidents. It was written in 1954 in German. Duerrenmatt was a total failure even in Switzerland. *The Visit* was a bitter drama portraying mankind as a tribe of selfish animals. A young girl, made into a whore, gets revenge by purchasing the souls of a village for a billion marks.

"The world made me into a whore," says Claire Zachanassian, "and now I make the world into a brothel. Those who wish to go down, may go down. Those who wish to dance with me, may dance with me."

It was a black picture of humanity, unrelieved by any of the usual religious or sociological edifications. Duerrenmatt held out no aspirins of hope. Like the other *avant-garde* playwrights, he held the world to be intrinsically meaningless, a chaos of absurdities imposed by hypocrites upon a senseless series of sensations.

Produced first in Zurich and then in Paris, the play had failed dismally. To say that *The Visit* had two strikes against it is an understatement. It had three. It was out. The ball-game was over. Duerrenmatt seemed fated to live a hand-to-mouth existence in Neûchatel, trying to get his pessimistic themes on paper while supporting his wife and three children on free-lance newspaper and magazine assignments. Then, in 1956, Maurice Valency asked permission to make an English adaptation of *Der Besuch die Alten Dame*. It was granted. The translation was made. It was turned down by many actors and many producers. It was turned down by the Lunts.

But the Lunts believed it was a "powerful play." They were haunted by the figures of the old lady and the old gentleman—she the sexually fascinating, power-driven, malevolent woman, and he the irresistible seducer destroying himself. They were always drawn to such figures. They could not put the play out of their minds, even in Paris that summer.

Peter Brook, one of the younger British directors, went to a party one day and got into a conversation with a French actress. She praised a play she had seen in Paris, which had failed, but was a beautiful play. Somebody should do it in English. Somebody like Peter Brook. He read the play, and caught fire. He told Roger Stevens, an American producer, about it. Stevens read the play. A perfect play for the Lunts! He spoke to the Lunts. They would have nothing to do with the play. They were on holiday. Stevens took an option on the play all the same. Hugh Beaumont liked the play. They formed a partnership. Surely, they would persuade the Lunts. There were telephone calls, back and forth, New York to Paris, London to Paris, Paris to London, but it was no use. The Lunts were adamant. Finally, Peter Brook went over to Paris and he got them to change their minds. They agreed to rehearse the play in England and open it in London, play it for a season, if it went, and then bring it to New York.

Lynn went about buying her clothes before they went into rehearsal. Madame Zachanassian was the richest woman in Europe. She would, naturally, wear the finest clothes. She planned to look over all the fall and winter collections. But she surprised Brook when she said, as they were entering Dior's, "We're not paying any of those fancy prices for stage clothes." The trio sat in the salon and M. Dior, personally, told them of his new conceptions as the mannequins displayed the styles.

Lynn said, "I love so many of the numbers, but your prices . . . well . . . simply fantastic . . . out of the question. . . ."

He thought he could perhaps make some adjustments. After all, it was a cachet to design clothes for Lynn.

"No, it is still too high. You don't know the theatre. I don't say your gowns aren't worth a thousand dollars. But an audience is so far away. Alfred, what was the play we did where I wore those simple cotton things and they looked so expensive?"

Alfred mentioned this play and that play and it dawned on Brook that they were improvising a play for M. Dior's benefit. They left and visited other couturiers. Word had gotten around the houses, and they all began competing for the prize. Castillo won it. By charm, insinuation, flattery, pretending that she needed cajoling, Lynn got Castillo to make her a stunning array of costumes and did not pay a single penny.

Alfred went about Paris, poking into pawnshops, old clothes stores and the flea market, to find the kind of shabby clothes Anton Schill might wear. In the end, he settled on his own old shoes and old suits, which were threadbare enough. With his usual attention to detail, Alfred not only wore a baggy suit, old shirt, and beat-up shoes, but his socks were darned at the toe and heel, though no spectator, nor even his fellow actors, would know his socks were old and patched.

Rehearsals began in London. "I never have worked with any actors more dedicated than the Lunts," Brook once told me. "You know, sometimes a married couple gives you trouble because after a rehearsal during which some things are agreed upon, they will go home and talk it over and come to new conclusions, which they bring in, and it creates dissension in the next rehearsal. Not the Lunts. And how courageous they were. Here she was playing an evil, coldhearted woman. He was a filthy, degraded old bastard. Now what would you expect two established stars to do? They would lose heart. They would compromise, soften the characters, adulterate them, sweeten them, bring it closer to what audiences expected of them, what they'd always played. For thirty years the Lunts have been having a love affair on the stage, flirting with each other and with their audiences. They knew how to make audiences love them. They knew they were now playing with fire in *The Visit*. But they didn't retreat or ask me to tone down the play. They explored every aspect of evil in it.

"If I had to sum up their qualities as actors, I'd say that Alfred reminds me of John Gielgud. Alfred, like Sir John, is a brilliant improvisor, who arrives at a role by intuition and trial and error. Lynn, like Olivier, works from her mind, meticulously, slowly, putting pieces together into a whole. How they complement each other!"

While playing Anton Schill, Alfred cut his own hair. And the other actors had to do the same. "You see," one of them complained to me, "we citizens of Güllen are poor people in a bankrupt village so how can we afford to get haircuts? He said there was no barber in Güllen any more. We had to cut our own hair."

They opened on Christmas Eve, 1957, at the Royal Theatre in Brighton. They were to play Brighton for a week and then open in London. A well-dressed and happy crowd filled the theatre. They came to see a vivacious comedy of love and laughter, of sex and sin, played by Lunt and Fontanne. Then the play began. As the brutal scenes of depravity unfolded, you could sense the tension in the air. Their beloved Lynn a monomaniacal bitch? Their darling Alfred an unshaven villain who had seduced a young girl and then framed her by false testimony? A small town, not unlike Brighton, selling its soul for a billion marks? Committing a municipal murder? It must be some joke of the playwright. A trick. They waited twenty, thirty, forty minutes, waiting for the early scenes to turn out a dream or a phantasy, for their dear Lynn and Alfred to become the darlings they were in a frivolous comedy. But the play continued to expose the blackness of humanity and ended with Alfred strangled and Lynn leaving the village in triumph, his corpse in her coffin. The curtain fell.

Total silence. Not a pair of hands clapped. There was not one sound at the first curtain call, so there was not a second curtain call. The audience trudged out. They were disappointed; but more than that, they were shocked, they were disgusted. They hated the play; they loathed the play; they wrote letters to the papers denouncing the play. They wrote letters to Lynn and Alfred, crying shame on their heads for letting them down in this filthy, dirty play. Suddenly there was no longer a theatre available in London.

Lynn and Alfred did not weaken. They met the crisis head on. This was not like the crisis with *O Mistress Mine*, when there were problems of pacing and revision to be solved so the play could be saved. No, this time the play was excellent and the production was superb and they were giving the best performances of their lives—and there was no theatre in London. Binky Beaumont, still fighting to get them a London theatre, arranged a tour of Blackpool, Stratford-on-Avon, Dublin, marking time. The Lunts insisted that their salaries be cut by fifty percent because the play was not making money.

In New York, meanwhile, Roger Stevens had learned of the dismal events. Stevens had other things on his mind besides *The Visit*: he was a director of The Playwrights' Company, one of the three directors of The Producers Company, and a Democratic Party treasurer. He headed a real-estate organization with interests all over the country, one of which was the City Investing Corporation, a syndicate that owned many New York theatres. They had recently purchased the old Globe Theatre, and it was now undergoing a massive renovation in, according to a publicity release, "the rococo style of the Potsdam palace of Frederick the Great." To transform a dilapidated theatre into a pastiche of a Potsdam palace is not an easy or inexpensive matter. A new stage was built. New seats were installed. A cantilevered mezzanine was added. The walls were lined with blue damask. Crystal chandeliers hung on them, and there was a giant chandelier hanging from the ceiling, which was further adorned with a 100-foot mural depicting the theatrical Muses, Melpomene, Euterpe, Thalia, and Terpsichore.

In February, Stevens flew to London. Beaumont was seriously considering closing *The Visit*; Stevens said in that event he would bring it to New York. Beaumont shook his head sadly. There was no hope, he said. Audiences simply detested the play, and hated the Lunts for playing in such a rotten piece of theatre. Stevens, undaunted, went on to Dublin, where the Lunts were playing at the Olympia Theatre. He arrived for a matinee. There was only a handful of people in the audience. The manager told him it was "a nasty little play. They've got a coffin on the stage. It's disgusting." But Stevens saw the play and found it beautiful. As he went backstage to see the Lunts, he decided that if his partners were agreeable, they should at once take *The Visit* to the United States and open it in the Globe Theatre. What if they were to give the imitation of the Potsdam Palace a brand-new name? What if they were to name it after Lynn and Alfred? Call it the Lunt-Fontanne Theatre?

It was a freezing day in Dublin, and Stevens found the celebrated stars down in the mouth. They occupied ratty dressing rooms. They were shivering and bedraggled, wearing long underwear. Stevens bucked them up. He thought it was a fine play. He liked coffins on a stage. He was not only going to open the new theatre with a loud fanfare but the first play in it would be *The Visit* and what did they think of a new name for the theatre—the Lunt-Fontanne Theatre?

"It seems completely mad," Alfred wrote Alan Hewitt, "but Roger Stevens is determined. I wonder if this is the play to open a grand new theatre? It's so sordid—half the audience hates it, and they will feel the same in New York—it's fascinating to act—but who cares about that except the actor. . . . We continue to get the most violent letters protesting against our acting two such frightful people in this bitter play."

Yet even those who were revolted were often moved. When they played Washington, D.C., later, columnist Joseph Alsop gave a dinner party in their honor where Alice Longworth told Lynn and Alfred, "Oh, it was horrible, the most horrible play I ever saw—but I enjoyed every minute of it!"

In New York, they rehearsed for a month and then took the play to Boston. One day, backstage, Alfred asked Peter Brook into his dressing room. He closed the door.

"Peter," he said, "I've been thinking over a new piece of business. How would it be if when I sit down I took off my shoe and shook some pebbles out? Like this." He slipped his shoe off and shook it and two pebbles fell out. He'd picked up a handful of pebbles in Boston Common and had been experimenting with the effect. It was for his opening scene entrance at the railroad station. Brook told him to go ahead and try it at tonight's performance. Suddenly, Alfred looked worried.

"Maybe it would be better with *one* pebble," he said.

Brook thought it astonishing that an actor should be so sensitive to nuances that he worried whether two pebbles or one pebble was the more effective.

In the second act, Lynn has a long and eloquent speech, which she delivers while sitting on the balcony of her hotel, puffing at a cigar. Brook wondered if the scene would not play stronger if the speech were cut out. An actor usually measures the importance of his role by the number of lines he speaks, but Lynn didn't demur. She played the scene without words in Boston, and played it silently with as much power as she had done with language—maybe more. She was a master of conveying a range of emotions and ideas by pantomime—even when she was immobile. James Agate, the great British drama critic, once wrote of Lynn's being a "mistress of the art of insinuation, extremely skilled in that hoodwinkery of quietism of which Duse was the arch-exponent. Hoodwinkery? Well, let me say the art of restraint suggesting the pent-up torrent, of avoidance hinting at virtuosity resisted." Desmond MacCarthy once defined "the peculiar beauty of Miss Lynn Fontanne's acting . . . as a kind of effortless but frank reticence, quite different from the crude art of obviously concealing emotion. . . ."

Wolcott Gibbs, of *The New Yorker*, described Lynn's "mannerisms . . . the fixed and regal deportment, the delivery of lines with a special, and apparently capricious, accent all her own, and the extraordinary economy of gesture—but somehow they gain new force from the fact that they are used to express a consuming hatred rather than the more comely emotions we have grown to expect. It is a brilliant exhibition of pure malice, and as the sustained mastering of an extremely difficult theatrical challenge (a villainess puffing away at a cigar is never very far removed from burlesque) it seems to me one of the most impressive of her innumerable accomplishments."

It was in the two scenes in the forest of Konradsweil that Lynn and Alfred brought to sublime purity their art of performing. Here they refined for themselves not only the essence of the play but their answers to the mysteries of existence. Madame Zachanassian has told the burgomaster that she wishes to be alone with Anton, to "visit our old haunts once again." In the forest, they sit on a bench as they did in their youth and listen to the sounds of nature and look around them. Suddenly they spy a fawn running through the forest. They raise their arms and in a synchronized motion their fingertips follow the fawn. Commenting on the forest scenes, Walter Kerr said they were "the rock on which the rest of the evening stands. The fusion of two personalities is in an instant complete: we understand what they have been to one another and why they are going to behave as they do. . . . The eerie strain of simultaneous union and a destructive separateness is sounded once more very late in the play. . . . Alfred is going to die at the hands of the townsmen yet he can rest his head on the shoulder of the woman who is draining his life away; Miss Fontanne can move with lightness and grace and the uncalculated innocence of the adolescent she once was. On the scaffold the condemned man speaks softly and warmly to the hangwomen. How the Lunts working with Peter Brook ever managed to find this cool place outside of Hell I don't know; I only know it is there on the stage, alive, defiant and astonishing."

In comprehending Claire Zachanassian and Anton Schill, Lynn and

Alfred came to comprehend his mother and his stepfather, and the hardness and sadness of her mother acting cruelly to her father and her father's failures and the lives of her sisters; and Laurette Taylor and Ellen Terry, blindly and self-destructively seeking love; and Claire Eames, who had broken Sidney Howard's heart when she ran away to Italy with a young lover; and Maxwell Anderson's weakness for young girls; and all the men and women in their lives who had died for love or money or power, or who had not had the love they craved, who had died for glory or for nothing; all the lives and loves and their own, as well. Into this play, they poured all the skill of their artistry and all their knowledge of life.

On Monday, May 5th, 1958, the new Lunt-Fontanne Theatre opened in a burst of glory. The audience was one of those great audiences on a New York first night, the leading spirits in every branch of society. It was to be, for most of them, the most shattering emotional experience they had ever known in a theatre. And when the play ended there were such cries of bravo and such thunder of handclappings as are rarely heard in a New York theatre.

Most of the audience then went to the Grand Ballroom of the Hotel Astor, a few blocks away, for there was to be a ball in honor of Alfred Lunt and Lynn Fontanne. About ten minutes after eleven, when the guests were all seated, Lunt and Fontanne entered the ballroom. A red carpet had been laid from the entrance to the head table. Slowly, they marched, arm in arm, down the length of the ballroom, looking so young and so alive and holding their heads so proudly and happily, and everybody there wept unashamedly. And then the entire assemblage, which included everybody of any importance in the American theatre, stood up and drank a toast to them; the mayor made a speech, and Mary Martin sang a song to them, and the Meyer Davis orchestra played a waltz composed for them, and Helen Hayes, holding up her glass of champagne, said, "We are all here tonight to express our love and our admiration for Lynn and Alfred."

And then after the champagne and after the supper and after the wonderful reviews in the morning papers, Lynn and Alfred went home to East End Avenue. They were talking about some new ideas they wanted to try in the first act. By then it was five o'clock and it was beginning to be light over the East River. They decided it was time for another glass of champagne and they drank it quietly, staring at the pearl gray horizon becoming lighter and lighter. Lynn said she was too excited to sleep but she thought it was really time for them to go to bed, and Alfred said it certainly was time for them to go to bed because they had to give a performance tomorrow evening and then there was the matinee on Wednesday. And so they went to bed.

ACKNOWLEDGMENTS

I WISH to thank the many friends and fellow actors and relatives and producers and playwrights of Lynn Fontanne and Alfred Lunt for the experiences they shared with me. I am grateful beyond words to S. N. Behrman, Marc Connelly, Noel Coward, Russel Crouse, Howard Lindsay, and Terence Rattigan.

Mrs. Karin Sederholm Bugbee and Mrs. Antoinette Fontanne Wilson gave me reminiscences of the childhood and youth of the Lunts, as did Ray Weaver, Andrew Weaver and Mrs. Andrew Weaver. Peter Brook and Rouben Mamoulian, the directors, were helpful, as were Ina Claire, Helen Hayes, Vivien Leigh, Ruth Gordon, Joyce Carey, Bretaigne Windust, Alan Hewitt, Robert Downing, Art Buchwald, Milton Berle, George Greenberg, the late Lawrence Langner and the late Theresa Helburn, Doris Olsson Bardsley, Alan Dent, Hugh Beaumont, Roger Stevens, Lady Juliet Duff, the late John C. Wilson, and Susannah (Mrs. Booth) Tarkington.

Marguerite Taylor Courtney gave me valuable insights and data into the relationship between Lynn Fontanne and Laurette Taylor.

I am grateful to Alexander P. Clark (curator of the rare book and manuscript collection at the Princeton University Library) for permission to examine the letters of Booth Tarkington and George C. Tyler; to the Houghton Library, Harvard, for the letters of Alexander Woollcott; to Donald Gallup, curator of the collection of American Literature, Yale University, for the Theatre Guild scrapbooks and letters.

I owe a debt of gratitude to John Mason Brown for making the correspondence with Robert E. Sherwood available to me. Ebba Johnson, librarian of *The New Yorker*, was helpful in tracking down some of the early Alexander Woollcott pieces written under pseudonyms. Kerrison Preston, friend and executor of the estate of W. Graham Robertson, was not only kind enough to make available to me the letters of Robertson and granting permission to use them, but he made the character of Robertson and his period come alive for me. Hamish Hamilton kindly gave me letters from Lynn and Alfred and remembered many charming stories about them. There must be many many others who have, at one time or another, told me a story, remembered an incident, recounted an experience, passed on some anecdote. Without realizing it, I have, during my career as a biographer of actors, been unconsciously gathering the raw material for this book—long before I made the decision to write it, and so, how I absorbed these materials, and when and where and by whom these stories were told to me—I do not always remember.

Maurice Zolotow.

Hastings-on-Hudson, N.Y.
June 1964

INDEX

Index